advance praise for

Learning in Free Fall

"*Learning in Free Fall* is one of the most compelling, engaging narratives about our broken education system to appear in years. Nicole Terrizzi offers us a raw, firsthand account of what it's like to work within the flimsy walls of a multi-billion-dollar school district, where that mammoth investment made no difference at all. Your heart breaks for the children caught in classrooms where violence, drugs, and emotional anguish are commonplace—and then you discover it's an elementary school. Despite it all, Terrizzi gives us hope, pointing us toward practical solutions already underway."
—Zachary Shore, author of *This Is Not Who We Are: America's Struggle Between Vengeance and Virtue*

"This book offers a nuanced, introspective look at life as an educator. With honest self-reflection, Nicole Terrizzi intertwines her personal struggles with the historical and political forces shaping education. *Learning in Free Fall* is a beautiful book."
—Michelle Kuo, award-winning author of *Reading with Patrick*

"In an America plagued by regular school shootings and a suicide epidemic, *Learning in Free Fall* is a must-read for educators, parents, and anyone who's ever felt alone in a classroom full of students. Nicole Terrizzi's story offers an honest and clear-eyed look at the challenges faced by teachers and students alike. She includes practical insight for approaching the education crisis from the inside out, taking into account voices rarely heard in the conversation."
—Tanya Rey, award-winning writer and author

"When I first opened *Learning in Free Fall*, I was immediately struck by Nicole's raw honesty about the emotional toll of teaching in a challenging environment. This book is a powerful reminder of how deeply race, economics, and mental health intersect in education. Anyone interested in the realities of inner-city schools, especially teachers and education advocates, should read this. The book reshaped my understanding of the struggles faced by both students and teachers. As someone who works in education, it has strengthened my resolve to prioritize emotional support and equity in all areas of my career."

—Evan Erdberg, founder and president of Proximity Learning and author of *#TeachersServeToo*

"Terrizzi's revealing account of teaching in an inner-city American school has educated me. *Learning in Free Fall* demonstrates how teachers and learners exchange essential life lessons in a symbiotic dysfunctional relationship. This work challenges readers to witness the effects of personal and societal pressures in our classrooms, which will bring awareness and inspire us to do better in supporting our educators and our children."

—Chris Davis, award-winning author of *Worthy: The Memoir of an Ex-Mormon Lesbian*

"*Learning in Free Fall* is a compelling memoir that explores the intersection between mental health and education. As a Teach for America recruit, Nicole faces systemic racism, poverty, and neglect, all while managing her own anxiety and depression. Her unwavering commitment to her students, despite the obstacles, shines through. This memoir is not just about teaching but also about resilience and survival. Nicole's story is an inspiring reflection on education, race, and personal growth, making it a powerful read for anyone interested in social justice and transformation."

—Jenn T. Grace, award-winning author
and founder and CEO of Publish Your Purpose

"From the opening sentence, *Learning in Free Fall* implores the reader to learn more. To learn why the student is acting out. To learn why the teacher expresses so much empathy. To learn why the most obvious solution also comes with the most baggage. Author Nicole Terrizzi releases a torrent of emotions conveying the tricky balancing act of providing an uplifting learning environment in an underfunded Kansas City school district while protecting her own mental (and sometimes physical) health along the way. Whether your circumstances connect more with Nicole's experience growing up in a small, predominantly white Christian town, or that of a seasoned educator working within a system that needs systemic change, this book is sure to fasten you to very real issues that may be difficult to stomach, but necessary to consume if you desire a deeper connection to the unsettled nature of education in America."

—Dustin Waite, author of
External and *Falling in Love with The Process*

Learning in Free Fall

Learning in Free Fall

A Testimony of Mental Health, Poverty, and Race in American Education

Nicole Terrizzi

RIVERSIDE PUBLISHING

Copyright © 2025 Nicole Terrizzi

All rights reserved. No part of this book may be reproduced, distributed, or transmitted in any form or by any means, including photocopying, recording, or other electronic or mechanical methods, without the prior written permission of the author, except in the case of brief quotations embodied in critical reviews and certain other noncommercial uses permitted by copyright law.

Paperback ISBN: 978-0-9796233-7-0
Hardcover ISBN: 978-0-9796233-8-7
LLCN: 2025900439

Published by:
Riverside Press Enfield, CT 06082
RiversidePressBooks.com
RiversidePressInfo@gmail.com

Cover Design by: Pete Garceau
Interior Design by: Timm Bryson, em em design, LLC

Disclaimer: This memoir is a work of nonfiction based on the author's personal experiences. While the author has taken care to present accurate accounts, certain names and identifying details have been changed to protect the privacy of individuals mentioned.

A portion of all sales of this book will be donated to a subset of the nonprofit organizations highlighted in the final chapter.

First Edition

For more information, please visit www.nicoleterrizzi.com or www.RiversidePressBooks.com

DEDICATED TO

the late Dr. William McKnelly, who saved my life;
Brian Chambers, who was my first reader and earliest advocate;
Zach Shore, Julia Scheeres, Chris Davis, Bailly Morse,
Brooke Maddaford, Lindsay Newton,
and the countless others who read drafts and provided
feedback, accountability, and motivation;
and my husband, Mick Terrizzi, my greatest support.

And a special thanks to my early readers, sponsors,
and supporters, without whom this book
would not have been possible:
Tommy Gill, Catherine Acevedo, Sheena Grove,
Dick Grosboll, Amy Bean, The Callaways, Janet Tinsley,
Jennifer Binning, and Lisa Shoulders.

CONTENTS

Chapter 1	1
Chapter 2	21
Chapter 3	37
Chapter 4	49
Chapter 5	61
Chapter 6	81
Chapter 7	97
Chapter 8	117
Chapter 9	137
Chapter 10	155
Chapter 11	175
Chapter 12	193
Chapter 13	211
Chapter 14	229
Chapter 15	247
Chapter 16	265
Epilogue	277

Endnotes, 289

"Not everything that is faced can be changed;
But nothing can be changed until it is faced."
—James Baldwin

chapter one

"I wish I was dead."

It was only the fourth week of school, and yet the seven-year-old boy in front of me was already one of my biggest concerns. I kneeled next to Samuel to have a private conversation.

"Hey, bud. Why would you say such a thing? What's going on?"

"I don't know," he replied nonchalantly as he continued to work on the addition problems in front of him.

I pressed further. "Do you know what that really means?

"I don't know," he continued, staring intently at his paper, filling in the numbers.

He was a gaunt, seven-year-old, Black boy who swam in his oversized, belted khakis and navy-blue, hand-me-down, polo shirt—the public school's uniform. He was tall, but his tiny, second-grade frame carried no more than forty-five pounds, and his buzz cut made his brown eyes appear even larger than they really were.

Samuel had originally seemed excited to be back in school, wiggling in his seat with his hand in the air as he eagerly waited to be called upon, and stuttering at times as he shared his excitement about reading *The Indian in the Cupboard*. But his eyes carried a weight—it often looked as though he could burst into tears at any moment.

I remained kneeled by his seat as the other students continued to work quietly. I put my hand on his shoulder.

"Hey, whatever it is, it's going to be okay. I'm here if you want to talk—anytime."

No response. He didn't even look up at me.

I was a first-year teacher, but that didn't keep me from realizing this kind of talk, especially coming from a second-grade boy, wasn't okay. I decided to consult with Mr. Kemper, our school counselor, as soon as I could.

I rose and continued circling the classroom, monitoring my class of twenty-five second-grade students. A recent graduate of a small liberal arts school in Iowa, I had made a two-year commitment to teach as part of the Teach for America (TFA) program. As an English and journalism major in school, my classroom experience was limited—let's be real, it was nonexistent—aside from the six-week training "bootcamp" I had gone through. I had spent my summer in Phoenix preparing, learning the basics of classroom management and curriculum and instruction, but I was already feeling the inklings that it may not be enough.

But I had seen *Dangerous Minds* and *Freedom Writers,* films that featured teachers working against all odds to provide opportunities for growth and immense change—to empower their students. I wanted to do the same.

I had prepared myself for Kansas City—the students, families, and the community; it was what I had trained for. Fewer than ten of the more than three hundred students in the school were white, a stark contrast to my upbringing in a rural Iowa town of 1,200. The school itself stood in stark contrast to what I had experienced growing up. Rather than classrooms filled with natural light, matching desks arranged in neat rows, and shelves upon shelves of activities and books, George Washington Carver Elementary School was a windowless, brick shell with largely mismatched furniture and chairs that often didn't even amount to enough seats for all the students in the classroom. The only books provided by the school were outdated textbooks, and a few other "free reading" books, all of which were in poor condition and many not appropriate for its kindergarten through eighth-grade learners. It was largely up to the teachers themselves to build their own classroom libraries.

I had quickly assumed my identity as "Miss C"—Cleveringa, my Dutch surname, had proven too difficult for most students.

Weeks of work had turned the pale-yellow partitions and movable brown walls of my classroom into a safe haven for my students. I had handcrafted many of the colorful posters that detailed our classroom expectations, monthly calendars, and reading strategies. I had everything in place for what I believed was needed for a successful classroom and school year.

Though there were a few bumps along the way, my first month of school had gone well. My class had quickly become a community, and my classroom was a safe space for learning and growth. We walked through the halls quietly and in a straight line—no small feat for a first-year teacher in what the nation deemed an "inner-city school." Working together over the past few weeks, we'd completed the get-to-know-you and team-building experiences I had meticulously planned.

They were Miss C's class, and they were proud to be part of it.

The previous week, my students had even received a coveted compliment from our principal, Ms. Rebecca King.

"Oooh! Look at all of Miss C's scholars," she'd said. "Working so hard, and so quietly too. What a great class!"

A grandmotherly Black woman with long, carefully coifed hair, Ms. King still wore heels to school daily. She had been in education more than forty years and I immediately admired her; I wanted to soak up all her knowledge and experience. And yet, it was clear her relationship with her job hadn't always been kind—there was an air of exhaustion only decades of work in education can bring. Her opinion of me and my class meant a great deal. The students wanted her affirmation, and I did too.

But even with Ms. King's accolades, my mind fixated on Samuel. He was quickly becoming a problem, but not because of his ill will toward others or his inability to complete the tasks I asked of him. He consistently gave me hugs each morning upon arrival to school, and again at the end of the day when all the students said their goodbyes. At this early juncture in the school year, he wasn't struggling academically. But something wasn't right.

Once I got my class settled at lunch, I cornered the school counselor, Mr. Kemper, in his office, and explained what Samuel had said earlier that morning. I expected an immediate response laying out clear steps to take for this type of behavior. I was sure there would be a protocol already in place on how to address this type of situation.

But, after I relayed the story, Mr. Kemper didn't even look up from his paperwork.

"Just continue to monitor him. Let me know if you see or hear anything concerning," the plump, middle-aged man responded as he continued to riffle through the papers on his desk.

Wasn't Samuel's statement itself concerning in its own right? I wondered.

"Well, should I call his mom and let her know what he said?"

"Yeah, that sounds like a good plan," he said absentmindedly, still not taking the time to even look me in the eye. With the fistfights and gang activity in the middle school, I knew there were larger, more immediate problems for Carver and its students, even at this early juncture in the year. He clearly didn't have time for things like this.

I went back to my classroom and used what remained of my twenty-five-minute lunch period to call Samuel's mom, Shantice.

"Oh, I'm sure he's fine. He's just getting adjusted to school again. I'll talk with him tonight."

"Okay, well, please let me know how I can support."

"I really appreciate that. Thank you, Miss C."

I placed the phone back in its cradle, wondering if I was overreacting. Even Samuel's mom didn't seem worried.

With my own diagnosis of anxiety at the age of nine, and the ongoing bouts of depression and use of antidepressants throughout my life, I had become empathetic and attuned to the struggles of others, particularly kids.

In the coming weeks, I grew more and more concerned about Samuel. I'd been keeping a close eye on him, analyzing his words and watching his engagement with other students. And though I didn't note anything out of the ordinary in his day-to-day interactions, his statements and actions continued to escalate in the classroom.

One day, as the students sat in their seats during a read-aloud, I caught Samuel pressing three sharp pencils to his neck. I tried to make as little fuss as possible, redirecting the other students as I attempted to handle the marks he was creating on his neck.

I immediately squatted down next to him. "What are you doing, Samuel?!" I asked, trying to mask my alarm.

I didn't wait for a response, and put my own hand over his to pull it back slightly so the pencil points were no longer making contact.

He didn't say a word.

"Samuel, I need you to stop. Can you give me the pencils?"

After a brief moment, as he seemed to be weighing my request, he released them into my hands.

"Miss C?" Rashad called out.

"Give me a minute," I responded, grabbing a crayon and passing it to Samuel.

He couldn't handle a pencil today, but I still needed him to write. I'd managed to largely avoid the attention of the other students, thankfully.

"Hey—let's talk later, okay?" I said to Samuel.

But we wouldn't get the chance as something else set him off later in the afternoon during music class and he spent the rest of the day in the office.

The smallest things would seemingly set Samuel on a tirade, causing him to lie on the floor, screaming and kicking anything or anyone in his vicinity. This occurred multiple times a week, and sometimes multiple times a day.

Was something going on at home? Was he bored? Was the material too hard? Were there students bullying him? What was I missing? Why wouldn't he talk to me?

During recess one day, Samuel wrapped a plastic jump rope around his neck and pulled it tight. Before I could rush across the blacktop, his lips began to turn a shade of gray. I grappled with his hands and the red plastic as I loosened the plaything from his neck.

"Samuel?! What are you doing?!"

Adrenaline had taken over, and I knew my frenetic tone came across not as concerned but angry.

His teary eyes looked to me and then the ground—he didn't say a word and his shoulders slumped.

I softened my voice, asking, "Buddy, what is going on with you?"

I waited for a response that didn't come. Samuel began to cry, staring at the ground.

"What can I do to help you?" I said, knowing I was asking myself this more than him.

By this time, sobs shook his scant body. I left the rest of my class under the supervision of another teacher, letting her know we'd need a few minutes. I brought Samuel to the office to sit with our school secretary.

"Can Samuel rest here until the end of recess?" I asked. She gave me a quick nod as she shot me a sympathetic look. "I'll be back in a few minutes."

I went back to my classroom and immediately called Samuel's mother, who again assured me everything was fine.

"I really appreciate you callin' me, Miss C. There's nothin' to worry about. I'm sure he's just playin'. I'll make sure to talk to him about it tonight," she said.

"Well, please let me know how I can help. I've been really concerned about him." I paused before broaching the question I had wanted to ask. "How would you feel about him spending some time chatting with Mr. Kemper, our school counselor?"

"Oh no, that's not necessary—he's fine. I'll talk with him tonight."

I had no doubt she would talk to Samuel, but I wasn't appeased. I didn't push the Mr. Kemper thing any further as I wasn't sure how much help he would be anyway—he hadn't shown much support of my advocacy for Samuel.

My suspicion was confirmed in a subsequent conversation with Mr. Kemper the next day. I'd tracked him down during my only prep period of the day and was laser focused on getting what I needed in the thirty-five minutes I had available.

I knocked on his open door and peeked my head in.

"Hi," Mr. Kemper said flatly.

I could tell he didn't know my name.

"Hi, Mr. Kemper. I'm Miss C. I wanted to check in as I'm really concerned about one of my students, Samuel Washington."

"Okay, well, what's going on?"

"He's been saying and doing some really disturbing things, especially for a second grader—like how he doesn't want to be alive. Earlier today he wrapped a jump rope around his neck until his lips turned blue, and only stopped when I physically made him."

"Did you ask him why?"

"I did, but he just cried."

"And have you been sharing these concerns with his family?"

"Yes, we've been in touch quite a bit."

"Well, you've done the right thing in calling home. This is now in his family's hands. Nothing more you need to do!"

That's it? I thought.

I wasn't convinced, so I decided to escalate things further without Mr. Kemper's input. I knew Ms. King had a lot on her plate with a school that hadn't met their state testing benchmarks in years, but I believed she should at least know what was going on with Samuel.

The next day, while my students were in music class, I took the short walk to the principal's office and lightly tapped on Ms. King's open door. The door opened to what felt more like a closet than an office: a four-foot-by-seven-foot, stark white, windowless box.

"Hi, Miss C. What can I do for you?" she said.

"Ms. King, I know you're really busy, so I won't take much of your time."

"Oh, it's okay. What can I do to help?"

I sat down in the aged, blue upholstered chair in front of her desk and noticed some gray-yellow foam escaping from a worn hole. The chair was the only place clear of debris as there were boxes stacked against the walls and leaning towers of file folders bursting with papers—I'd never been claustrophobic before, but this tiny room was the definition.

"Well, I just wanted to fill you in on one of my students, Samuel Washington. He's been saying some really concerning things and acting out in class. I've been keeping his mom, Shantice, informed, as well as working with Mr. Kemper—"

"Well, you're doing all you can, then," she interrupted with a tone that told me her focus was on other matters.

"Yes, but I at least wanted to let you know he's been threatening suicide, and yesterday he wrapped a jump rope around his neck; his lips turned gray before I could pull it from his hands," I said desperately.

As soon as I said the word *suicide*, she looked up from the paperwork in her hands and *tsk*ed her teeth in disapproval.

"Oh, well that's too bad," she said, looking me in the eye. "But you're doing the right things, working with Mr. Kemper and Samuel's mom. Thanks for letting me know, but it sounds like you've got it under control."

I appreciated the affirmation, but I sure didn't feel like I had things under control. In fact, I didn't feel like I had any clue what I was doing.

"Okay, well, I just wanted to be sure you knew what was going on."

"Thank you, Miss C. You're doing just fine."

Realizing that was my cue to leave, I rose from the blue chair and thanked Ms. King for her time.

At the end of the school day, I pulled Samuel aside from the group of students who had stayed in the impromptu after-school program I had created. The three other students in the classroom plunked away at the desktop computer in the corner, playing games and doing activities, as I sat Samuel down at the table with his book. Before we started reading, I prodded him with questions, trying to decipher what I could do to help the little boy in front of me.

"I'm angry," he admitted as he stared at his book, glancing up to look me in the eye.

Okay, that's something, I thought. *At least he's telling me how he feels.*

"Why? What's going on?"

"I don't know," he said immediately, now refusing to look up.

Dead end.

"Are you sure? Is there someone, or something, that's been upsetting you? At school? At home?" I pressed, hoping I wasn't pushing him too much but knowing I needed more information to help him.

"I don't know," he said, shrugging.

This phrase was becoming his mantra when he spoke, an easy out.

"Well, let's think about what we can do to make things better. It makes me sad to see you upset."

Over the next few days, Samuel and I created a shared plan for what to do when he was feeling angry. We set up a desk for him in a secluded area of the classroom where he could go when he first started feeling upset. I told him he could use the space to write, draw, or read, with the hope that some physical distance from the other children would help him regulate his emotions. We also decided that he could utilize the hall pass whenever he needed to take a quick walk, and I coached him on focusing on his breathing, getting a drink of water, and then coming back to class.

We implemented the plan, and it worked for about a week. Soon after, his comments and actions began a downward spiral. He threatened to hurt himself. He lay on the floor and continuously kicked a chair into the wall, screaming, wailing, crying, and disrupting not only our class, but anyone in earshot.

"I hate my life! I hate this school! I want to die!" he screamed.

Many students giggled at Samuel's outbursts. Others ignored him, probably because this type of behavior wasn't outside of the norm in their elementary school.

I tried everything I could think of: First, acknowledging Samuel's needs, and then—when that didn't work—trying to ignore him and do my best to execute my lessons with some semblance of normalcy. I didn't know what the best path forward was.

In my mind, this was my job—to take care of these kids, which included taking care of Samuel. But I felt as though I was failing Samuel already.

I continued to call Shantice, chat with Mr. Kemper, and talk with Ms. King. And yet, nobody seemed to share my intense concern for this seven-year-old boy threatening suicide.

And then, one Monday in October, everything changed.

The morning had started uneventfully. It was just before lunch, and my second graders were working on their math. I was circling the room, passing out small yellow math blocks for a hands-on activity where I'd help students identify, count, and model the ones, tens, and hundreds places. Even with explicit instructions about how we were going to use the little blocks, the tiny pieces were just too enticing for a second grader not to play with them.

Over the past few weeks, students had realized that, if they antagonized Samuel, this would result in having less time to focus on their work—with a strategically timed insult, a stolen pencil, or a poke to the ribs, it was if a bomb would explode.

Khalil, a boy who had started the year with fairly good behavior, had begun to establish himself as someone I couldn't ignore. He had begun to take advantage of Samuel's emotionally fragile state, agitating him at opportune moments.

It was as my back was turned that Khalil flicked one of the tiny yellow math cubes across the table, hitting Samuel—and pulling the pin from the grenade.

Suddenly, Samuel went into meltdown mode, lying on the floor wailing, "I hate this school! I hate Khalil! I wanna die!"

Carver Elementary School was constructed during the open-classroom movement in the 1970s. This meant my classroom's pale-yellow walls were not really walls at all, but movable partitions made of aluminum and plastic; my classroom didn't even have a door.

The school's open floor plan meant we could hear everything that was happening in one another's classrooms, which was supposed to empower teachers and students. But, in practice, the open concept only resulted in everyone being easily distracted. Whoever thought open classrooms were a good idea must not have spent much time in an urban classroom.

As such, for many of us at Carver Elementary School, success meant keeping the kids quiet. As I rushed over to Samuel, my face flushed with shame because I knew everyone could hear that I couldn't properly manage my second graders, namely Samuel.

I tried to console Samuel but to no avail. Deciding to ignore him for now, I got the other students started on the task at hand: modeling numbers with the blocks in front of them.

With the office right down the hall, our vice principal, Ms.

Hartley, must have heard Samuel's wails because she popped her head in to see if she could offer some assistance.

The short, portly woman eyed me questioningly as she made her way over across the room to Samuel, straightening her glasses as she said calmly, "Samuel, I need you to get up off this floor right now."

He continued to wail, not even acknowledging the request. I'd noticed before that most of the kids ignored Ms. Hartley as her voice didn't carry much weight, both literally and figuratively.

Samuel began kicking the partition wall. My students persisted with their work, disregarding what was becoming a familiar experience. Khalil glanced at me sheepishly, allowing his shoulder-length braids to fall in front of his eyes as he hid a smile. I knew he knew he was the cause of the wailing boy on the floor.

"Miss C, go ahead and give Shantice a call," Ms. Hartley said without pause.

Even Ms. Hartley was on a first-name basis with Samuel's mother.

At the mention of his mother's name, Samuel abruptly stopped his wailing but continued the thud of his feet against the aluminum and plastic partition that served as our wall.

I picked up the phone and dialed the familiar number. Two rings later, Shantice was on the other line.

"Hi, Shantice. This is Miss C at Carver Elementary. I'm so sorry to bug you. Samuel is having a bit of a rough day. I'm wondering if you would be willing to chat with him?"

"I'll be right over."

"Oh, I don't think you necessarily need to come in. If you'd be willing to just check in with him, that would be great."

"Nah, I'll be right there."

The classroom was silent, and I could see my students lingering on every word I said, likely imagining what had been said on the other line.

I heard the click of the receiver and placed the phone back in its cradle.

Carver was a neighborhood school, so I knew Samuel's home was minutes away, within walking distance.

Seemingly thinking the problem was taken care of, Ms. Hartley left my classroom.

My students miraculously stayed quiet and continued to work with their place-value blocks as the unrelenting thump of Samuel's foot against the partition wall provided an unwelcome soundtrack.

I continued circling the classroom, stopping to work with Alexis, a petite girl with a tiny poof of a bun on top of her head.

Before I could fully comprehend what was happening, Shantice rushed into my classroom and yanked Samuel off the floor by his arm, dragging him out the doorway and into the staff bathroom across the hall.

My classroom was silent as my students and I looked to the open partition where a door would be.

Suddenly, Samuel's screams were followed by loud, desperate sobs.

Then we all—my classroom of second graders, the teachers and students in the surrounding classrooms, and me—heard an unmistakable, horrific sound that resonated through the hall: the crack of a belt. Then came multiple, consistent cracks, almost in a sick rhythm. *Crack, crack, crack, crack, crack.*

I lost count. I couldn't count. And then it was silent again.

Oh my God. What am I supposed to do? I worried, frozen in fear.

My students shifted uncomfortably in their green, plastic, small children's seats. My voice broke as I attempted to shift their attention to the little yellow blocks.

"Hey guys—let's all do problem number nine together. If you're not quite there yet, or have already done it, it doesn't matter. Let's get the answer together."

I stumbled over my words, choking back the lump in the back of my throat and hearing my voice shake.

Did they hear it? What am I supposed to do?

I glanced over at Ebony, the first of my students whose eyes I caught before she shifted them to the dingy blue carpet. I noticed how neatly her five, twisted-braid pigtails were arranged around her head as the tears began streaming down her face.

Where are the other teachers? Did no one else hear it?

The school office was right next door. Surely they had heard the muffled screams, the crack of the belt echoing through the hallway.

The class snapped to attention as we all heard the squeak of the wooden bathroom door opening across the hall. All of us stared at the doorway, anticipating who would come through.

Shantice strode into the classroom with the looped, black leather belt and its gold buckle gleaming in one hand, and Samuel's arm in the other. Some students watched as they approached me at the front of the room; others pretended to continue their math work. My eyes were wide, heart pounding, short of breath.

"Samuel has something he'd like to say to you," Shantice said, scoffing.

I don't remember what Samuel said next, but it was wrong. Or maybe he did something incorrectly or hadn't followed her directions, I'll never know, but this time my twenty-four second-grade students and I watched the black leather belt come across Samuel's face, his arms, his back.

It was if we were suspended in time. Was it five seconds? It felt like hours.

The crack of the belt happened in slow motion, the echo reverberating through my classroom and down the hall.

"Please stop! Please stop! Please stop!" I begged, suffocating on my own sobs, tears in my eyes, hands out in front of my body willing the belt to stop.

And then, finally, it did stop.

"I'm really sorry you had to see that, Miss C. Samuel will be on his best behavior the rest of the day."

Shantice pulled Samuel to his feet, her spindly arms still holding the belt as she used her thumb to wipe the trickle of blood that trailed from his nose.

Her short hair was just long enough to cover some of the intensity in her eyes as she gave Samuel a kiss on the head and gruffly stated, "Be good," before walking out.

My ears rung in the silence she left behind as my tears streamed and I realized my students were crying, or stifling sobs. I stood there with Samuel down on his knees in front of me.

Why hadn't I stepped in, gotten in the way of the belt? Why hadn't I gone into the bathroom and stopped it to begin with? How had nobody else heard what was happening? Why had nobody come to Samuel's aid, or to help me?

What am I supposed to do? I thought as I pulled myself together, wiped the tears from my eyes, and grabbed some tissues, focusing intently on the little boy in front of me.

"Hey—are you okay?" I whispered as I knelt to look into Samuel's eyes, handing him the tissues.

"Yeah."

I guided him back to his seat, looking around the classroom and surveying the damage, trying to act normal. I glanced at the clock.

We're late for library class, I realized.

I didn't know what to say, and I was shamefully grateful for the out provided to me by our schedule.

"Alright guys. It's gonna be okay. We need to get ready to head to the library."

Many students looked blankly at the thin, tear-stained face of the twenty-three-year-old white girl standing in front of them. I knew they weren't buying a word that was coming out of my mouth.

It was silent, except for a few muffled sobs. I wondered if the tears from my students were because they were scared or because they identified with Samuel's experience.

"Hey guys, we're going to have some time to talk about this but, right now, Ms. Brooks is waiting for us in the library. Can I get table three to show me how to correctly line up in Miss C's class?"

I wasn't even fooling myself, let alone my kids. The group of four slowly got out of their seats and got into line.

Everyone was visibly defeated and quiet as we walked down the stairs into the basement, heading toward the library.

"You're late," Ms. Brooks, Carver's librarian, scolded me.

"I'm sorry," I responded, unable to muster the energy to say anything more.

I dropped off my class, went back into my classroom, put my back to the open partition that should have housed a door, and sobbed as quietly as I could. I gave myself a moment, and then held my breath. I looked into the fluorescent lights to stop my tears, then took out my compact and a Kleenex to rid myself of the mascara raccoon eyes I had created.

Moments later, I was in Ms. King's office, sure she would know what to do.

This time I didn't announce myself; I pushed the door open.

I explained what had happened, eyes glassy with tears again as I described how Shantice had first beat Samuel in the bathroom with the belt, and then in front of the class.

"I'm so sorry. That sounds just awful, Miss C. I'll handle this from here."

"Thanks so much, Ms. King. Please let me know what I can do to help."

The rest of the school day was a blur. I shared the experience with my two friends at the school—Melissa and Rachel, who were also TFA teachers—during our lunch period. They'd had their fair share of intense experiences with their middle schoolers, but nothing on this scale.

I tried to talk to my class about what they'd witness during the afternoon, but I didn't really know what to say. The safe space within my classroom that I had created for my students was gone. They had seen quite visibly I couldn't protect them. We went through the motions of our science lesson and finished the day with writing. I didn't keep any of students after school that day, deciding instead to circle back with Ms. King to see how I should progress with my class and what steps she had taken.

I found her in the hallway, saying goodbye to the final students who were leaving the building for the day.

"You have a good night now, Dajuan," she said, pulling shut the heavy blue door and looking to me. We walked back to my classroom together.

"Well, Miss C, after completing my investigation this afternoon and talking to Samuel, I don't think Shantice is an abusive mother," she proclaimed.

I was taken aback, the surprise painted all over my face as I stuttered in my steps.

"But, Ms. King, it's not speculation. I saw her whip Samuel with her belt. He still has welts on his arms and back. She gave him a bloody nose," I stated accusingly.

"Well she really shouldn't have done that, and I've spoken to her to make sure that doesn't happen again, but my investigation shows me this is just a one-off incident."

My eyes narrowed and face flushed—I could not believe what I was hearing.

"I'm not so sure that's the case. Samuel has been having a really tough time—"

"I've completed my investigation," she interrupted. "There will be nothing more. I appreciate the passion you have for your students."

And so, just like that, the conversation was over. The leader of the school, the one person who was supposed to support me, particularly as a first-year teacher, was, in so many words, telling me to "mind my business."

We arrived at my classroom's doorway and Ms. King turned to walk back to her office, abandoning me in the empty hall.

As Samuel's teacher, I felt, deeply, that it was my responsibility to help him, especially because he was so clearly asking for it. But how?

chapter two

I grew up in a town of 1,200 people, and was in the fourth generation of a family of immigrants from the Netherlands. My grandparents' farm in Sioux County, Iowa, had been in the family for more than a hundred years. In a state where pigs outnumber people eight to one, we were people of the land, raising grains used for livestock feed (not human consumption).

Every year, my grandfather planted a few rows of sweet corn at the edge of the field—more than enough to sell door-to-door during the late summer months. I'd frequently ride my bike through the neighborhood for a few hours in the morning, writing down orders in a spiral-bound notebook that was small enough to fit in my back pocket. In 1995, it cost $1.25 for a baker's dozen.

Around noon, I'd return home and meticulously count the thick ears of corn, then break off the excess stalk at the bottom to line them up neatly in brown paper bags. For the homes that were close enough, I'd deliver my family's bounty via red wagon. For those that were farther away, or for orders that were large enough, my mom drove me in our family's gray Astro van in the late afternoon. All earnings at the end of the summer were put into my savings account, which was my college fund.

Alton was surrounded by a patchwork of fields of corn and soybeans with a railroad line that cut through the fabric of the land, with towns dotting the blacktop roads that further checkered the area. Our town was secluded but idyllic in many ways. With a small swimming pool; softball and baseball fields, and teams; a bowling alley; and numerous creeks, ponds, and parks, we had our own slice of Americana. Main Street was framed by a single stoplight, a small post office, the town bar, and a shoe repair store. The town's solitary restaurant was aptly named the OK Cafe; it was where I held my first job at the age of fourteen, and where I realized I would always be "Jim's granddaughter" or "Dwane's daughter" if I stayed in my hometown.

Though Alton provided a familial experience, there wasn't much diversity in any sphere—cultural, racial, religious, or even in divergence of experience or thought. Our nearest movie theater was a thirty-minute drive away and getting to the mall took more than an hour, but I didn't think much about any of these things as I was growing up. I didn't know anything different.

Of the ninety-nine counties in the state of Iowa, Sioux County was then, and remains now, one of the most conservative.

Religion was woven into the very fabric of the community, with sixteen churches in just six square miles. I was baptized in the town's Catholic church, but in an attempt to find our church "home," we attended church in four denominations before I reached the age of twelve: Catholic, Presbyterian, Lutheran, and Reformed, in that order.

In addition to saying the Pledge of Allegiance every day at school, in fourth grade, my teacher facilitated a vote and we, as a class of nine- and ten-year-olds, decided that we would say the Lord's Prayer before each meal. Looking back now, it doesn't seem like a very democratic decision, nor one that is appropriate for a public school.

I attended our church's weekly youth group on Thursday

evenings, year after year during elementary and middle school, and went to the Teens Encounter Christ (TEC) conference—and multiple other Christian-based weekend experiences throughout middle school, always working on building my relationship with God.

Like everyone else in the town, Christianity played an important role in my life, but I had a secret: I couldn't "feel" God's presence or hear him speaking to me in the ways my friends described. When I was younger, I'd asked my Sunday school teachers about how to feel closer to God. As I got older it became more difficult for me to admit, but by sixth grade I went as far as to ask our pastor directly.

"What . . . what if I'm struggling to feel God's presence? And I'm not able to hear his guidance or understand his will for me," I said, taking a deep breath.

My pastor spoke gently. "That may be a sign you need to spend more time studying his word. I think you should focus on 'blooming where you are planted.' Do you understand what that means?"

I hate that scripture, I thought.

I always had. I felt like it meant I was supposed to stay stuck in my small town and refuse to dream bigger. Of course, I didn't say that.

"To get involved in what's here and now?" I responded.

"Exactly. God is speaking to you, young lady. You just need to be open and ready to accept it."

I had always felt I didn't quite fit the mold of Northwest Iowa, even as a little girl. The first time I really understood it was in second grade, when I was out on the swings during recess and Kevin Devries asked me, "Why don't you ever smile?"

Additional differences started coming into focus: I'd get pulled out of class once a week to go to Mr. Namuth's office to talk about my feelings. Mr. Namuth was our school counselor who was known for sporadic visits to classrooms to read special books and offer fun activities. I never fully understood what led to teachers identifying me—at the age of eight—as needing a counselor's one-on-one support, but it could have been a multitude of things from my overly quiet demeanor to my refusal to finish all the food on my school lunch tray—the expectation at my small public school—or maybe it was my lack of laughter on the playground. Whatever it was, it was enough for all the other students to understand I was different.

My thoughts were always focused on much bigger things than what was the norm for a child of my age, and my feelings weren't something I was able to identify, let alone share with anyone.

My relationship with my dad was based on sporadic engagement: the occasional summer evening playing catch as he had a great appreciation for baseball (I've always suspected he wished I, his first born, had been a son); engaging in nature, which was both his passion and his job as an avid hunter and conservationist; and, on the exceedingly rare occasion, accompanying him on a trip to the local watering hole.

I didn't fully understand it at the time, but I did know my dad's nightly tradition of going to the bar was something to be revered. Riding in the front bench of his little, white, Chevy S10 pickup, I would often bounce in my seat as we drove the five blocks downtown. My dad would hold the country-blue door open for me, and I'd step in just far enough to wait for my eyes to adjust to the dark. I could hear pool balls cracking together, breaking up Lynyrd Skynyrd's *Free Bird*. When my vision returned, I'd see my grandpa in the corner. After waiting for my dad's go-ahead, we'd walk across the room as I waved to announce my presence to the bartender and my grandpa.

In the thirty minutes it would take my dad to drink a few beers, I'd excitedly dangle my feet from the sparkly red, patent leather bar stools, sipping fountain Coca-Cola from a plastic red cup while I sat between Dad and Grandpa. I knew if I was there, my dad would moderate his intake.

But when we got home there was more Budweiser, the "king of beers," with dinner, and a few more after too. Once my brothers and I were in bed, the yelling would start. It wasn't every night, and it never got physical, but it was enough that I stayed awake, devising excuses to go downstairs and make it stop.

First, I'd "need" a drink of water. The fighting would stop for a while, until I needed to go back downstairs to use our home's only bathroom. This was the intermission to the cacophony. Then I'd creep back downstairs because I was "hungry." By this point, the yelling would turn to me.

"Go back to bed, Nicole—and stay there! I don't want to see you up again!" she'd shout.

For a nine-year-old, this was a dangerous game of playing middleman, refereeing their fights without fully understanding the rules.

But I didn't really have anything to compare my relationship with my dad to. My friends' dads were largely farmers and laborers who played the role of breadwinner. Dads were to be feared when they came home. Mine didn't feel any different.

The library, my books, and school were my refuge. The library was a mere three blocks from our house, and I walked to the brick, two-story building and climbed the worn, blue-and-black, carpeted stairs multiple times per week.

I'd pore over the small selection of books they had. I started with *The Boxcar Children* and books by Beverly Cleary, sitting on the floor and soon flipping through the titles to try to find the ones I hadn't yet read. I quickly graduated to reading the *Choose Your Own Adventure* books, ultimately reading every page to learn all the possible outcomes. Then it was on to the entire *Baby-Sitters Club* series, *Sweet Valley High* books, and Lurlene McDaniel's books; I often read multiple books at once.

By the age of ten, I had largely read all the books I could find at my level. So, I went on to magazines, going up into the small loft area where all the old copies were archived to leaf through pages and pages of makeup tips, teen fashion, and kissing tips and tricks. At one point, I even began reading the encyclopedia, writing my own "term papers" on topics I deemed worthy: animals I hadn't seen in real life and, after discovering *The Diary of Anne Frank*, any topics related to the Holocaust and WWII.

After learning about Anne Frank I began journaling in earnest, finding it therapeutic to write down my innermost thoughts and feelings.

I think Eleanor Brown, the town's librarian, saw me more as an oddity than anything else as I was often the only patron there, or at least the only one who would spend hours there so often.

By my early teen years, I was checking out Danielle Steele and Dorothy Garlock, authors of historical romance novels whose book covers often depicted women looking longingly at the skyline. I always made sure to let Eleanor know, as I checked these books out, that they were for my mother (though we both knew otherwise). I spent so much time at the library that, by the time I was fifteen, I was volunteering to help with children's programming and shelving books. Finally, they asked if I'd like to be paid for my time and put me on the payroll.

But the escape wasn't enough at age nine or really at any point thereafter. I'd worry about implausible things happening to my family: that I'd come home to find the house burned down with only the ashes of my brothers and my mom left behind. Or that my dad was going to get struck by lightning while driving the tractor at my grandfather's farm. I didn't want my mom to drive to go get groceries because I was convinced we were all going to get into a car accident and die. It was too much to carry for a third grader.

All these worries unsurprisingly turned into tears as I struggled to share my deepest fears with my family.

"What is wrong, Nicole?" my mom asked again, one time when I was about nine, clearly exasperated with the situation.

I tried to choke back the sobs, biting the sides of my cheeks and holding my breath as I willed my breathing to go back normal.

"You're going to make your brothers cry if you keep this up. They're going to think something's wrong."

As if on cue, my one-year-old brother looked to me and let out a wail.

"This is the third night this week. I just don't understand why you're crying for no reason. I just can't handle it anymore. I'm taking her to the doctor!"

"And what do you think they're going to do? They're not going to give a third grader antidepressants. You need to take her to a counselor," responded my dad.

My parents talked about me as if I weren't even there. And at the doctor's office, it was the same.

"How long has she been having crying spells?" the doctor said.

"I'd say four or five months at this point," my mom responded.

"Any big changes she's gone through recently?"

"I guess Andrew being born, but that was more than a year ago at this point." Mom shifted my baby brother to her other hip.

Dr. Bakker finally turned to me, asking, "How are you feeling today, Nicole?"

"I'm fine," I murmured.

"And how about the last week or so? Are there times you feel sad or worried about things?"

"I worry about everything," I responded, ashamed I was causing so many issues for my family.

He looked to my mom, then said, "Well, I'm sorry to hear that, Nicole. We're going to see if we can set you up with someone to talk to about how you're feeling, in hopes you can feel a bit better, okay?"

My dad was right—he wasn't going to give a nine-year-old antidepressants.

Unfortunately, due to our rural location, the closest specialist for someone with my needs was almost ninety minutes away in Sioux Falls, South Dakota. I could only imagine the frustration my mother felt, having to take a weekly trek across state lines with a baby, a toddler, and a nine-year-old whose anxiety was running amok.

But the counselor was just what I needed. Marshall Dapper's name always made me giggle, and though I didn't think he lived up to his name—with his long, salt-and-pepper, feathered hair and thick-framed glasses—he quickly became one of my favorite people in the world.

His office was small and dark, without any windows, and the only light came from two small lamps—one on his desk and another on a side table. But the dark green, Persian rug and overstuffed chairs provided an environment in which I felt safe and secure.

I cherished our sessions together—our weekly engagements felt like a haven. He encouraged me to continue journaling, taking stock of each day, a practice I've continued through most of my life. Often what I wrote was just for me, and was typically just a reflection on the day's happenings, but sometimes I even shared what I had written with him.

But one of our most impactful sessions was where Marshall taught me about the "circle of worry." I watched as he drew, on a yellow legal notepad, a stick figure of a little girl at the top of a circle.

"This is you," he said, pointing to the figure. At the bottom of the page, he drew two more stick figures. "And these are your mom and your dad."

As he drew an arrow around the circle, pointing to the stick figures of my mom and dad, he explained, "When you worry about your family, they in turn worry about you"—he completed the circle—"which makes you worry about them, and them worry about you." He completed another circle. The pen flew faster and faster around the paper as the circles of worries continued, resulting in a mess of circles on the page. My nine-year-old mind understood the main idea—this wasn't helping anyone. It is a learning I carry with me to this day.

Marshall was a constant in my life for almost two years, offering stability and a safety net as I navigated my anxiety. But then Marshall let me know our next meeting would be our last—he was leaving private practice to go back into the elementary school setting. And so, I was back at square one.

Instead of finding another counselor, my mom made the strategic decision to take me to the psychiatrist in the building next door to where I'd been meeting with Marshall. This setup meant I only needed to make the trek to Sioux Falls once a month to maintain access to my antidepressant prescription. Over the course of a few months, I tried a few medications, eventually landing on Paxil.

I didn't share that I was taking the medication with many people as I was somewhat ashamed that I needed to take medication in order to be "normal" or happy.

It felt as though it was a secret, not only for me, but for my family as well. Many of my friends had stay-at-home moms, doting caregivers who carted them from activity to activity and picked them up from school with snacks in hand.

My mom was an in-home daycare provider, hustling to make ends meet and managing three kids mostly on her own. I so badly wanted my mom's love and approval, and antidepressants sure weren't helping my cause.

I remember one friend in particular who walked into our fifth-grade classroom beaming one morning.

"I had the most amazing experience last night. I shared with my mom that I was committing my life to Jesus. We stayed up super late talking about what this meant for me and how proud she was of this step I had taken," she said.

I had had my own revelation recently, but I kept it to myself: My relationship with my mom had never been what I had hoped—we weren't close. Was committing my life to Jesus what she had been waiting for from me? Was this why she had been frustrated with me, and so unengaged? If I took this step, maybe I'd get to spend the wee morning hours connecting with my mom as she shared her pride in my decision. Although I worked diligently to say the right prayers and attend the right church services, I'd never quite felt God's presence. Maybe this would help.

That night, I waited until I could tell my brothers were sleeping in the room next to mine. Then I snuck downstairs to where my mom was sitting at the kitchen table.

"Mom?" I said tentatively, hopefully.

"Yeah, what do you need, Cole?"

"I've decided to commit my life to Jesus," I proclaimed proudly, smiling as I waited for her affirmation. This had to be what she had been waiting for.

She looked away from the TV screen for a moment and paused before saying, "That's nice. Go to bed."

My heart sank. I turned around and walked back through the dark living room, trudging up the stairs. That wasn't the golden ticket I had hoped for after all.

I'd always felt my mom thought I should just be able to get over it, whatever "it" was, and that my tears were ultimately a sign of weakness, even at such a young age.

I stayed on the antidepressants through seventh grade, and did as well as an awkward middle-school girl being raised in an alcoholic household could do. But things at home changed pretty drastically when my dad decided to go to in-patient, Christian-based treatment for his alcoholism. He was gone throughout the month of December, which meant he missed Christmas. It was most definitely not the most wonderful time of year, that year.

He came back home on January first—a new person in a new year. But all of a sudden my dad was sober, and wanting to be involved.

He was home and fully present for dinner at night.

"How was your day, Cole?" he asked one time.

"Fine," I responded, trying to hide my annoyance at his questioning.

"What are you learning about in English class right now?"

"I don't know," I responded, not wanting to engage.

I didn't know what he wanted from me. Coupled with me being an angsty thirteen-year-old, the daily questions were new territory, and I wasn't happy about it.

"What would you guys think about going roller skating this

weekend in Sheldon? I've got some new friends I'd like you to meet. One of them has a couple of kids about James's age."

My brothers couldn't contain their enthusiasm. But it sounded awful to me—meeting new people, especially people that were in "the program," with kids who were more than four years younger than me? No thanks.

But this was my new dad—gung ho about taking his kids roller skating on the weekends.

There were more changes: Dad slept on a cot in our toy room in the basement, which served as a daily reminder for my brothers (who were then five and nine) and me that something wasn't quite right.

That summer, without school to distract me, I cried uncontrollably throughout the day, sporting swollen eyes and dealing with sobs racking my body at inopportune moments. My mom, who was by then a teacher and home with my brothers and me during the day, hit her breaking point a few weeks into our summer break.

The air was sticky with the heat and humidity that is typical of an Iowa summer; cool air only creeped into the evening hours.

"What is wrong with you? You've got to stop," my mom commanded me as I was crying uncontrollably yet again.

"That doesn't help anything," my dad told her.

I choked back a sob, looking at the floor.

"If you don't stop, I'm going to take you to the hospital," she threatened.

I didn't have anything to lose.

"Let's go," I retorted.

I meant it, and so did she. So my brothers stayed home with my Dad, and my Mom and I drove the ninety minutes to the psychiatric hospital in Sioux Falls, South Dakota. My stay was short-lived, but the twenty-four hours I was there were formative. I learned that shoelaces could be a device of death and were taken away upon entry, and that "crazy" people didn't always look crazy—they were just like me.

After spending the night in the hospital, the next day my mom and dad appeared for a meeting with my new doctor—I didn't know his name. I wondered where my brothers were. We sat at a long, mahogany table with black leather chairs. The doctors in their white coats sat across from us, and I was situated between my parents. I felt small.

"How are you feeling, Nicole?"

"I'm alright," I responded.

I kept my answers short, especially with this doctor I didn't even know.

"Why is it that you think you're here?"

"Because I cry a lot of the time and worry about things that don't really happen."

"What do you worry about?"

"Everything."

"And what do you cry about?"

"I don't know."

The doctor looked to my parents. "And what's going on at home? Any potential causes for anxiety?"

They got into the details of my father's alcoholism, his "abandonment" of the family during treatment, and his unsatisfactory return, at least according to my mom, who wasn't willing to forgive him.

"I don't get any support from him," she told the doctor.

"Well you need to figure things out, and quickly. Because you're tearing this girl apart."

The doctor looked to the young woman beside him in a white coat, to me, and finally to my parents.

"Are you going to work at this or aren't you?" the doctor demanded.

It was silent for a moment before my mom responded: "I want a divorce."

It got quiet.

"Would you mind if I spoke with your parents for a few minutes? Jessica would love to talk to you in the hallway," the doctor asked me.

I looked at the young woman next to the doctor. She didn't look like a doctor, aside from the white coat. I nodded my head and followed this brunette girl in a blue sweater and a white coat out the door where we sat on the green carpet.

Making small talk was easy—I've always been able to do surface level.

"So, what do you like to do for fun?" my new friend Jessica asked.

"I really like to read, and I play basketball and softball too."

"Oh! I played softball when I was little and all throughout college," Jessica replied.

Although I couldn't distinguish the words, I could hear my parents screaming at each other over the doctor in the white coat.

"How about we go for a walk?" Jessica asked.

I followed as she stood up, and then we walked down the hall to the nurses' station as I considered what I'd heard.

Once the doctor had helped my parents to the decision of divorce, I was discharged from the hospital, anticipating a new normal to come in the weeks and months ahead.

On the ride home, I heard Harvey Danger's *Flagpole Sitta* for the first time:

> *Put me in the hospital for nerves*
> *And they had to commit me*

You told them all I was crazy
They cut off my legs, now I'm an amputee,
   God damn you
I'm not sick but I'm not well
And I'm so hot 'cause I'm in hell[1]

My thirteen-year-old brain had never related to a song so well. My parents got divorced a few months later, and my dad moved to a tiny apartment in the neighboring town. We attempted normalcy for months, with my brothers and I moving between different homes within our small town. We saw my dad on Tuesday nights and every other weekend, until my mom, my brothers, and I finally made the big move away from our home town.

Even in the late nineties, divorce was a stain on my mother, my brothers, and me in our insular, Christian, conservative community. If my dad had been abusive, she would have had a socially sanctified reason to leave. But she didn't have that luxury.

I think we were often considered "at-risk" kids in many people's eyes and, in some cases, our friends' parents didn't want their kids to interact with us. Others friends' parents thought of us as charity cases, and gave us special dinners and playdates.

So my mom made the decision to leave. We moved near Des Moines, a city of 250,000 people, which was the biggest city in the state. After packing up our home for the sixth time, we moved four hours away from my dad and the only town I had ever known.

I didn't know it at the time, but the fresh start was exactly what I needed, and what my family needed. I'll be forever grateful to my mom for making that decision.

But even with the move, I maintained my anxiety, depression, and need for control. Growing up in an alcoholic home, I never knew what to expect. I'd learned that I could stop the fighting by going downstairs at night, and that, if I went to the bar with my dad, I could monitor his drinking and do my best to control the situation. I carried this weight with me wherever I went, and it played a role in all aspects of my life, even into adulthood.

School was how I gained the affirmation I so desperately sought. I wasn't an amazing athlete, but I played basketball and softball, and kept stats for the boys' soccer team. I signed up for speech, student government, and choir. In high school, I became the junior homecoming queen and the senior class president, and, in college, I was the student body president—the first and only female to hold the title in more than a decade.

My mom never seemed to be impressed, and in some cases she wasn't even supportive of my activities. She worked long hours and sometimes multiple jobs to support three kids, so an afternoon softball game wasn't often a priority. My vanity, coifing my hair daily and perfecting my lip gloss, definitely wasn't high on her list of things to validate.

My dad, on the other hand, was the epitome of the midwestern farmer, and ensured I knew that humility was of the utmost importance. "If you need to tell someone you're the best at something, you're probably not. Let other people tell you," he'd say.

And so that's what I did. I happily received my affirmations and accolades from others: my teachers, my friends' parents, school leadership, and my coaches.

Throughout high school, college, and beyond, my mental health remained relatively stable. If I could control everything—my appearance, my grades, my "status" among my peers—I felt okay. And I managed to do so successfully, leaning on medication and counseling when needed.

But after the moment Samuel's mom walked into my classroom with that belt, nothing was the same.

chapter three

Shantice would know it was me.

But I knew what I had to do—I had to make the child abuse report to Child Protective Services (CPS), even though I was certain she would know I was the one who had made the call.

It was only a few hours after the abuse had taken place, and my vision of what I believed to be right and wrong was clear.

My tears flowed freely as I dialed, my voice cracking as I explained the situation to the stranger on the line as best I could.

"Ma'am, you have nothing to be worried about—this is an anonymous call."

"I know, but I know she's going to know it was me who made the report."

"I can assure you no details about who provided this information will be supplied."

"Thanks."

"Is there anything else you'd like to share today?"

Aside from my disdain for the systems that allow things like this to happen and the inexplicable lack of support I've received? I thought.

"No, that's it," I said, swallowing.

The school system had failed Samuel. Mr. Kemper and Ms. King had failed him too. I felt it was my responsibility as his teacher to ensure he was safe. I needed to trust that the CPS system would protect him because, ultimately, I couldn't do it on my own.

By this time, I'd shared Samuel's story multiple times: with two trusted teacher friends at school during lunch; the teacher whose room was next door to mine (she'd heard the abuse but, despite being a veteran teacher, she said she didn't know how to respond in the moment); both of my parents; my roommate, Anna; and my TFA program director. I'd also told Mick, another TFA teacher who taught at a different school and was quickly becoming a friend. Sharing the story helped me process what had happened, though I was surprised by the varied responses I received.

My roommate, who was in law school, had asked: "You know you're a mandatory reporter, right?"

Rachel, a middle-school teacher at Carver who was also with TFA, had responded: "What the actual fuck? Are you for real?"

My TFA program director had offered this helpful advice: "Well, you're going to have to decide if you're going to report it or not—I can't tell you what to do."

Mick was incredulous. "That," he paused, "is insane. What are you going to do?" he asked.

Ultimately, I knew in the pit of my stomach exactly what I needed to do. I made the call, both literally and figuratively, and knew I had done the right thing. But I sure didn't feel any weight lifted from my shoulders. If anything, I slept more poorly that first night, thinking through the potential repercussions of what I had done.

The next day, I decided to share my experience with one last person at my school. I tracked down Mr. Robertson, one of the school's paraprofessionals, in the morning before school started. Sharing the experience with him was strategic: he was six-foot-two and two hundred and fifty pounds, so I hoped he could offer me protection should I need it. I was embarrassed to ask, but he seemed to understand.

"I can't say for certain I'll be able to stay close, as ultimately Ms. King tells me where to go and what classrooms need me most, but I think I should be able to make the ask if I need to, to stay in your classroom even if it's just before and after school the next couple days," he said.

I knew the day after the incident would be too soon for CPS to have shown up at Samuel's house, but I sensed the impending storm, the thunder rolling in the distance, as I anticipated an onslaught of anger. Having Mr. Robertson hanging around offered some peace of mind, albeit small.

My classroom had definitively shifted since the experience with Shantice. My students had been visibly shaken, as had I. I went through our daily routine attempting normalcy, and the day concluded without anything atypical. Maybe things were going to be alright.

When the school day was over, I walked over to Miss Eleanor's small, pink home, which was across the street. Miss Eleanor provided in-home daycare to numerous students at the school, as well as their siblings. Twice a week, with permission from their parents, I would go and pick up four of my students—Alexis, Marquand, Anton, and Samuel—and bring them back to the classroom for ongoing tutoring and support. This wasn't something I was getting any extra compensation for. We had been taught in our TFA summer training that if we wanted to ensure significant academic gains for our students, not everything could be done in a normal school day. We needed to be relentless.

The students all walked hand in hand with me in the center as they eagerly shared their plans for how they wanted to spend their personal hour with me.

"Miss C, can I use the computer to play a game?"

"Miss C, you still got those markers that are smelly? Can I draw with them?"

"You guys can absolutely have some free time, but we're each going to practice each of your reading books first," I responded.

The four simultaneously moaned.

Samuel seemed a bit more withdrawn but it was hard to tell. In the six weeks I'd known him, he'd had flashes of excitement during what was typically a pretty sullen demeanor.

"Miss C, are you going to come back and teach us next year?" Anton asked.

"Oh, we're not even halfway through this year yet!" I replied, knowing I hadn't really answered the question.

The truth was I couldn't think about next year quite yet—I had to get through this one first. And I didn't feel right lying to a second grader but I didn't actually know if I'd be back.

Our after-school time was a nice reprieve from the day and always flew by. I felt like the students saw me as more of a person during small-group or one-on-one work—there was something about the school day, when the class was at critical mass, that just felt so different. I spent fifteen minutes with each student, saving Samuel for last. There were so many things I wanted to ask him, but I followed his lead.

"How are you doing, Samuel?" I asked.

"Fine."

"What book do we have to read today?"

"*The Three Wishes.*"

"And what do you think this book will be about?"

"Wishes."

So, it was going to be like this: strictly business. As much as I wanted to learn more about Samuel, and to support him in whatever ways he needed, I couldn't force him to open up.

We read the book together, working through the challenging words and preparing for the reading test later in the week.

My after-school tutoring group finished our time together and began shutting down the computers and cleaning up. I packed my backpack, and the five of us walked arm-in-arm back across the street to Ms. Eleanor's home. Marquand, Anton, and Alexis chattered incessantly among and over one another, while Samuel shuffled his feet.

Marquand creaked opened the gray aluminum door of Ms. Eleanor's home, pushing the heavy inner door over the brown shag carpet. The four disappeared into the darkness as I stuck my head inside, eyes adjusting to the light.

"Ms. Eleanor!" There was no response. "Ms. Eleanor, they're back!" I called out.

I heard Ms. Eleanor's padded slippers walking across the kitchen linoleum, her heavyset body swaying into focus in the door frame.

"Alright, thank you, Miss C! We'll see you next week—have a good weekend!"

"Sounds great. Thanks, Ms. Eleanor. You too!"

I could tell she was still undecided about me, but I was slowly gaining her trust. It probably helped that I was offering an additional hour of free childcare. Ms. Eleanor always had a varying number of kids, from infants to teenagers, that she was responsible for watching throughout the week—and, for all I knew, through the weekends as well.

I walked back across the street to the Carver parking lot, tossed my backpack in the backseat of my small white car, and headed home.

I had another fitful night of sleep with my anxiety running rampant. It was only Tuesday, which meant there was plenty of time for Child Protective Services to show up before the end of the week.

What if Shantice came to my classroom and got physical with me? I was athletic, but there was no way I'd really be able to defend myself against her. What if she brought a weapon? My thoughts swirled as I fought to find rest.

Unlike the majority of the schools in the district, Carver didn't have an off-duty police officer or even a security guard, and although we had a security system to buzz people in, the front office staff wouldn't think anything of a parent coming by. I hadn't told Ms. King about my report, and I wasn't going to flag it for the front office. So I was on my own. If Shantice wanted to confront me, she would definitively be able to do so.

I did what I could to cope. I was in the habit of journaling when I felt overwhelmed, recounting my days and the frequent lunacy of what I experienced. So I prayed, asking for God's guidance, that his will be done, and that he protect me from harm. I read the Bible, immersing myself in the word so that I might more clearly see the path I vehemently wanted to believe God laid before me. I hadn't found my church home in Kansas City, but I knew I needed the community.

On Wednesday, I cried as I drove to school, not because I was overly sad or upset, but because it was a cathartic release that had almost become a daily ritual. The twelve-minute drive—from my apartment on the cusp of the old town, trendy, Westport neighborhood to the school—was not nearly long enough to flush out my emotions, but it would have to do.

The drive was disheartening as I witnessed concentrated race and poverty, the crack cocaine epidemic running rampant, and a plethora of overgrown lawns and chain-link fences framing vacant homes and empty lots.

In the early mornings it was quiet, birds chirping as the sun rose, dew still on the grass as I drove down the one-way street. By evening, there were groups standing on porches and near multiple cars in gravel driveways and in front of homes, bass bumping as they watched the young white girl drive through the 'hood, likely wondering what purpose I served.

While I lived in the city from 2008 to 2010, it was estimated that one in ten homes were vacant and, in some neighborhoods, including where Carver was situated, that figure rose to one in four.[2]

Kansas City has a rich history, and not all of it is pleasant. Within my first week of being in the city, all the members of the TFA–Kansas City corps learned about Troost Avenue—the city's tangible racial and economic dividing line. The physical land itself has a dark history, first being traced back to the Osage Nation as a canoe trail in the 1700s. Upon the native peoples' displacement in the early 1800s, the area around Troost Avenue was sold to the Reverend James Porter, before Kansas City was even formally established. This large swath of land later became a slave plantation where between forty and one hundred slaves worked to clear the land of the forests that would subsequently become "millionaire's row" after the Civil War, as Porter parceled out and sold his land.[3]

Seeking to appeal to a larger consumer base, Porter began building moderately priced homes during the real estate boom of the 1880s, but when the economic crisis of the early 1890s hit, housing prices dropped, forcing the sale of many of these homes to people in the Black community. The community continued to grow, and was one of the only areas with access to education beyond elementary school for Black families.[3]

By the 1930s, redlining—the illegal practice of banks and government refusing to provide financial services to an individual, typically someone in the Black community—began. Blockbusting also found a foothold in the community, with real estate moguls instilling fear in white families that minorities would move into the neighborhood and decrease property values, which then led to white people selling their homes at low prices. These white families began fleeing to upscale communities and subdivisions, like that created by J. C. Nichols, that not only boasted parks, sprawling lawns, and one of the nation's first shopping centers, but that also included racially restrictive clauses in the deed restrictions—covenants that quite literally prohibited Black families from moving into certain neighborhoods.[3]

The outcomes of these practices could be seen with a keen level of clarity in the neighborhood surrounding Carver Elementary, where the large majority of the school's students resided. In the 1930s, the neighborhood was a thriving community of mainly white, working-class families. With the desegregation of schools in the landmark Brown vs. Board of Education decision in 1954, and Troost being one of the boundaries of the school district, white flight to the suburbs burgeoned and continued for decades. By the time the 2000 census occurred, the neighborhood was 96 percent Black.[4]

This was definitively reflected in the student population at Carver where less than 1 percent of students identified as white. As a young woman who had grown up in a largely homogenous, white, Christian, conservative community, teaching in this environment was a shift nobody could have prepared me for.

After pulling into the empty school parking lot that Wednesday morning, avoiding the potholes as best I could, I turned off the ignition and just sat for a few moments, taking a deep breath before opening the door and heading toward my classroom. I used my key to open the heavy blue door, and held it open for my friend Rachel who had pulled into the lot shortly after me.

Rachel taught eighth-grade science, and her year hadn't started off smoothly either. Although her classroom was downstairs, she followed me upstairs to mine to talk.

"How ya doing?" she asked as we walked.

"Ah, I'm fine, hanging in there, I guess! How about you?"

"Same. Any news on that student and his mom?"

"No. Well, not really. Ms. King said she didn't think the mom was abusive, but—"

"Are you kidding me?" Rachel interrupted me.

"Yeah, so, don't share this please, but I ended up making the call to CPS as we're mandated reporters."

"Wow, that's heavy." I could hear the sympathy in Rachel's voice.

At least she *gets it,* I thought.

"Yeah. I'm pretty anxious about the mom knowing it was me," I admitted.

"Oh, I'm sure you'll be fine. There's no way she could really know it was you. You're not the only one who knew about it. A kid in the class could have even told their parents."

I nodded. "Thanks. You know, we should drive to work together some days if our after-school schedules align," I suggested.

Our condos were only two doors down from one another. In fact, there were six TFA teachers in our complex, three of whom worked at Carver.

"Yeah, I'd totally be game. Let's chat!" she said.

"Great! Well, have a good day! It's hump day, but who's counting days, right?" I tried to force a chuckle.

Rachel laughed and waved goodbye.

As I walked into my classroom, I thought about how grateful I was that I'd found a friend at Carver. Then I unloaded my bag and started preparing for the day by writing the day's objectives on the board in chalk, double-checking that I had the correct books and materials ready and easily accessible, and pulling down the small chairs from the tops of the desks and arranging them neatly.

Destiny, one of my most vocal students, walked into the classroom and proclaimed her presence: "Good morning, Miss C!"

She ran over and gave me a hug before putting her coat and bag inside the small movable coat closet that housed all the students' things. She then began helping me take the chairs down off the desks.

Slowly, more students began to trickle in. I realized I had forgotten to track down Mr. Robertson since I'd been more focused on my interaction with Rachel than with a potential run-in with Shantice.

"Destiny, have you had breakfast yet? Can you make sure you head down with the others?" I asked.

Before she could respond, I saw her look to the doorway as Shantice barreled toward me with Samuel in tow.

"What gives you the right to talk to anyone about how I discipline my son?" she shouted as her eyes shot daggers. By this point, her face was inches from mine and her hands were clenched as if she was ready to pounce.

In a venomous voice, she hissed, "You don't have anything to say?"

My heart was in my chest—I couldn't breathe, and I certainly couldn't speak.

My students continued to enter our classroom, now quietly and curiously watching to see how this was going to play out.

No longer holding back, Shantice yelled in my face: "Who do you think you are?!"

"Shantice, I'm going to have to ask you to leave," said Mr. Robertson, who was suddenly at my side.

Shantice turned to him. "Do you even know what she did?" she scoffed.

"This is not the time or place. I need you to go," he said, motioning to the door.

"Don't you touch me," Shantice said, looking at his hand as if it were on fire, and then looking at me through narrowed eyes.

The kids were all watching with dumbfounded looks on their faces. I felt exactly as they looked.

Ms. King walked in the door as students walked by my room, conspicuously glancing in to see what the noise was about.

"What seems to be the trouble in here?" asked Ms. King.

"Shantice was just leaving," Mr. Robertson explained, as Shantice brushed past Ms. King without a word and walked out the door. The other students slowly began to file into the hallway—now that the show was over, they wanted to get their breakfast before it was too late.

Ms. King looked to me for an explanation, her eyes intense and expectant.

"I-I made a call to CPS to report what happened on Monday. I had to. I'm a mandatory reporter, and I needed to protect my students."

She *tsk*ed her teeth at me and looked at the floor before looking me in the eyes. The shame was immediate, even though I was an adult being scolded by this elderly principal.

"I'm really disappointed in you."

I had wanted her approval so badly, and now I didn't know what to think. My eyes welled with tears as I clenched my jaw, doing everything I could to not cry in front of Ms. King, Mr. Robertson, and the students lingering in the classroom.

"You talk too much. You sure didn't need to share this with Mr. Robertson or anybody else."

I didn't have a response for her—there was nothing to be said. Instead, I used all the energy I could muster to contain the sob that was building in the back of my throat.

Ms. King turned and walked out the door.

"Are you going to be okay?" Mr. Robertson asked, looking at me with sympathy but also with the fear of a young man who wasn't sure what to do with the girl on the verge of tears in front of him.

The tears finally welled over. "Fine," I replied as I quickly wiped them away. "Thank you. I don't know what I would have done without you."

"It wasn't anything. I'll try to stay close, but I really don't think you have anything to worry about moving forward. It's unlikely she'll be back."

"Truly, thanks again, Mr. Robertson."

And then he turned and was gone, and I was left with the remaining students, many who had seen every moment of the critical event that had transpired in the previous ten minutes. More students began to trickle in the door as we neared our start time.

It felt as though any authority I had somehow maintained after the first incident with Shantice was gone. The day became another battle for my students—and for me, frankly. It had been my job to create a safe space for them, to ensure they had access to opportunities to learn and grow, and I had already failed. I called in sick the next day and then again on Friday—I needed the time to figure out if I could go back.

chapter four

I hadn't started my service for Teach for America at George Washington Carver Elementary. In fact, after accepting my placement in Kansas City, I had originally started my time with TFA with an understanding that I would be a kindergarten teacher at a bougie charter school. This original placement wasn't quite what I had anticipated or even signed up for, but I wasn't going to complain.

Before that, I had taught kindergarten to a demure group of summer school students in Phoenix, Arizona. It was a shock to learn—a few weeks before school started—that my placement had changed to Carver and that I'd been bumped to teach second grade. All preparations had been for naught.

But I need to go back even further to share the real ambition behind my desire to teach.

It all started when manual labor seemed better than going home to my mom's incessant questioning. As a junior at a small liberal arts college in central Iowa, I knew if I went home for spring break I wouldn't hear the end of it: What are your job prospects with an English major? And why journalism—how is that going to help? You need a job that gives you benefits, and you don't get benefits as a writer. You need to find something stable. I just don't know how you're going to make it with a liberal arts degree. You don't want to be a nanny for the rest of your life, do you?

None of these questions had answers that would satisfy my mother, and often the next question had begun before I was even done answering the first.

With another year before I would graduate, I figured I had some time to figure that out. I'd stacked my classes and course loads, double majoring in English and journalism/mass communications. To my mother's chagrin, I'd also added two extremely practical and marketable minors: music and women's studies. I was on track to graduate within four years but I had no idea where I was headed, and that was a problem.

The desire for perfection was very real for me, and only compounded in college. I maintained a 3.8 grade point average, was elected as a class representative in student government year after year (and was student body president my senior year), and was appointed the copy editor of my college newspaper.

After serving as a resident assistant (RA) my sophomore year, I was promoted to student hall director, which included managing thirteen sophomore RAs. This meant I had my own room, albeit in a freshman dorm.

With all these activities, including working as a nanny for a local family—not to mention, you know, attending college classes—I was stretched thin. I had weaned off Paxil, my antidepressant of choice, the previous year. I didn't like feeling like I needed to take medication to be happy.

I felt the familiar creep of anxiety more and more often and fought it by seeking control anywhere I could find it.

Things came to a head as I led the planning for what we called Safe Block, where we invited the community into our dorms so students could pass out candy for Halloween. There were an overwhelming number of variables we needed to consider before welcoming local children into our college dorms.

I thought about all of them as I hopped into the shower and prepared for another marathon of a day. I mentally ran through my itinerary: classes in the morning, drive to Des Moines to nanny in the afternoon, back to campus to our basement computer lab to copyedit our college newspaper and ensure it was ready for print, then homework and prep for the same thing the next day.

The hot water provided some relief as I dove into the logistics of Safe Block, thinking through the budget and associated costs, and all the what-ifs that could occur with kids walking through the dorms. It was a lot to handle, and I didn't feel particularly supported by my boss.

I turned the water off, wrapped myself in a towel and stepped onto my rug. As I did, my eyes began to go dark, as though I'd entered a tunnel. I grabbed the shower door and slowly lowered to my knees, and then my back. At first, I thought my shower had just been too hot, but this was different.

My heart felt like it was pounding out of my chest and, as I lay on my back looking at the ceiling, I realized I couldn't move. In the moment, I honestly felt like I was going to die, and my mind went to those who would find me lifeless on the floor wearing only a towel.

I don't know how long I lay on the floor, but it felt like an hour—in reality, I'm sure it was minutes. I managed to get my breathing to calm, which in turn calmed the physical response my body was having. I was able to sit up and get a drink of water. I put on my clothes and makeup, grabbed my books and backpack, and walked to class as though nothing had happened.

I wouldn't realize until months later that I'd had a panic attack.

I sat alone in my college dorm room as Rihanna's "Umbrella" softly played from my desktop computer speakers. I leaned back in my chair, popping another Sour Patch Kid into my mouth.

The day before spring break was the peak of the semester, and I was more concerned about the prospect of spending a week at home with my mom in the coming days than I was at the blank, white, Microsoft Word document on my computer screen staring back at me. I was supposed to be finalizing an eight-page paper on Thackeray's *Vanity Fair* for my Victorian literature class.

Most students avoided Professor Lisa McCandless's courses if they could. And after she gave me the first two *B*s of my academic career, I was determined to do better on this *Vanity Fair* paper.

But, first, procrastination. What else could I focus on other than Lisa McCandless's midterm? I opened my email and there, sitting in my inbox, was my out.

ALTERNATIVE SPRING BREAK TRIPS! LAST CALL!

Although my parents were able to help a bit with my tuition, I wanted to keep my loans at a minimum. So I'd scheduled my classes back-to-back as much as possible, in either the mornings or the afternoons, and nannied for a local family during the hours when I wasn't in school. I had originally planned to spend my weeklong spring break working my two jobs—nannying and staffing the kitchen of the same nursing home where I'd worked during high school—at full-time hours.

An "alternative spring break trip," as labeled by our religious life community, was doublespeak for manual labor of some sort.

And yet, that was somehow more appealing than spending time at home and managing extended work hours. So I did something irresponsible and hit "reply."

> *If there's still a spot available, I'd love to be part of the trip to Mississippi.*
> *Thanks,*
> *Nicole*

My small, liberal arts college in Iowa was big on volunteerism. I wasn't. My ties to the religious life community who sponsored the trip weren't deep. I'd tried again and again to "build my relationship with God," but I still didn't experience "him" in the ways my peers did. I'd finished reading the Bible through, in its entirety, and didn't feel any wiser spiritually.

I wasn't quite sure what I was signing up for with this trip, who I'd be spring breaking with, or what I hoped to gain from the experience. I did know it wasn't home.

The mom of the kids I nannied for would understand.

I pressed "send."

My mother wasn't thrilled with my change in plans, especially because it meant I wouldn't be bringing in additional money. I'd grown up in a home constantly pressed for money, so my financial situation always concerned my mom.

But, two days later, I was crammed into a fifteen-person passenger van with people I vaguely knew, rubbing elbows and making uncomfortable small talk on a cross-country road trip. The sleeping bags and duffels were piled so high that they obscured the view of our trip leader and driver, who was only a few years older than the college kids seated behind her.

The interstate system cut through the plains of Iowa and Missouri, leading to and through St. Louis and Memphis, which were bigger cities than most of us had seen. Sixteen hours later, the changing landscape told us we were entering into the aftermath of Hurricane Katrina—which was, at the time, the largest hurricane ever to make landfall in the U.S.—in southern Mississippi.

Although the town was thirty miles inland from the coast, the effects of the hurricane were devastating: the roof of the local community college's art building had been ripped off, and debris was scattered for miles. The repercussions from the storm continued to ripple through the community in various ways after the storm, even though we arrived eight months after it occurred. With the nearest movie theater more than fifty miles away, a car full of teens had been killed in a nighttime auto accident just a few weeks before. This was one of the reasons we were there: to build a central community space for teens to gather, so they didn't have to travel fifty miles to find a place to hang out.

In the five days I spent in Mississippi, I cleared debris—mostly fallen trees and branches—and helped build a barn that was to be a gathering place for area youth. Four of us deemed ourselves the "chainsaw gang," taking on the work of clearing an overgrown area in front of the barn. There were hours filled with the buzz of the idling chain, the screech of the laboring engine as it pulsed through wood, and the familiar crack of trees and branches as we sawed them into pieces that could be moved and disposed of. Within forty-eight hours, we had completed the work they had assumed would take five days.

I was exhausted by end of each day, and yet, when we came

home to the small white house where we were staying, I wasn't ready to go to sleep.

The ten of us were in sleeping bags and on couches in the sparsely furnished living and dining rooms. The sleeping arrangements led to late-night guitar playing and walks through the tiny town. As this was a trip sponsored by the college's religious life community, there was no shortage of worship songs and discussion about God. And though I'd wanted to escape any discussion about my future, we undoubtedly landed on conversing about what made us happy.

Looking back, I know now that I was in a heavy bout of depression before signing up for this trip. I didn't know myself well enough to understand what made me happy, but I did know this trip and this experience was the happiest I'd been in a long while.

I quickly built friendships with my college acquaintances as well as with the local students and church members. It was one of the first times I had traveled outside of Iowa to a community that was different from where I had been raised. I fostered relationships with individuals who didn't look or speak the way I did, and whose thoughts and life experiences were very different than my own.

I sipped my first taste of sweet tea on a columned, wrap-around porch at a beautiful, Southern estate that had been spared from Katrina's wreckage. For the first time, I gorged myself on macaroni and cheese that wasn't from a blue box, tried black-eyed peas and collard greens, and rejoiced in sweet potato pie.

There was Mr. Travis and Ms. Georgia, our hosts, who were the epitome of Southern hospitality—with frequent iterations of "y'all" and "bless your heart" and "fixins"—offering a direct vision into a different culture than the homogenous town of 1,200 in which I had spent most of my existence.

There was Jamal and Lamonte, two Black students from the

local church. Given the limited diversity on my small college campus in Iowa, just spending time with them and getting a glimpse into their experiences at Gulf Coast Community College was eye-opening.

And then there was Mr. Curtis, who I met the first night we pulled up to the small white house where we would spend the next five days. He was standing on the porch with the others who had come to welcome us.

Mr. Curtis was mute, though his eyes and handshakes welcomed us all the same. He carried a small notebook where he would feverishly scratch out what he had to say, and often communicated his feelings with his hands and his eyes. He was cared for by the church.

As the week progressed, our whole group learned more about Mr. Curtis. We found out that he had remained after the evacuation orders had been given, and that he hadn't spoken since the experience of Hurricane Katrina. There were others we met who had lost their homes, even their livelihoods, but Mr. Curtis had lost his voice.

The following day, we left the little white house for the last time and began our drive to the coast. The group chattered excitedly about all the fun we'd had, how sore our muscles were, and how excited we were for our pit stop on our drive home—Memphis! Beale Street and the Coyote Ugly Saloon (because of the 2000 movie) were high on my list of places to visit.

But as we approached the coast, the chatter was stifled as we all began to experience a much more face-to-face vision of Hurricane Katrina's devastation.

We drove the grid of concrete slabs where houses used to sit, with brick stairs leading to homes that were no longer there. Driving past skeletons of brick buildings, churches, and businesses was sobering—for many, their life's work was gone, as it had become a true "boulevard of broken dreams."

Countless trees were uprooted, leaning against one another, bundled together after the water had left them behind. Many of the trees left standing were marked with a large, green, spray-painted X, indicating they would be removed in the coming months when it became a priority. Branches had been pruned by the intense wind and twenty feet of surging water, leaving behind a shadow of what a tree should be. The branches that remained held debris from the homes they used to shade.

The flagpole in front of the school was bent into an *L* from the strength of the wind. Someone had attached an American flag after the storm.

Despite it being more than eight months after the hurricane made landfall, there were still people living in tent communities—or, if they were lucky, FEMA trailers. These people were the ones who had come out on the other side with their lives; more than 1,800 others had not. These folks had survived Katrina—after either staying behind to bear the brunt of her force or leaving for safety, only to return to nothing. All who remained were determined to rebuild.

It wasn't until after this experience that I would fully comprehend the sheer breadth of the destruction Hurricane Katrina had caused; at the time, she was the most destructive and costly hurricane on record, causing $125 billion in property damages alone, with the total economic impact in Louisiana and Mississippi estimated to be more than $250 billion.

As the van approached the coast, the bobbing heads began to

let go of some of what we had seen. We drove past dozens of wood posts sticking their heads out of the water, no longer supporting docks in the harbor, boats nowhere to be seen.

We found a little parking lot and stopped. I could feel the energy shift as the group excitedly climbed out of the van. For many of us, including me, this would be our first time experiencing the ocean.

All the movies I'd seen had prepared me for a sunny sky reflecting off the clear, blue, sparkling water, the picturesque light waves from the surf creating a series of small crashes as they raced to shore.

But after seeing what she had done with Hurricane Katrina, the gray drear of the sky that day seemed to perfectly reflect uncharacteristic stillness as the water quietly lapped to shore. Losing the sky in the gray and austere expanse of the horizon, I felt small, not because of the immensity in front of me or the beauty of the gray blue, but because of the rage I knew she was capable of.

I've never been a stranger to work, having grown up in a farming community in Iowa, but my experience in Mississippi, was different. While on my grandfather's farm, the work I did ultimately supported me and my family; trudging through the muck and mire of rural Mississippi, and hauling wood and siding to help build a barn for families that had lost so much to Katrina, was supporting a cause much larger than myself. I was helping those who needed it.

I left Mississippi, in that fifteen-passenger van, a different person. I had purpose; it was the happiest I'd ever been.

As soon as we got back to campus, I began researching ways to continue the altruistic high I had experienced.

I found an opportunity to travel to Jamaica, with a church group out of Kansas, which meant I was largely with people I'd never met. I spent most of my time working at a home for troubled teenage girls, and on one of the days we went to an orphanage. When we walked in, multiple crying toddlers tugged on my shorts, asking to be held. I picked one up, but the others still grabbed at my legs. I wept. One of the employees came up to me and told me I needed to stop—the kids didn't understand why I was upset.

I tried to control myself—I was ashamed of my tears, but I was overwhelmed.

When I returned home, I lined up my next experience, and then the next. I volunteered as a staff member at a women's shelter multiple days a week. I helped build a house in Mexico. I volunteered for political campaigns in support of the causes I was passionate about.

These experiences became my job prospects: the Peace Corps, AmeriCorps, the Fulbright scholar program, Teach for America.

I felt like I'd finally discovered what made me happy.

After narrowing my search and application process, I was accepted into both the Peace Corps (to teach English in Turkey) and Teach for America (to teach kindergarten in Kansas City). I accepted the TFA position.

Kansas City was a mere three-hour drive from my home—how different could it really be?

chapter five

"Nobody would blame you if you quit," my mom reassured me after I'd told her what happened with Shantice and Samuel.

"I've never quit anything before, Mom. Part of me thinks this is what I signed up for. Nobody else has quit—I can't be the first."

"How are you going to go back into that school after what happened to that student?" my mom implored.

I paused. It was hard to hear the worry in her voice because I'd asked myself this exact question, and I didn't have a good answer.

"I don't know. But I feel like I have to. It's not these kids' fault. And I'm partway through my master's," I responded, knowing Mom was always one for the logical, prudent argument and that she liked that part of the TFA program included earning my master's degree at a discounted rate.

"Besides, ultimately, I don't want to quit," I said.

The conversation with my dad wasn't much different.

"You don't have to go back; you can just come home," Dad said.

"But Kansas City is my home now. I can't leave Anna without a roommate, or the other teachers, or realistically, the students. Did I tell you they had something like ten long-term substitute teachers the year before I came?"

"Do you think there was a reason for that?"

I couldn't help but chuckle. "That's not fair . . ."

"I'm just saying, it's okay to say you tried your best."

"But if I leave, that's not my best."

"Well," he said, then paused. "Then I think you have your answer."

I had the self-imposed long weekend to waffle between anxiety, guilt, and ultimately dread on Sunday evening as I prepared my lessons for the week.

But when I went back to school on Monday, my students were thrilled to see me, greeting me with hugs galore and what felt like a chorus of "We missed you!"

It's a funny thing, both loving and loathing your job at the same time, but I'd decided I couldn't shirk my commitment. So I focused on one day—and sometimes one hour—at a time.

As days turned into weeks, there were moments of pure insanity. It was hard for me to believe a second-grade boy would even *know* what a condom was, let alone bring one to school to show off to his friends, but Rashaad did. Then there was Ebony, who brought a toy gun; and Izaak, who brought a cigarette. Khalil lashed out often and in multiple ways—climbing on top of student desks and kicking pencil holders and spewing sharpened pencils across the room—in addition to slapping and biting his classmates. He finally broke down during a one-on-one chat.

"I want to be good, Miss C," he wailed as he hit himself in the head with his fists.

I grabbed his arms to prevent him from hurting himself and then, when that wasn't enough to keep him safe, held him tight against my body to physically restrain him.

"I'm stupid. I'm a faggot!" The tears streamed as he wailed.

"Khalil, you aren't any of those things, buddy. Why are you saying that?" I responded with compassion and genuine confusion.

I could feel his anger melt as he quietly responded, "Because, Miss C, I'm a faggot."

It was heartbreaking and overwhelming and incredibly frustrating, all at the same time. I wasn't sure he knew what the word meant, other than that it was always flung in hate. I'd heard the middle school students use the word often, and I knew he did as well.

Later that day, I received a construction paper card with a rose drawn on the front. Inside was a hand-drawn picture of Khalil and me, and a note:

I Love Miss. C. I like Miss C. She is my Friend. I like her. I want to be good.

My heart needed that card. But it still felt like everything I tried to do to help my kids—first Samuel, then Khalil, and then others—floundered.

The physical violence in my classroom, and at Carver Elementary as a whole, began to escalate. The younger, elementary-aged students on the first floor learned of fist fights in the upper grades from their older siblings, or by witnessing them firsthand in the hallways. It wasn't long before punches were thrown in my classroom, by two of my favorite students: Damian and Destiny.

I tried to respond to these incidents in the best way I knew how, by trying to keep as much peace as I could in my own classroom, by talking things out one-on-one with individual students whenever possible, and by providing as much love and support as I could muster.

Amidst the chaos, there was learning too. Teaching students to add—and seeing the lightbulbs go off as they got the hang of their math facts, and more feverishly and excitedly scribbled down the correct answers—was unlike anything I had experienced before. Alexis had come into my classroom with a rudimentary understanding of phonics, but after three months of receiving additional help after school, she had learned to read. It was incredibly rewarding.

This was my classroom, and these were my students. I was determined to do everything I could, day in and day out, to empower them, to ensure they had access to resources, opportunities, and the best education I could offer them. I told myself that even if I wasn't successful at anything else, at least I could be a source of consistency and love.

I had met most of my students' parents during the first few months of school, many at Back-to-School Night, and others via phone as I called home to report both positive and negative behaviors. As we entered October, I wasn't too concerned about the pending parent-teacher conferences, aside from the prospect of seeing Shantice.

I had sent home forms detailing each student's assigned conference time, and mostly looked forward to reconnecting with parents, and sharing the kids' "wins" and areas where they could grow.

On the night before conferences, it was quickly approaching six o'clock when I realized I was one of a few remaining teachers in the building. Janitorial staff had already come and gone, but I had stayed late to make sure my physical classroom reflected the work my students and I had been putting in. The next two days would be full, and I wanted to be sure everything was in order. Each student had a folder with work they were most proud of, including my progress reports and handwritten notes.

As I packed up to go home, I saw the errant form on the floor under a desk. I knew immediately it was one of the notes I had sent home to the parents confirming the time of their parent-teacher conference. My heart immediately dropped. As I walked over to pick it up, the feeling in my gut already told me who the owner was: Samuel Washington.

"Fuck," I muttered aloud.

Of course, the conference time noted was the next morning. Now what? Was this an opportunity to allow the conversation to just "fall through the cracks"? It wasn't my fault—I'd given the form to Samuel. Done all I could. I knew he'd already been picked up from Ms. Eleanor's, so it wasn't possible for me to give the form to Samuel to bring home.

But, again, my moral high ground got in the way. I knew if I didn't call Samuel's house and confirm the time, I'd have to live with the knowledge that I'd done something that ultimately wasn't best for one of my students.

"Fuck," I said, louder this time since there was nobody there to hear me.

I put my bag back down, plopped heavily into the faded, worn, blue office chair, and pulled out the list of family numbers from my desk. I took a deep breath as I began dialing the Washington household.

One ring, two rings, three rings.

Maybe I'd get lucky and it would be Samuel's dad or, even luckier, an answering machine or no response at all.

"Hello?" It was Shantice.

My heart began racing and my breath quickened. Say something, I commanded myself.

"Hi, Shantice. This is Miss C at Carver Elementary, and I just wanted to let you know that unfortunately I found Samuel's parent-teacher conference confirmation form here at school, and wanted to be sure to let you know that his time is tomorrow at 10:30 a.m.," I said so quickly that I suspected she hadn't had time to register it was me.

It was silent for what felt like forever.

"Oh. Okay."

I heard the receiver being placed back in the cradle.

Coulda been worse? I thought.

I grabbed my bag and headed home for the evening—my good deed done.

Carver, on paper, was considered a failing school. In 2008, we were in the midst of the implementation of No Child Left Behind, a law that significantly increased the role of the federal government in holding schools accountable for increasing student achievement. By testing students in grades three through eight, schools' goals were measured through Adequate Yearly Progress or AYP. I had already become very familiar with the chorus of AYP.

"This is the year," Ms. King boasted. "We're going to meet our AYP. We've got full-time teachers in all our classrooms, the supports we need—I just know it. This is the year."

I appreciated her confidence but, upon discovering Carver's track record, I wasn't so sure. We hadn't met AYP in more than five years so the most serious sanctions—Level 5 School Improvement Continuing Restructuring—were already in place. Schools in this phase were permitted to respond in the ways they deemed best, but this could mean replacing staff (yearly staff turnover was awful, which is why there were already eight alternative-certification placements at the school); working with an expert consultant (we had several special, "proven" curricula in place with associated experts to implement them); or reconfiguring school administration and operations.

We had to inform Carver parents of our "restructuring" and Level 5 status, ensure they knew they could attend other schools, and provide additional tutoring services and supports for those students who stayed. Unfortunately, despite implementing all of these changes, I didn't see it making a difference at Carver because the system itself was broken.

Moreover, the school district was the first school in the nation to lose its accreditation in 2000, by failing all Missouri's performance standards.[5] This wasn't a Carver Elementary problem, but seemed a wholly entrenched systemic failure in the city as a whole.

Given these realities, I was surprised by the number of parents who showed up for parent-teacher conferences that day—that long, exhausting day. I'd anticipated that they'd take a long time, but I underestimated how emotionally draining they'd also be.

I appreciated that my most feared conversation—with Samuel's family—was scheduled to happen early in the day because that meant I didn't have to anticipate for hours. And I was even more grateful to see an unfamiliar face, with soft eyes, enter the classroom at 10:30 a.m.

"Hi, I'm Samuel Sr.," he said as he extended his hand.

"I'm Miss Cleveringa," I responded as we shook hands. "Please, feel free to have a seat."

I sat down in the faded, worn, blue office chair, while Samuel's dad sat at the horseshoe table in front of me, in the same seat where his son sat during our tutoring sessions. I pulled out Samuel's folder and opened it as I slid it across the table. I wasn't quite as nervous as I'd thought I'd be—Samuel Sr. seemed to be just as shy, soft spoken, and kind as his son. And I was thrilled to be talking to him one-on-one.

"Well, as you'll see from the progress report, Samuel has been doing well academically, though, as I'm sure you've been made aware, we have had some difficulties with his behavior initially. There have been a number of incidents that have concerned me," I said.

I tended to cut to the chase, and this situation didn't feel like it warranted much small talk. Realistically, with fifteen minutes maximum to be spent discussing each student, we didn't have the time.

"Oh, Shantice has kept me well informed. I know Samuel Jr. may have said some stuff that could have concerned you, but you don't need to worry. We've talked and he's just playin'," Samuel Sr. responded.

"I appreciate that, but this has been ongoing, since the first weeks of school. He looped a jump rope around his neck a few weeks back—"

He cut me off. "Yeah, Shantice let me know. I know he was just playin'. I know my son, and you don't have anything to worry about, Miss C."

"Okay, well I'm happy to support in any way I can—please just let me know what I can do."

"We will sure do that, Miss C."

"I've had a really good time getting to know Samuel. I think we've both really enjoyed the extra tutoring sessions on Tuesdays and Thursdays after school."

"I know he's enjoyed that time as well," Samuel Sr. said kindly.

"And I really have seen improvement from these sessions. As you'll see on his progress report, his reading scores have consistently been climbing. It's great to have him in my reading class."

"That's great, Miss C. We really do appreciate all you do for Samuel."

"I know things have been a little tricky here over the past couple weeks in particular," I said, alluding to the report I had made to CPS about what I had deemed to be abuse.

"You know, Shantice was really surprised to hear from you last night."

Is he changing the subject? I wondered.

"Yeah, I can imagine. I knew it would be unlikely that you'd come if I didn't confirm this time with you though. And I knew I had to do what was best for Samuel," I said.

"And we sure appreciate that, Miss C." He began to rise, picking up the progress report folder and Samuel's work.

I stood up as well, extending my hand to give him a final handshake, and then he walked toward the doorway.

Samuel Sr. looked back before exiting, saying, "Thank you again, Miss C."

"Of course."

And he left.

The remaining parent-teacher conferences over the next forty-eight hours led to a multitude of emotions.

Damian's mom sang my praises, telling me, "You have been a wonderful teacher for Damian, and I could not ask for anything more."

Meeting Rashaad's mom, who was the same age as me, was a bit overwhelming. She asked me when he should be going to bed, what she should do when he talks back, and how to best discipline her son. I felt totally ill-equipped to offer the type of parenting advice she was seeking.

Izaak's dad asked me multiple personal questions during the conference, which I navigated as well as I could. Then he very coyly ended the conference by asking, "Have you been able to get any Arthur Bryant's BBQ yet? Because I'd love to take you."

I kindly declined.

I closed the books on my first parent-teacher conferences, feeling like, all in all, they went okay. The following week, we'd enter the month of November, which meant I was more than halfway done with my first semester of teaching. Better yet, there were multiple school breaks in sight.

The world in 2008 wasn't a particularly stable place to be, particularly as a recent college graduate, with the collapse of the housing bubble and the Great Recession. I was one of the lucky ones who found a job after graduating, and I felt fortunate that I'd be accepted into the competitive Teach for America program.

Though my first months of teaching hadn't been kind, I was learning to manage my new reality and, with Barack Obama's historic victory that made him the forty-fourth president of the United States, momentum seemed headed in the right direction.

I had never been particularly lucky in my romantic relationships, and this was most apparent when I compared myself to the majority of my high school friends who had married their childhood sweethearts or found their partners in college, but things were looking up in that arena.

Mick was also a Teach for America teacher, but I hadn't made the greatest first impression. I had embraced the mantra of "work hard, party harder" while in college and I had continued that trend in my postgrad life. After a night of particularly drunken shenanigans at one of the first TFA parties, I had stupidly thrown myself at him knowing full well he had a girlfriend.

He very gracefully declined my advances. Mortified, I apologized profusely the next day, as I had unfortunately not blacked out during the blatant rejection.

And yet, I'd felt comfortable with Mick quickly, sharing the details of my experience with Samuel, his family, and the ongoing repercussions. He'd been a big support, talking me through my emotions and outwardly encouraging me to "choose to do the right thing."

Mick had very quickly become a normal and welcome presence

in my weekend party crew, and we strategically ensured we were at the same places at the same times.

It's important to understand what type of person joins Teach for America as a corps member. In 2008, the organization received almost 25,000 applications and, after an extensive screening and interview process, fewer than 7 percent of those who applied were accepted into the program that year. Many, if not most, of our fifty-person, Kansas City corps had stereotypical, type-A personalities, which meant we were all extremely motivated and competitive high achievers—and were all in one place, together.

Drinking, for many of the teachers, was a release of the incredible dysfunction we experienced daily in our classrooms and within our schools.

"We made it! Another Friday!" Tess said as she hugged me.

Tess was a third-grade teacher at Carver and had quickly become a fixture in our weekend crew. We were at Tomfooleries, again, a bar that had quickly become a regular spot for several of our corps members.

More and more teachers filtered in, and each empty hand quickly filled with a drink.

"Man, this week was a rough one," Rachel shared as she pulled up a chair to the small table we'd commandeered.

"Anything in particular?" I prodded.

"Honestly, just the normal: kids walking out of class, refusing to engage, and Ms. King's complete lack of support. She is the worst," Rachel confessed.

"I'm glad I'm not the only one who thinks so," I said in solidarity.

I felt a hand on my shoulder and looked back to find Mick. I stood to give him a hug.

"So great to see you!" I said.

"You too! I'm gonna go grab a drink. Save a seat for me?" he asked.

"You got it!"

Tess gave me a knowing eyebrow raise while Rachel jabbed me in the ribs.

"Looks like that's going well, huh?" Rachel joked.

"Just friends." I laughed, secretly hoping for more.

I had never liked beer but found a quick affinity for the local Boulevard Wheat from Kansas City's Boulevard Brewing Company. My drink of choice was usually still a dirty Shirley Temple—gin, Sprite, and grenadine—but I'd often mix the two, downing four or five drinks in a night, which was quite a bit for my small frame. This night was no different.

By midnight, Mick was offering to host an after-party at his apartment with the small crew that was remaining.

"You wanna come?" he asked me.

"Sure," I said, trying to play it cool.

It was only Rachel, Anna, me, and Jason (one of Mick's close TFA friends) remaining. The five of us walked back to Mick's place where we continued drinking and listening to music.

I began to live more and more for these weekends with Mick, seeking to leave the dysfunction of the week behind.

Despite it feeling incongruent with our weekend debauchery, I also began spending more and more Sundays at church, trying multiple ways to release the heaviness of the work week .

A friend from my past had re-emerged in Kansas City. Mindy had come to Kansas City to become part of a Christian evangelical movement at the International House of Prayer, or IHOP for short. Based on a mission focused on offering prayer and worship twenty-four hours a day, seven days a week, IHOP sought to "proclaim the beauty of Jesus and his glorious return."[6]

Our fathers had grown up together in Northwest Iowa, so our friendship had always felt like a natural continuation of theirs. I began attending IHOP with her, seeking to build my relationship with God with the hope of coping better with my daily experience at Carver Elementary School.

I continued to struggle to feel God's presence in the same ways I had growing up, but IHOP was definitively a different type of experience than what I'd been experiencing regularly on Sundays in Kansas City. There were tearful testimonies, prayer groups where people experienced visions and shared them—often speaking in tongues—and proselytizing.

Mindy was very involved in the "community," an offshoot of IHOP where young people shared a home, pooled their money, and studied with one another, all fervently committed to Christ's work.

It all seemed extreme, but so was this TFA experience. I had been taught that adversity in life can be how God works to accomplish his will in your life. Hard times ensured we were pushed to lean on him.

Maybe Teach for America and these struggles were all part of God's plan, and how I would come to know him better. I wanted it to be that easy.

Teaching in "inner-city" Kansas City with a predominantly Black community was a vastly different experience than what my TFA training had prepared me for. I had taught kindergarten in Phoenix, but that was with three other co-teachers from Teach for America, a full-time teacher in the classroom to support us, and a TFA coach in a classroom largely filled with Latino students.

Teaching in Kansas City required more than jumping into the deep end of the pool on my own—it was diving into the middle of the ocean with a buoy of tools that were impossible to use because I just needed to keep my head above water.

There was just so much at Carver we were working against, in many cases even the administration and leadership itself. I'll never forget one of the first real conversations I had with our vice principal, Ms. Hartley, which happened after school in early November.

We stood next to each other chatting in my doorway, saying goodbye to the straggling students as they walked down the hall

"Goodbye, Shawn. Have a nice night!" she said loudly.

She leaned over to offer her wisdom as a decade-long teacher and administrator, lowering her voice to ensure any remaining students in the hall wouldn't hear.

"You should know that there are a number of students at Carver who are homeless and squat in the vacant homes near the school. You'll learn who they are. A lot of times they don't have electricity or water," she said to me in a hushed voice.

"Is there anything we're able to do for their families? Any services or referrals we can make?"

"We've got a resource list but, honestly, it's not very helpful. The best you can do is keep some extra clothing, hygiene items, etcetera. And if they say they have a stomachache, don't even bother sending them to the office—they're hungry, not sick. I'd just buy granola bars in bulk to have on hand," she admitted.

I'd already spent a lot of my own funds on books, classroom decor, and even some furniture. Now I was going to be providing food, clothing, and hygiene items as well? I kept listening.

"You should just be happy you're a second-grade teacher—you've still got a chance at that age. By the time they reach middle school, they're a bit of a lost cause if they can't read or even fill out a job application. I don't even worry about those ones anymore, though, because they probably won't make it to sixteen anyway," she said.

This was our school leadership. It was so depressing. Looking back now, there are so many ways I wish I would have responded:
How are you in education?
I don't think I've ever heard something so cold.
What the fuck?
In reality, I didn't say anything at all.
"Good night, Shaniece! We'll see you tomorrow!" Ms. Hartley said loudly, sharing her farewells to the walls just as much as to our students. "Well, Miss C. We'll see you tomorrow as well."

"Thanks, Ms. Hartley," I forced myself to say, feeling grateful I was more than halfway through my first semester of teaching and quickly approaching my first real break: Thanksgiving.

It was another Thursday afternoon after a particularly rough day. Students hadn't accomplished nearly as much learning as I'd hoped, due to many distractions that I couldn't control: There was pinching and hitting, breaking pencils and tearing up papers set in front of them, loudly cursing (yes, even among second graders) to provoke fits of laughter, and even total defiance of most requests I made.

I tried diligently to remain firm, set and reset expectations, make phone calls home to report positive behavior, introduce positive behavior supports focused on incentivizing and rewarding good behavior, and implement individual and class punishments. Writing students up and sending them to the office was a last resort that was becoming all too common—I didn't know what do anymore.

The tutoring sessions with the small group after school had become a bit of a saving grace for me. I enjoyed offering one-on-one support to Samuel, Alexis, Marquand, and Anton, and it gave me hope that I wasn't a complete failure.

I walked across the street to Ms. Eleanor's house and rapped my knuckles against the aluminum screen door. A kid I didn't recognize appeared and pushed it open for me, allowing me inside. As my eyes adjusted to the light, I saw eight kids scattered across the floor, couches, and chairs, some doing homework or reading, others playing some type of hand game with their younger counterparts.

"Hi, Ms. Eleanor!" I called out, trying not to be too loud.

"Hi, Miss C! I'm ready to go!" Marquand said as he rose.

Then Alexis and Anton appeared with Samuel and Ms. Eleanor trailing behind. Alexis ran up and gave me a hug, though we had only last seen each other fewer than ten minutes before.

"Well, hello, Alexis!" I giggled.

"Thanks so much, Miss C. You'll drop them off at the normal time?" Ms. Eleanor said.

"I'll see you then!" I responded.

The four of us walked through the maze of kids on the floor, and then we all held hands as we crossed the street. I used my key to allow us back into the school.

"Miss C, can I use the computer first?" Marquand implored.

"You know, Marquand, I believe you got to use the computer first on Tuesday—"

"But Miss C!" he protested.

"I think we'll let Samuel use it first today."

"Yessss!" Samuel exclaimed quietly.

"Miss C, Marquand got in trouble in Miss Irving's room today," Alexis told the group.

"Tattletale!" Marquand proclaimed.

"Well, you did," Alexis said sheepishly.

"Santa might as well put me on the naughty list," Marquand said to everyone.

I couldn't stifle my laughter. "Oh Marquand, it's okay! You can choose to have a better day tomorrow! There's still plenty of time before Christmas!" I chuckled.

"You really think so?" he asked, clearly concerned.

I felt bad for giggling because I could see this clearly was a serious subject, and ensured my next response was sincere, saying, "I *know* so."

I caught him smiling.

After we got to the classroom, three of my crew went to their desks and Samuel beelined to the computer. The time always flew by and, before I knew it, Samuel was standing in front of me for the final fifteen minutes of the hour.

"How are you doing, Samuel?" I asked.

"Fine."

"What book are we working on today?"

"*Is There an Alligator in the Pond?*" he responded.

"Great! And looking at the cover, what do you think this is going to be about?"

"I've already read this."

"Well, then can you summarize it for me based on your memory before we read it?"

We were going through the motions, him explaining, me asking the questions I was supposed to.

But then I asked a question that struck a nerve: "Samuel, how are you doing *really*?"

"I'm fine," he insisted.

"Have you gotten into any trouble at home lately?"

He took a moment, looked at the ground, and said, "Yeah."

I pressed further, knowing I was probably overstepping my bounds.

"What happened?" I asked.

"Well, I got in trouble for talking back to my mom, and I had to kneel on rice for a long time. It really hurt my knees."

What could I do with this information? Honestly, probably nothing. So what was the point of pushing further? I'd already seen what reporting behavior I deemed to be abuse did for Samuel, for my classroom, and for me.

"Miss C! It's time to go!" Alexis yelled.

I ignored her for the moment, looking Samuel in the eyes. "I'm really sorry to hear that," I said sincerely. "Please know you can talk to me, and I'll do my best to support you."

"I know," he replied, sounding like an old man.

The others had already shut down the computer and put away their activities, and were now heading toward the door.

"Hold on guys—we've got everything put away already? You're ready to go?" I asked.

"Yep!" the three replied in unison.

"Me too," Samuel said.

"You guys are so fast!" I said, quickly packing up my bag. "Alright, let's head back to Ms. Eleanor's!"

The group began to chatter again as we walked down the hall.

"Errrbody in the club gettin tipsy," Anton sang.

"Anton, do you even know what that means?" I asked, but before he could answer I stopped him by saying, "You know what, I don't want to know. Let's choose another song to sing."

"How about 'I kissed a girl and I liked it'?" Marquand sang.

"You know what, how about 'Single Ladies'?" I suggested.

That's safe, right? I thought.

"If you like it then you shoulda put a ring on it," Alexis sang before I had even finished. The boys laughed and joined in as well as we crossed the street to Ms. Eleanor's house.

Marquand opened the door and entered, and the three others followed. I stuck my head inside. As my eyes adjusted to the darkness I saw many more people than normal, and assumed they were family members of the students who stayed at Ms. Eleanor's every day after school.

I caught the nearest adult's eye. "I'm so sorry to disturb!" I explained. "I'm Miss C. I work at Carver across the street. Would you be willing to let her know that—"

"Hey Miss C!" Ms. Eleanor said as she waltzed into the living from the kitchen, a floral silk wrap holding her hair in place. "Why don't you come on in for some dinner? I've got some catfish and homemade macaroni and cheese. There's plenty left for you."

"Oh Ms. Eleanor, you sure don't have to feed me."

"I won't take no for an answer."

I was surprised by her insistence.

"Well okay, then! It sounds like I don't have a choice!" I laughed.

I walked toward the light in the kitchen, weaving my way through the kids and adults spread out on the floor. This was the furthest I had ever been into Ms. Eleanor's home.

There were more than twenty people in her home, all eating. It only took me a few moments to realize I was the only white person there.

Ms. Eleanor handed me a heaping plate of food.

"This looks delicious, Ms. Eleanor. Thank you so much for having me," I said.

"You're welcome, baby," she said kindly.

As Ms. Eleanor made conversation in the kitchen, I slowly walked back into the living room, feeling like an anxious kid entering the lunchroom and looking for a suitable spot.

"Miss C, please come sit on the couch," said a voice I couldn't place.

A middle schooler quickly moved from the couch to the floor.

"Oh, I don't want to make anyone move!" I responded.

"Already done. You're our guest—you're not going to sit on the floor."

"Well, thank you so much," I said, making eye contact with the middle school student who had moved to the floor, and nodding my gratitude.

The paper plate sat in my lap, light grease from the catfish soaking through. A piece flaked off into my hand as I placed it in my mouth. The crunch of the exterior melted in my mouth; the distinct taste of the fish was not foreign to me but was more buttery than any I had ever experienced.

"Wow," I exclaimed.

"Good, huh, Miss C?" Samuel said, looking up to me from the floor.

"It sure is!" I agreed.

No wonder nobody was talking much—this food was business.

The macaroni and cheese didn't disappoint either, with its creamy, milky cheddar coating wide elbow noodles. It reminded me of the macaroni and cheese I had during my trip to Mississippi; this was only my second experience with the dish outside of the Kraft blue box.

Being invited to dinner at Ms. Eleanor's—in addition to including some of the best catfish and macaroni and cheese I had ever experienced—more importantly felt like formal acceptance into the Carver Elementary School community.

I wasn't an outsider anymore. It was going to be okay.

chapter six

Mick and my relationship started as friendship that was based on a failed romantic endeavor, and quickly blossomed into much more.

Our weekly, Friday night, group dates evolved into checking in with each other via text multiple times a week. Though we were teaching at different schools our stories were similar, and we took comfort in supporting each other.

The Friday nights quickly became sleepovers at Mick's since his place was within walking distance of our typical hangout spot. We'd sit on his balcony with blankets and look at the stars, talking until the early morning hours.

Being from California, Mick's life experiences were so different than my own. He'd share about growing up in San Francisco, just a few blocks from the Pacific Ocean, while I talked about what it was like to spend your childhood knowing almost everyone in your small town that was surrounded by fields of corn and soybeans.

Things progressed quickly as we both shared more about our lives and our battle stories from our respective classrooms. We talked about our families, our very different college experiences— Mick had attended a large state university that was considered a party school, which was worlds away from my small, liberal arts school where the professors called if I missed a class. Soon we shared more about our personal passions.

"I played drums and toured with a band in college," Mick told me.

"That's so cool! What kind of music?" I swooned.

"We sounded a bit like Evanescence, if you know them."

"Of course I do! Do you have any recordings? I'd love to hear you!"

"Absolutely! I'll share some with you. I was under twenty-one, which was challenging at times. Sometimes I'd only be allowed into the venue to play the show, and then I'd have to leave," Mick admitted.

"Oh wow! That's crazy!" I said, laughing. "I was a music minor in school. I'm a singer. My school has an amazing opera program—like, they've produced multiple, professional opera singers."

"So—you sing opera?"

"I try, though honestly I was only a minor," I admitted.

"What do you mean 'only a minor'? You were in the program?!" Mick asked.

I laughed again. "Oh, definitely! The music program was just so hardcore at Simpson. I always felt like I knew my place, as *just* a minor." I made air quotes as I said the word *just*.

"Well, I'd love to hear you sing. I have my recording stuff here if you'd ever want to record."

"That would be amazing," I gushed. "I've never done anything like that."

"I have the perfect closet for it!"

"I'm in. Maybe I could record something for my dad for Christmas. He'd love it."

"Done. It's a date," Mick replied.

It was the final days before Thanksgiving break, which I hoped would provide a welcome respite from the insanity of Carver and an opportunity to see my family. My mom and brothers were a three-hour drive away, while my dad lived five hours away. I was looking forward to seeing everyone, but mostly to spending time out on the farm with my dad.

For the moment, I'd take advantage of the twenty minutes of recess by chatting with Carver's other second-grade teacher, Toni, as we watched our students run across the vast expanse of old, cracked, black tarmac. The small climbing structures and grass were reserved for the kindergarten and first-grade students, so the second and third graders were left to make their own fun from the limited playground balls, jump ropes, and faded yellow outlines of schoolyard games that had been painted on the blacktop a decade before.

"Miss C, what are we doing in class next?" Destiny asked.

She had become my shadow, sticking close to me throughout the day and even more at recess since there was so little to do.

"We're going to start brainstorming for our next writing assignment," I said.

"Oooh! That sounds fun. Do you wanna walk with me around the blacktop a little bit, Miss C?"

"Sure, Destiny," I responded.

As we walked around the playground, I monitored the students who were remarkably able to create their own fun with so few materials.

"Cornell—not so rough," I yelled at a child across the expanse.

My shoe kicked what I assumed was a small rock, but the copper sheen caught my eye. I followed the path it had taken with Destiny in tow. I picked it up and quickly examined it.

"What's that, Miss C?" she asked.

"I'm not sure," I said as I pocketed it.

But being a Midwest farmer's daughter who had done her fair share of shooting, I had a hunch.

When I finally had a spare moment at lunch, I took the dull orange piece from my pocket and confirmed my suspicions. This wasn't a bullet casing; this was the projectile—a copper bullet that had been fired from a 9mm pistol and landed on our school playground. I put it back in my pocket and rolled it between my forefinger and thumb, refusing to believe it was real. But again and again, throughout the afternoon, I slipped my hand in my pocket and touched the piece.

When I had first been placed in Kansas City for my teaching assignment, I thought I had lucked out. It was a mere three hours from home and a Midwest city. I had never been to Kansas City, but how different could it be?

It was surely less unknown than Turkey, which is where the Peace Corps had invited me to go. My mom was much happier with a position so close.

But I would learn very quickly about the decay and corruption of the city's schools, and the entrenched history of racism and violence that has consistently ranked (for decades) Kansas City within the top ten of cities with the highest crime rates in the United States.

Nicknamed "Killa City,"[7] the murder rates in Kansas City in 2008—when I was a teacher there—meant it was safer to be deployed as a soldier during the Iraq War than it was to be on KC's streets as a young Black man.[8]

Kansas City's gang presence wasn't always organized and violent, but it was introduced in tandem with crack cocaine. Jamaican street gangs first brought crack to Kansas City in the mid-1980s, but after successful suppression by local police, the Bloods and Crips gangs from Los Angeles filled the void. With widespread competition for drug sales in Los Angeles, gangs began to migrate to cities across the nation, creating satellite operations that boasted markups of up to 300 percent, with local talent executing on the sales. This led to the organization and further creation of Bloods and Crips gang affiliations in Kansas City neighborhoods, with drive-by shootings rising from fifteen in 1989 to almost three hundred in 1990.[9]

The 51st Street Crips became a dominating force in the area, with Steven "Moody" Wright Jr. being recognized as one of the city's most notorious gangsters for his extreme violence. Cornell "Fat Tone" Watkins came to the helm thereafter, and was widely recognized as the killer of Andre "Mac Dre" Hicks, a Bay Area rapper.[10]

Carver Elementary sat in the middle of the territory of the Tre Side Bloods. In 2016, it was estimated that there were over 3,000 gangsters in more than one hundred gangs in Kansas City.[11]

We had earned the night out. Thanksgiving break was upon us, but before heading back to our respective homes, Rachel, Tess, Anna, and I had plans to go out and celebrate. We'd all survived four months of our respective commitments; my roommate, Anna, in law school and the rest of us in Teach for America.

My phone rang as I drove back to my apartment to prepare for the evening. It wasn't a number I recognized, but I hit the accept key and put the phone to my ear.

"Hello?"

"Hi. Is this Nicole," the speaker said, and then paused. "Cleveringa?" she said, struggling to pronounce my last name, which was common.

"This is."

"Hi, Miss Cleveringa. This is Pam from the Missouri Department of Social Services, and I wanted to call to update you on the status of the child abuse report you filed a few weeks ago."

My heart started racing. "Okay," I said.

I hadn't expected a call—I didn't know if there was any follow-up.

"We wanted to let you know that after completing our investigation, the report was deemed to be unfounded, but appreciate your taking your status as a mandated reporter seriously."

I didn't know what to say. "Okay, thanks," I managed to squeak.

"Unless you have anything else, I'll go ahead and let you go. Thank you for your time," she said.

"Okay, thanks," I said as I pulled up to my apartment, put the car in park, and broke down crying.

What the fuck?

Was I so far removed from this community that I didn't even understand what abuse was? Who did I think I was, anyway? A white girl, coming into a Black community—very clearly an outsider—making judgements. I had to do what I thought was right, and I had done exactly that.

Unfounded?

So that was it—case closed—nothing more to be said.

I heard my army dad's voice echoing in my mind: *Stick your ass up and it's gonna get bit.*

I'd be lying low moving forward, that was for sure.

I did know one thing: It was time to *drink*. I walked through the front gate of our apartment and through our front door, and dropped my bags on the couch. I went straight to the refrigerator, cracked open the screw-cap bottle of Riesling, and poured myself a healthy glass. It only seemed appropriate.

"You're starting early," Anna said as she walked into the kitchen. After seeing the fresh tears, her tone changed. "What happened?"

"I just got notified the abuse report I made was unfounded."

"Wait—Samuel? You're kidding me. I'm so sorry," Anna said as she came over.

She gave me a hug and I awkwardly balanced the wine glass while hugging back, not willing to set it down.

"Yeah, so—drinks! Want some wine?" I said as lightly as I could muster.

"I'll grab my red," she responded.

The two of us drank as we got ready. I took very little time to do so, and then I sat on the stairs, chatting with Anna and texting Rachel and Tess to see about their status, as Anna finished primping.

At Tomfooleries on the Country Club Plaza, a privately owned shopping district, the four of us ate dinner and I quickly caught Rachel and Tess up on the day's happenings.

"Insanity. It doesn't make any sense," Rachel said, shaking her head.

"Is what happened in your classroom not the literal definition of child abuse?" asked Tess, incredulous.

We headed upstairs to a bar-only area and ordered another round of drinks, waiting for the other Teach for America corps members who were bound to show up.

I was already three drinks deep at this point, but I'd earned it after the week I'd had.

"Look who the cat dragged in!" Rachel boomed inside the still relatively empty bar space.

I glanced over to see Mick and his friend Jason, another Teach for America teacher. I had let Mick know, earlier in the day, that I was going to dinner with the girls—and that we'd likely head upstairs after and that I would love to see him.

"Hey! How are you doing?" Mick asked as I stood to give him a hug.

It was standard practice now—we always greeted each other with a hug.

"Good. So glad to have a bit of a break. How are you?" I responded.

"Same—can't wait to let loose a bit tonight."

"Me too. It was a bit of a rough ending today."

"How so?"

"Well, you know I reported what happened with Samuel."

"Of course."

"Well, I got notification from the state that the abuse was unfounded."

"Seriously?"

I nodded.

"Well, let's get you another drink!"

I laughed, and happily accepted.

The night was just what I needed: time and space to let loose with a crew who were quickly becoming some of my closest friends. Mick and I remained part of the group conversation, but snuck in playful glances and sometimes brazenly brushed our hands over each other's legs under the table. And suddenly it was midnight. By then the bar was packed, and it was clear the table we had procured very easily earlier in the evening was the envy of many. We decided to give it up. Our numbers were dwindling, and we were starting to acknowledge that none of us would be staying too much longer.

Rachel weaved her way through the crowd to find Mick and me.

"Hey, lovebirds, what are you having?" she asked.

I blushed and glanced to Mick. He had a big smile on his face.

"I'll take an Irish coffee," Mick said.

"I'll have our usual," I responded.

"And what's that?" Mick asked.

"Basically, a dirty Shirley Temple made with gin."

Mick laughed. "How did you come up with that?"

"Rachel!" I said, laughing in reply.

"Hey, after this drink, would you wanna walk back to my place and watch a movie?" Mick asked.

"Yeah, I think that sounds fun!" I said.

Mick only lived a few blocks from the Plaza, in a spot I could have only dreamed of affording. The apartment complex had its own sauna and outdoor pool, and happened to be where many of the Kansas City Royals' players lived. Compared to where Mick was from in the Bay Area, rent in Kansas City seemed cheap.

"Here ya go!" Rachel said, carefully maneuvering the three drinks, which we grabbed.

"Thanks so much, dude!"

"Love you!" Rachel gave me a one-armed hug, as she sucked from the small straw in her drink.

"Careful, that's a double," she whispered.

"Good grief, I think that should be enough!" I giggled, at this point feeling the culmination of the night's festivities.

Two young men we didn't recognize came up to our trio. "Hello!" said one of them

"Hi, guys! How are you?" Rachel said.

"Great! Definitely enjoying our evening. I'm Jared, and this is Brian."

"Awesome. I'm Rachel, and this is Nicole."

I was grateful Rachel jumped in.

"I'm Mick. Great to meet you guys," Mick chimed in.

"Awesome, what are you guys up to tonight?" asked Jared.

"Just enjoying the evening," Rachel responded. "Excited for the Thanksgiving break. We're all teachers!"

"Oh wow! At the same school?" asked Jared.

"Rachel and I teach at the same school, Mick at another, though we're all part of the same program," I said.

"Super cool. Jealous of the summers off."

"I wish they were really summers off," Rachel said, brave enough to clarify a common misunderstanding that drove teachers nuts.

The small talk continued until Mick had finished his drink.

He leaned in to me and said, "Hey, I'm gonna go get rid of this, hit the bathroom, and then you wanna head out?"

"Sounds good," I replied.

"How long have the two of you been together?" Jared asked loudly.

I felt myself blush and hoped Mick couldn't tell in the gray light of the bar.

We both spoke over each other, attempting to clarify that we weren't actually together, while laughing awkwardly.

The truth was that I didn't even know if Mick was still with his California girlfriend. I hadn't wanted to broach the topic.

As Mick left to go to the bathroom, Brian looked to me.

"So, if you're not together, can I have your number?" Brian asked.

I shifted a bit, feeling uncomfortable. Mick and I weren't officially together, but sometimes it felt like it.

"I'm flattered, but I don't give out my number anymore. I can take yours," I said.

"But the real question is, will you actually call me?" Brian asked.

"That's a hard no, dude." Jared laughed.

I looked to Rachel, saying, "Well, he tried?"

I never knew how to tell someone no, but I was glad Brian and Jared took the hint and cleared out before Mick got back.

We said goodbye to Rachel, and Mick and I ventured out into the night with the lights of the Plaza glowing and the pitch black beckoning.

"I don't think I'll ever get used to these temperatures," Mick said.

"This isn't even the worst of it!" I laughed. "It hasn't even hit freezing yet!"

And yet, the brisk air seemed to stand still as we listened to the sounds of the bar fading behind us. Mick slipped his hand into mine, as we shivered toward his home.

We quickly made our way through the locked gates and into the complex.

"I'll turn on the fireplace as soon as we get inside," Mick told me.

Once we got settled in, I knew the likelihood of me making it home at this point was slim.

"What movie do you wanna watch?" I asked.

"How about you pick three from the collection I've got, and then I'll choose one."

"Great!" I agreed, browsing his titles for the most girly options available. I held three out and proclaimed: "*Moulin Rouge, Unfaithful,* or *Chicago.*"

"*Moulin Rouge,*" he said quickly.

"I'm joking," I said.

"What?" He looked confused.

"I literally picked the three girliest movies you have on your shelf. I'm joking. I'll give you my real decisions now." I laughed.

"Oh my God—you so had me!"

Mick pulled his futon mattress to the floor, creating a little nest of pillows and blankets as the fireplace warmed the room.

We landed on *Flyboys*, a WWI drama with James Franco—something we both could enjoy. But we didn't end up watching much of the movie anyway.

When we woke in the morning, we walked over to a local diner for breakfast. After eggs, bacon, toast, and greasy hashbrowns, he walked me to my car and gave me a kiss goodbye, promising we'd chat again later.

I drove home basking in joy. By this point in my life, so many of my friends were already married with kids on the way. Had I found my happy ending?

As I swung open my front door and was overcome with emotion, I plopped down on our stairs and couldn't help but cry.

My roommate greeted me from the kitchen and walked into the living room where I sat with my head in my hands.

"What in the world is wrong with you?" Anna asked, concern in her voice.

I was embarrassed. "I think I'm in love."

She laughed as she sat down and rubbed my back. "That's a good thing!"

"I know." I laughed. "But I'm scared. I've never felt like this before—so out of my control. And it's so fast—I haven't even known him that long," I said.

"And that's okay too," she told me.

This was new territory for me.

Going home for the holidays to be with my divorced parents and spending hours on the road carting my two brothers around the state wasn't easy, but it was better than Carver. I drove the three hours to my mom's house to spend Thanksgiving Day there with her, my brothers, her new boyfriend, and his two, high school–aged boys. Thanksgiving always meant a lot of food, but the Iowa fare did not offer anything fresh or light.

As I was still getting to know my mom's new boyfriend and his sons, the dinner felt full of small talk with a bunch of strangers. I excused myself quickly after dessert—I had made plans to go out with old high school friends to catch up. Though I found myself just wanting to go to sleep, I went anyway.

"I hope you're not drinking and driving," my mom said accusingly.

"One drink, one hour—I won't be out late," I reassured her.

The discussion with my friends didn't really feel any different than the one I'd had at home. I shared my "war" stories, watching their eyes widen and mouths fall open as they hung on every word describing the harrowing experience of watching a mother beat her son with a belt in front of a room of second graders.

"That's just awful," one friend said.

"I don't understand—if this school is so bad, why don't the families just move?" another asked.

"It's a little bit more complicated than that," I explained.

But I didn't want to expound further. They didn't get it.

We shifted the conversation to more palatable topics: who was newly dating whom, who was sleeping around, shopping and hair-coloring mishaps, and sister fights.

I sipped my wine, nodding my head in agreement to whatever they were saying. It all felt so trivial. I stayed true to my word and said goodbye after the single drink.

"Aw! You just got here! Do you really have to go?" one friend asked.

"I'm really tired," I responded.

And I was. I was physically tired, but I was also tired of feeling like nobody understood what I was going through.

"I can only imagine. It's going to be okay. Hang in there, Cole," a friend said kindly.

But I didn't want pity—I wanted understanding, and I wasn't going to get that here, or from my family either.

I headed out, feeling disappointed. I couldn't help but cry as I drove the short way home, bearing a heavy cloud of solitude in my experiences.

The next morning, my brothers and I left a bit later than we'd planned, drove the four hours to my dad's house, and arrived just after noon.

I quickly got to work, baking a pie from the ingredients I had asked my dad to purchase the day before.

"You know I could have just as well bought the pie and saved you the time," Dad said.

"And I know you know I like doing this for you and the boys—and this will taste better anyway," I said.

Baking was my labor of love and is still one of the ways I show people I care.

It felt a bit more normal at my dad's, and he hadn't done too badly on the Thanksgiving dinner. He'd come a long way with his bachelorhood-cooking skills. It was just the four of us this time, and the pace at the farm was just so much slower, particularly in the winter months. I was sure my dad would find some wood splitting for us to do.

There was so much nostalgia in this space. The home was first my grandparents' and then, after they passed, my dad took over the house and all the work that came along with it.

After we finished dinner, my dad and I moved to wash the dishes as my brothers got the fire restarted in the fireplace downstairs.

"Feel good to have a break?" Dad asked.

"Yes—I'm already dreading going back," I admitted.

"Don't let tomorrow ruin today. One day at a time," said Dad, leveraging one of the mantras he'd learned from AA.

"I know. It's just been a bit weird coming home too. I went out with some friends last night, and it just feels like everything has changed so much since I've been gone. And I haven't even been gone all that long."

"You realize it's not everything else that's changed," my dad posed as he rinsed a plate and handed it to me to put in the dishwasher.

Right, I realized. It's not them, it's *me*.

"Yeah, I guess not. I just can't believe four months could have such an impact. I know it seems silly to say, but I feel so much harder already."

My dad chuckled. "A bit of a taste of the real world, eh?" he said gently.

"I know I'm lucky to have a job with the economy tanking, and I know this is what I signed up for, but I guess I didn't anticipate getting knocked down so fast and hard."

"Everyone has the curtain pulled back for them at some point, and it sounds like you're gaining that experience a bit more quickly than your friends."

"I guess so," I said.

We left it at that. Even if this *was* what I had signed up for, I hadn't anticipated this pit in my stomach at the mere thought of going to back school.

Maybe church would help. We always went with my dad when we were home with him. I knew I needed to trust in God. If I called out to him, he would be the support I needed. Or at least that's what I'd been taught.

chapter seven

As we entered the final month of the first semester at Carver, it was becoming more and more clear that the greatest measurement of success wasn't always related to how much the students learned. If you couldn't keep them quiet with academics, it was expected that you kept them quiet with other things—Ms. King didn't really care what you did.

I saw one teacher line her students up in the hallway, where they waited during what should have been their class time, as she copied page after page of coloring sheets and word searches. Another played the movie *Amistad* at least once a week.

I was becoming more and more disenchanted.

And I was having a tough enough time keeping my classroom under control, let alone quiet.

I definitely wasn't the only one having trouble—the school's track record of success was pretty abysmal. Only 12 percent of Carver's students tested at grade level for both math and reading, which meant that, of the three hundred students enrolled, only thirty-six students *total* were where they were supposed to be academically. The achievement gap was alive and well at Carver, especially regarding both racial and economic disparities: 89 percent of Carver's students received free-and-reduced lunch, and 99 percent of the student population identified as students of color. The odds were stacked against our kids for so many reasons.

But, to be fair, the odds felt like they were stacked against pretty much any student in the school district. In 2000, the district was the first in the nation to fully lose their accreditation after failing all eleven of the performance standards. Though other schools around the nation had experienced state takeover, Kansas City was the first to lose their accreditation *wholly*, which meant not only was the district forced to pay tuition and transportation for students who wanted to transfer elsewhere,[12] but the diplomas received by its high school graduates were essentially worth less than the paper they were printed on.

The school district was also the scene of a significant experiment examining what access to more and better resources could do for student achievement. Due to the segregation that redlining, blockbusting, and white flight of the 1960s and '70s had caused, in 1977, on behalf of its students, the district sued the state of Missouri, federal agencies, and the surrounding suburban school districts. In 1985, the court found the state liable for the unconstitutional segregation that existed within the district,[13] and ordered the state to spend about $2 billion over the next two decades to improve integration in schools, boost test scores, and repair classrooms.[14] The hope was that these changes would attract more white students from the suburbs.

In essence, the district had been issued a blank check, and the transitory leadership saw it as such, building an Olympic-sized pool and indoor track that rivaled those on college campuses, and a courtroom to host mock trials.[14]

Though the district had the best per-pupil expenditure and teacher-to-student ratio as any school in the nation, test scores didn't rise, the Black-white achievement gap did not diminish, and there was more, not less, segregation as white students stayed in their suburban school districts.[14]

By the time I had joined the Carver team in 2008, money and resources were dwindling, along with the district's student population, and I didn't see any benefits reflected in our school, aside from an aging, largely unused auditorium.

From my vantage point, there wasn't much to show for $2 billion that had been spent.

Ms. King stuck her head in my room, saying, "Miss C, I need you to keep your class quiet. I can hear them from my office."

"I'm sorry, Ms. King. We'll do better, right class?" I looked at my kids.

Some of the students nodded their heads, while others smirked.

"Okay, guys, we're going to continue with our mock interviews, but we'll need to make sure we're using our indoor voices so we're not disturbing any other classes or Ms. King."

Before I could even finish my sentence, Orion and Cornell bolted out the door. This was becoming the new normal for these two. After seeing their older siblings wandering the hallways freely, I assumed the two had gone downstairs to find them—or wreak whatever havoc they could in the empty gym or another classroom.

I sighed.

"Miss C, who should I work with now that Cornell is gone?" Efrem asked.

"How about you and Rashaad work together for the rest of your mock interview questions? Destiny, I'll be right with you, and we can start."

I called the office to let them know Orion and Cornell had left my classroom, just to cover my own ass since I knew they would not respond in any way. I motioned for Destiny to come up to my desk.

"I'm so excited you're my partner, Miss C!"

"Me too, Destiny!" I said, smiling.

I had created a project where students interviewed each other and then wrote a short biography about their partner, but since there was an odd number of students in the class, Destiny and I were partners.

"Okay, Miss C, I'll start! What is your favorite subject in school, and why?"

"That's an easy one! I always liked English class, and writing in particular. I studied both of those subjects in college because I liked them so much!"

"Okay, give me just a minute to write this down."

I thought back to Orion and Cornell roaming the halls. I'd call their parents at lunch, just to check in, though it wasn't likely Cornell's family would answer. I had never met them since nobody showed up to his parent-teacher conference. On the other hand, Orion Sr.—and his daughter Trinity, who was an eighth grader downstairs—and I were on a first name basis.

"Okay, Miss C! It's your turn."

"Alright, let me see. Destiny, what do you want to be when you grow up?"

She bit on her thumb nail. "I think I'd like to be a veterinarian, because I really like animals, and I would like to help them."

"I think that would be a great job for you, Destiny, because you're so caring," I said as I jotted the note down, planning to write my own biography on Destiny to be sure she was part of the full experience.

She smiled a grin of self-satisfaction.

"Okay, Miss C, my turn again! Who is the most important person in your life and why?"

"Oh, that's a really good question, Destiny. I would say my dad, because I think he's a very wise person, and I love him a lot."

"You talk about your dad a lot."

I laughed. "Do I?"

"Yes, he sounds like he's really smart."

"I think so. Hey, give me just one minute, Destiny," I said, turning to the class. "Okay class! You have two minutes to ask your partner one more question and finish taking your notes." I looked at Destiny again. "Okay, one more question for you, Destiny. If you had one wish, what would it be?" I asked.

"To live with you," she responded, without missing a beat.

"Oh, Destiny," I said, stalling. "That's so sweet, and I think it would be so fun to live with you, but I know your family would miss you so much!"

"I doubt it. . . ." she said, looking down.

"I know it." I gave her a hug.

"Alright class, it's time to go ahead and finish up in five, four, three, two, one—pencils down. When I say go, I would like you to quickly and quietly gather your materials, walk back to your desk, and prepare for lunch. Whatever table is seated—quiet and ready to go—first will get to lead us."

Students started to move prematurely.

"Oh, hey! I didn't say go yet!" I said, and they froze. "Go!"

The class knew how to run like a machine when they wanted to—I just couldn't get any consistency with them. As the class was moving and preparing for lunch, Orion walked back into the classroom with blood down the front of his shirt. I rushed over.

"Orion—what happened!? Are you okay?" I asked.

He opened his mouth to show the gap next to his front tooth. "Cornell punched my tooth out," he said, a sense of pride in his voice.

The other students watched as I ran to the corner of the room to grab a bunch of tissues, and quite literally shoved them in Orion's mouth. The blood on his shirt had made it look worse than it was, but this obviously still wasn't good.

"Here, let's get these here to stop the blood. Do you feel okay? Was the tooth already loose?"

I knew I had done what I was supposed to do by calling the office to let them know Orion and Cornell had left, but I also knew I was still going to be held responsible for this.

Desks continued to open and closes as the rest of the class prepared for lunch.

"It's fine, Miss C. It was loose," Cornell said.

"Well, let's get you to the office to have them check you out. You head there, and I'll meet you after I get the rest of the class to lunch."

With his mouth full of tissues, I watched as he slowly meandered down the hall toward the office. I looked back to the rest of the class, who were waiting impatiently to be called on to go to lunch.

"Great job, guys! Looks like Rashaad's group is ready."

"But they weren't ready first!" Aiyden yelled.

"But they're showing me they're the most ready now. Who's next?"

I got the group downstairs for lunch, and rushed to the office to check in on Orion, knowing I likely wouldn't have time to eat any lunch with only a twenty-five-minute period. As I approached the office, he walked out with Ms. King in tow.

"Hi, Miss C," Ms. King said. "I just spoke with Orion. You'll want to call his dad and let him know what happened. I'll walk him down to the lunchroom."

"Okay, Ms. King, I'll do that right now."

"I'm not sure why Orion was out of your classroom, but I guess we'll discuss that later," Ms. King said accusingly.

Now I for sure won't have time for lunch, I thought as I dialed the phone.

Orion Sr. picked up right away. "I'll have Trinity pick him up today after school to make sure he doesn't get in any more trouble, Miss C. Thanks for letting me know. And I'll make sure to talk to him tonight as well," he said, clearly unconcerned about the fight.

And then it was time to go and pick up my class. Thankfully, the rest of the afternoon went by smoothly: group reading after lunch, PE (with a teacher who always made sure to tell me—in front of the students—how much he disliked teaching my class, which was infuriating), math, and then a short social studies lesson.

As we packed up for the day, Trinity walked into the classroom.

"Hey, Miss C. Can I grab Orion?" she asked.

I looked to Orion, who was still packing up. "Yep! Just give him a minute and then he can head out with you."

"So sorry he had a rough day. My dad texted me."

"Yeah, I'm sorry it happened too."

"I'll talk to him. But I can tell you care, Miss C. Orion is lucky to have such a nice teacher."

"That's really kind of you to say, Trinity. I'm trying my best..."

"Orion, let's go!" she barked.

Poof! The nice moment was gone.

I called Mick, wanting to share the story of a second grader knocking out his classmate's tooth.

"You'll never believe what happened today."

"Tell me."

"Orion and Cornell walked out of class again—nothing new there. But this time, Cornell knocked out Orion's tooth."

"Holy shit!" Mick said.

"Thankfully, it was already loose, and I have a good relationship with Orion Sr., who didn't blame me. But obviously I feel some responsibility, as they were supposed to be in my class."

"Do any other teachers at Carver have students who walk out of their class?"

"Yes," I admitted.

"And are you doing the best you can?"

"Yes."

"Then try not to beat yourself up," Mick insisted.

I had started to feel as though I was unloading more and more on Mick, since he was one of the only people who understood my experience at Carver.

"How was your day?" I asked him.

"It was actually a pretty good one. Some of the normal craziness, but I found a bunch of drums in a closet at school. I'm thinking about starting a drumline for the kids to participate in as a sort of incentive program."

"Oh my God, that sounds amazing! That's so perfect!"

"Yeah, I've gotta get it cleared, but it's always been a dream of mine to open a drum school of some sort in the future. This could be the beginning!" Mick said, sounding hopeful.

"That's *so* exciting," I said genuinely. "And are you so excited to go home and see your family for Christmas?"

"I am. I need a break." He sighed.

"I totally hear you there."

"I know this break is only going to be two weeks, but I'm going to miss you!" he said.

"I'll miss you too." I could feel myself blushing, and was grateful this was a phone call. "You leave first thing Monday?"

"I do, but don't worry. We'll see lots of each other this weekend before I go," Mick reassured me.

I planned to head home Monday as well, and would split the time again between my mom's house and my dad's house, and visit high school and childhood friends in each place. I was determined to not share the stories of my classroom so readily—it was my experience, and the trials and tribulations were my own to harbor. I didn't want to see mouths agape or hear gasps in awe of what had become my new normal.

The two weeks of holiday break went quickly. I was already anticipating 2009, and wasn't feeling particularly positive about what the year would bring.

January was a cold reality, both literally and figuratively. The seasons in Kansas City brought extremes, and the winter months often dipped below zero. I found very quickly that some of the toughest months of teaching were January and February; aside from the bleak weather, it was the midpoint of the year, which brought the longest stretch of teaching without any break in sight. The nearest interlude—spring break—was more than eleven weeks away. By the middle of January, I felt guilty that I was already thinking about my next break, but I wasn't the only one.

"Wanna take a sick day together soon?" Rachel asked one day early in January as we drove together to school.

The two of us had started sleeping over at each other's places, serving both as early morning cheerleaders and drill sergeants in alternating sentences.

"Uhm, yes. 100 percent," I responded.

"How about next Friday?"

"Perfect!"

It offered something to look forward to—our little secret. The plan was to lie in bed, watch movies all day, and start the weekend (drinking) early. We figured we deserved some time to unwind even if our holiday break hadn't been that long ago. Neither of us had used any time off at that point. As a teacher, no matter your tenure, there was an unwritten rule: You don't take time off. If you did, the administration would surely let you know they weren't happy about it.

We put our sick-time request into the online system on Thursday evening, knowing this would offer the best chance for a substitute to pick up our classes for the following day while staying within a believable timeframe for realizing we were "sick" (though both of us being out on the same day probably raised some suspicion).

After sleeping in Friday morning, we saw both of our classes had been covered, which granted us a much needed, guilt-free, Friday indulgence. We stayed in our pajamas, and started our movie marathon with *27 Dresses*, then moved to *Step Brothers*, and ended with *Saw V*—the film trifecta of romance, comedy, and horror. We sipped on Dr Pepper and rum all afternoon, munched on chips and candy, and talked and laughed the entire day. As another Midwestern girl, Rachel and I had a ton in common outside of teaching at Carver. Our final movie of the day ended with the walls closing in on our Agent Strahm in *Saw V*.

"Literally, my worst nightmare. I hate horror movies," Rachel said.

"Ahhh! I love them!" I admitted, laughing.

It wasn't just the afternoon filled with rum—this was the best I had felt in weeks. But that bubble burst when I got a text at the end of the day from Tess, who taught third grade at Carver.

> *The subs totally bailed on both of your classes, so Ms. King split the students among the rest of the school.*

I looked to Rachel, mouth agape.

"What's wrong?" Rachel asked.

"Tess just said our classes got split between the other teachers because the substitutes left before end of day."

"What!? Are you serious?!"

She had to be joking. But I texted Tess back, and she confirmed.

Unfortunately, not kidding.

"Brutal," I said.

So much for a guilt-free day off.

"Hey, I think I'm just gonna go back to my place and call it an early night," I told Rachel.

"Oh, okay! Do you wanna do dinner?" Rachel asked.

"Thanks, but I'm not even hungry after all the junk we ate today. Thanks so much for hosting an amazing day off!"

"Absolutely! I'd say let's do it again, but it sounds like that won't be likely in the future," Rachel said.

"Dude—seriously. Sorry to end it that way!"

We found out on Monday that, due to Carver's reputation, substitute teachers were known to leave early or even cancel before the day started.

I also learned that my students had been put into small groups and spread across the first-, second-, and third-grade classrooms, which meant they'd lost a full day of instruction. And I could only imagine my colleagues were none too thrilled with me, despite my leaving well-organized lessons plans for the substitute.

January ended even more poorly than I'd anticipated as I had to take more time off, and for a horrible reason: My grandfather passed away. The funeral involved a five-hour drive back to my childhood home.

I was grateful and surprised when Mick offered to go with me.

"I'd love to be there to support you," he said.

"I'm so appreciative, sincerely. But you really want the first time you meet my family to be at a funeral?"

"I really don't mind, if they don't. I know your grandpa meant a lot to you, and I'd love to be there as you make the trek home."

"Well, I think you're incredibly sweet. Thank you—it means a lot."

So we made our first trip back home and Mick met my extended family. My mom has four siblings, so there was a *lot* of family there.

My cousins couldn't get enough of him, and I fielded all sorts of questions: California boy, huh? He's cute—is he a Teach for America teacher too? Does he have a brother?

Both my mom and dad were a bit more skeptical. I hadn't brought many boys home, and never to my childhood home, so this was a novel experience in its own right. Nothing much was said by either of them but, considering the occasion, I didn't think much of it. My mom had just lost her dad.

The one true embarrassment was yet to come. Growing up in such a Christian, conservative community, my dad wouldn't allow Mick and me to sleep in the same room even though we were both adults. So my brother slept on the couch and Mick took the bedroom next door to mine, sleeping in a twin bed that still donned Ninja Turtle sheets we had gotten secondhand after my parents' divorce more than a decade prior.

Regardless, Mick held my hand at all the right moments, said all the things I needed to hear as I mourned the loss of my family's patriarch, and kept my mind on positive things during the long drives to and from my childhood home—I couldn't have asked for more. He was an incredible support, and it was clear I was becoming more and more dependent on him.

But back in Kansas City, the experiences in the classroom and utter lack of control I felt was beginning to take a toll.

I wasn't new to anxiety or depression—I knew the signs: I didn't have an appetite anymore. I'd never been much of a breakfast eater, and I rarely had time for lunch—that twenty-five minutes was often spent engaging with a student in some way. I fibbed to a friend about why I couldn't go out one night, preferring to stay home alone and drink a bottle of wine by myself. During the weekends, I'd begun to spend the majority of my days asleep so I didn't have to think about things.

But the worst part was the return of crying spells. My eyes would well with tears as I drove to school, during lunch, and as I put together my lesson plans each night.

I knew from previous life experience that people didn't want to deal with me when I was like this, so I did my best to hide it and handle it myself.

I took the appropriate steps.

It took a while, but I found a new counselor and began going to see Shanna weekly. I'd seen almost a dozen counselors in my twenty-five years of life, so I knew to cut to the chase in my first session by sharing my laundry list of childhood "traumas," including an alcoholic father and emotionally unavailable mother. I'd learned how to set the stage early with a new therapist, explaining whatever shit show I was currently experiencing, which I was sure was brought on by my own decisions and inability to recognize the causality in my own emotions.

It felt good to share the insanities happening in my classroom with someone who didn't judge me and who offered a lens of consistent support.

And yet, my classroom wasn't getting any better. I spent hours lesson planning, putting the ownership of the failures in my classroom solely on my shoulders. Our Teach for America training had stressed that "teacher actions dictate student outcomes." I'd been taught that it was my fault if I couldn't keep my students engaged, or that they felt it was okay to hit each another or run out of the classroom. I clearly hadn't set high enough expectations or made the learning fun or exciting enough.

In addition, we were pushed to make "significant gains" each year. Because so many of our students, even kindergarteners, were behind on their academics, we were pushed to help our kids improve by metrics showing at least 1.5 years of growth or more each year.

When the new calendar year started, I had a new student join my class from the other second grade. Nolan was one of the few white students in the school, but it wasn't his race as much as his comb-over, navy-blue, collared sweaters, and overly empathetic demeanor that made him the target of relentless bullying. After the first semester was over, Nolan's parents had requested for him to shift to my classroom.

I'd heard the rumors that Nolan's family was threatening to sue the school for neglect and assault because Nolan had been hit multiple times in the other classroom. As devastating as this was to learn, it was honestly affirming—I wasn't the only Teach for America teacher having troubles at Carver.

Ms. King had first tried to place Nolan in Ms. Washington's third-grade classroom because Ms. Washington was a veteran teacher and Nolan didn't know many of the third-grade students, which seemed positive. But there was one key misstep: Nolan wasn't a third-grade student, and therefore wasn't receiving an education that best met his needs. After a few weeks, somebody in a position of authority let Ms. King know this couldn't continue; Nolan needed to be in second grade.

So when Nolan joined my classroom, Ms. King made very clear

that it was my job to keep him safe, and I was doing my best. But a few weeks after the second semester started, Nolan was punched in the face by Orion after Nolan "accidentally" kicked Orion's shoe. I wrote up the incident and sent them both to the office.

Things weren't going well.

During one particularly rough day in February, Ms. King walked into my chaotic room with a handwritten form. As pencils and insults flew across the room, she formally reprimanded me, which meant it would be added to my teaching record, for failure to control my classroom.

She laid the form on my desk, and then said, "You can leave if you want to. We'll just split your kids up into other classrooms. You're not doing anything to help us meet our AYP today."

This insult laid bare my inner self in front of my eight-year-old students, and the embarrassment and tears came quickly. As always, the most important thing was our Adequate Yearly Progress.

"I'm doing the best I can," I forced myself to say.

"And that's not good enough today. This isn't working right now. You can leave, and we'll send your kids to different rooms, or you can just pick some and we'll send them out," Ms. King said firmly.

"I guess . . ." I trailed off, not knowing what to say.

"Figure it out. Are you staying or are you going?" said Ms. King without a hint of empathy.

"Staying," I responded.

Leaving would give away any thread of control that remained in my hands.

"Khalil, Orion, Cornell, Ebony, Aiyden, and Samuel, please follow Ms. King," I said.

As the six students walked out, some giggling, I couldn't hold it in anymore and tears started streaming down my face.

Stop crying! I told myself, knowing this had become a common occurrence.

I turned my back to the class, trying to contain myself, and felt a hand slip into mine.

"Miss C," said a small voice. I looked down to see Destiny next to me. "You should just quit. This isn't fair."

That made the tears come faster. An eight-year-old, one of my own students, had just given me permission. No, it was more than that: She encouraged me to quit.

"Destiny, I don't want to leave you guys. I'm doing my best. I want to be your teacher," I said.

She began crying as well as she hugged me. I wiped away my tears, and turned to see the rest of the class. Jabris was at his desk, also crying.

A few minutes later, our vice principal, Ms. Hartley, walked into the classroom. I was sure she had been sent by Ms. King. At this point, all the students were quietly working on the assigned task, but I was still visibly upset.

Ms. Hartley focused her attention on me and said, in a low voice, "You need to get it together, bring up your self-esteem as a teacher."

If only it was that easy, I thought, realizing she was playing the "good cop" to Ms. King's "bad cop."

I said nothing and just nodded, feeling totally defeated.

"We're going to make you the Positive Behavior Support Team leader for the school. Hopefully that will help," she said, unconvincingly.

I had no idea what that was, but hoped maybe I'd get to miss school for some sort of training.

"Sure, I'm open to learning more ways to better support my class," I responded.

"Great, I'll talk to Ms. King."

Thanks for the pep talk, I thought sarcastically.

I felt an obligation to these students, to this school, to my commitment to Teach for America, to myself—I don't quit. But it was beginning to feel like I was going into battle each day.

Ms. King's formal reprimand, and the embarrassment of paring down my class, was just another fight in the war. I mentally worked through my battle plan: I'd call my Teach for America program director after school. She'd help me come up with another behavior plan, and maybe she'd know what this Positive Behavior Support Team thing meant. I'd try something new on Monday.

In the meantime, I just needed to get through the day, which should have been easier since I'd strategically reduced my class by six students. But I couldn't shake the shame of knowing my colleagues had to take portions of my class because I couldn't handle them.

The rest of the day was fine, until the final period when our Youth Friends Mentors stopped in for their weekly visit with their students.

I hadn't had much engagement with the two older white women who'd come into my classroom each week. I didn't really need to as their focus was on the students they worked with. The nonprofit had partnered with Carver for many years so I hadn't been given a choice in how to engage with the program, but I was happy that the experience seemed to be positive and provided some good, one-on-one mentorship for Destiny and Efrem.

We were just beginning our final lesson of the day, which was focused on writing. With the six students still missing from my classroom, it was smooth sailing. I walked around the classroom as the students were silently writing, stopping here and there to offer guidance and words of encouragement.

"Alright guys, I want you to put your pencils down and close your folders in three, two, one. Thank you for ending the day so well! When I say go, we're going to go ahead and put all of our materials away and start getting packed up for home."

The class waited in anticipation until I said, "Go!"

The students followed their end-of-the-day routine as the two mentors came back into the classroom with their students. They motioned for me to come over.

"Hi! How can I help?" I asked.

"Hi, Miss C. I was talking with Destiny today, and I'm sorry to hear it sounds like it was a rough day in here again," said one of the women.

I clenched my teeth and took a breath.

"Yeah, it was a bit of a tough day, but we're keeping at it!" I responded.

Her eyes softened. "You know, I feel like God is using me as his instrument here. There are some people who are made for this and others who aren't." I could sense the pity in her voice. "I'll be back next week, but I sincerely hope you aren't."

She patted my back and walked out of the class before I could respond.

What the actual fuck?

I stood near the door, stunned, as the class continued to prepare to leave around me. Was this God's plan? For me to quit less than halfway through what I committed to do? I wasn't so sure. God didn't seem to be anywhere near Carver Elementary School.

The six students who had been placed in other classrooms streamed back into my room, followed by Ms. King. As the class continued to pack up, following the procedures I had put in place, Ms. King walked back out without saying a word.

"Miss C! Our table is ready first!" Efrem said joyfully as he tugged on my hand, bringing me back to the moment.

I put my finger to my lips and, without saying a word, got my class to quiet down as my tears begged to spill over. I steeled my eyes and took a deep breath. It didn't matter if Ms. King had lost her faith in me, that the mentor I barely knew had told me to quit, or that my students were probably questioning my ability to continue.

I'd prove them wrong. I wasn't going anywhere.

chapter eight

Nolan remained a concern due to the bullying, but after a few weeks of stability, I was feeling pretty good about how I'd been managing a pretty tough situation. After his fight with Orion, I'd been monitoring Nolan's every movement, and most of the students in my class seemed to intuit Nolan had some sort of special protection and generally steered clear of him.

Nolan didn't have many friends, so he often engaged me in conversation.

One day, lightly spitting as he spoke, he said, "Miss C, did you know that I caught a big toad in my back yard last night? I know it was a toad because it was rough and bumpy, and not slimy like a frog. It was this big!"

He flipped his brown hair out of his eyes as he excitedly modeled the size of the toad with his thumbs and index fingers. He closed one of his eyes as he made sure his fingers offered just the right measurements, and finally looked to me for approval.

"I did not know that, Nolan! That sounds like fun! Where did you find him?"

"He was hiding in the grass in the back yard. He was hopping, and my mom didn't notice him, but I saw him right away. I wanted to keep him, but my mom said no."

"Oh, that's too bad. But that way it will make sure that he lives a long and healthy life, hopefully in your back yard!"

"Yeah, I guess so."

I could tell this wasn't quite the answer he had hoped to receive from me. "Maybe you can share about your toad in writing class later today, but right now it's time to take our seats so we can start our morning meeting."

"Okay—I'll talk to you later, Miss C," he said excitedly as he ran back to his seat.

Because of the target on his back from his peers, Nolan gravitated toward interacting with the teachers, and I couldn't blame him. But unfortunately, that isolated him from the others even more.

"Alright class, it's time to start our day! I need you all in your seats as I count backwards, and then I'll call your table-groups up to the carpet for morning meeting."

My routines weren't flawless, but I continued to set high expectations and, in large part, students were rising to them.

"Khalil, I need your bottom in your seat."

"Miss C, *my* bottom is in my seat," Nolan said playfully.

Several students rolled their eyes and sighed with disgust.

"I see that. Thank you, Nolan."

Sometimes I could tell why the students singled him out, but I didn't know quite how to nudge him in the right direction. I didn't know how to tell him, *Hey Nolan, if you could try to be a bit less Goody Two-shoes that would be helpful.*

Amazingly, the class flawlessly executed their morning meeting and were soon off to their reading classes, which were organized by reading level. A few kids stayed from my homeroom, but this shuffle meant I had a new class to teach with some first graders who bumped up and other third and fourth graders who came down to the second-grade reading level.

The education-reform model that Carver followed, called "Success for All," was a scripted curriculum that dictated word-for-word what you were to say and when you were to say it. It was so strict that we were told by Ms. King, "I should be able to walk into your classroom with the guide and know the words that are coming from your mouth."

Not exactly my idea of effective instruction.

"This stupid, Miss C," one said as he watched the puppets on the television screen.

The ninety-minute reading block wasn't something I needed to prepare for, which might sound idyllic given the environment we were in, but there was also no room for creativity—the program assumed teacher autonomy was a deficit.

I'd actually gotten into a public argument with our Success for All trainer during our new-teacher orientation over the summer. I hadn't known any better—just like Nolan, I seemingly knew how to put a target on my back from the very beginning. It started with an innocent enough question.

"If we find our students are struggling with certain concepts or materials, is it okay to substitute supplemental activities?" I'd asked.

That received a canned answer: "The Success for All curriculum is stand-alone. You will not need to supplement with any additional materials. Numerous studies have been completed, and time and time again the Success for All curriculum has been shown to work."

"But what if it doesn't?" I said, seeing I'd struck a nerve, knowing my naïveté was showing.

"So you think you know better than numerous learning scientists who have doctorates in education? If you follow the curriculum as written, as I've trained you on, you won't need to supplement a thing," she'd responded.

One of the reasons Teach for America had hired me was for my persistence.

"But these learning scientists don't know my students, or their experiences," I'd said.

I'd gotten on my soapbox before I'd even met my class, and received one of my first bell ringers in response.

"You need to understand you're now a cog in the wheel of teaching, and there's nothing you can do about that."

My face flushed. I kept silent, more disheartened than angry. This was just the beginning.

"Point – Ready – Read," from my Success for All script, became my daily mantra, and there was nothing I could do about it.

Once our reading block was over, students went back to their homeroom classes.

As my homeroom students filtered back into our classroom, I immediately noticed something was wrong with Nolan. There was a scrape and bump on his head, and he nervously went directly to his seat.

I made a beeline over to him.

"Hey Nolan, what happened to your head?" I asked.

"I fell."

The normally verbose young man was hiding something and I didn't buy it.

"Where? Are you sure that's all that happened?"

"I just fell on the carpet."

"Okay, well, I'm going to send you to the office to get an ice pack. That's a decent bump. We'll want to make sure the swelling goes down."

I called the office and let them know Nolan was coming with a bump on his head, and that I couldn't get any more information out of him. We had to take care of his physical wellness first. I'd try to get information later.

Nolan came back to the classroom, ice pack in hand. He almost seemed proud of his shiner at this point.

"I feel a lot better, Miss C," he said.

"Okay good, buddy. Just let me know if anything changes, and you don't feel good, okay?"

He agreed and we continued with class, moving into our math lesson as I wholly forgot about the bump, until Alexis spoke up.

"Miss C! Nolan's lips are turning blue," Alexis shouted.

Sure enough, I glanced over to see Nolan's lips were a light shade of blue.

"Nolan, are you feeling okay?"

"Yeah, I'm okay, Miss C."

"Well, I'm going to call the office and have Ms. King come just in case. We'll see if the nurse is here today."

I followed protocol and called the front office, telling our school secretary I needed Ms. King or Ms. Hartley as soon as possible for a medical emergency, and that this had to do with Nolan. The school secretary said she'd send someone right away.

I looked back to Nolan and his skin color had changed to a pale yellow-white.

"Nolan, are you okay, buddy? Keep that ice on your head."

"I'm okay, Miss C. Just tired," he said.

I called the office again and asked for help. Ms. Hartley walked in as I was hanging up and escorted Nolan to the office.

Just fifteen minutes later, because of my classroom's proximity to the main office, my entire class heard the stretcher's wheels and seatbelt harnesses bang over the front door's threshold. A few of my students ran to the doorway. I quickly shooed them away, but used their faux pas to my advantage, watching as Nolan was strapped to the stretcher.

Little did I know, this would be the last time I'd see Nolan.

He didn't die, but his family had, understandably, lost all faith in Carver Elementary's ability to keep him safe. I'd failed him; Carver had failed him. It felt like this system I was working in was one failure after the next.

I would later provide a statement to a police officer under Ms. King's direction. I couldn't help but feel responsible, even if the event hadn't happened in my classroom. I would never find out what had truly happened to Nolan, nor how he was doing. I can only hope he found a classroom and a school that provided him what he needed.

I called Mick. I knew I'd be seeing him later in the evening, but I just had to get off my chest what had happened with Nolan. I laid out bare the conclusion of Nolan's story: the bump on his head, the white-as-a-sheet moment, the lack of support from the office until he had to be taken away on the stretcher, and the immense guilt I was feeling.

"It's not your fault," Mick said.

I paused. I didn't know how to respond.

"You know this isn't your fault, right?"

Tears welled. "I feel like I should have been able to . . ."

"No, Nicole. This isn't your fault."

I unsuccessfully tried to hold back a sob.

"Hey, it's okay. Would you wanna stop at my place before we go out tonight? Then we can spend some time together just the two of us?" Mick said.

I pulled myself together, responding, "That sounds great. I'll text when I'm on my way over—it'll probably be a couple hours."

"See you then."

It was great to spend some time with Mick one-on-one, and when we showed up together at the bar there was no doubt that we were together, even if we hadn't had a conversation about being "boyfriend/girlfriend."

"So, pregaming now together too?" Rachel nudged when she got me alone.

"Honestly, it was such a tough day. Mick just invited me over beforehand to spend some time."

"Well, that's sweet. But what happened?"

"Nolan—it's a long story."

"We got time!"

I shared my story, and Rachel and Tess had their own from the week. We took a shot together in solidarity.

As the night moved into the early morning hours, Mick made eye contact from across the room. I knew what he was asking and nodded in agreement.

"Hey guys, I think I'm gonna head out," I told my friends.

"Off to Mick's?" Rachel asked.

I didn't even try to play coy.

"Yep," I said.

Mick and I walked back to his apartment hand-in-hand, our exhalations visible with each breath through the below-freezing night air.

We crawled into bed together, snuggling up to each other in the dark as we began to fade into sleep.

"I love you," Mick said.

Suddenly I was more awake. My breath quickened.

"I love you too," I said.

It had come naturally.

I wasn't sure how much alcohol he'd had, or if he really meant what he said. We fell asleep in each other's arms.

We woke as the sun began to stream through the open portion of his curtains and snuggled up to each other again.

"Do you wanna grab breakfast at Winstead's?" Mick asked.

"That sounds great. Pancakes are a necessity."

"I don't think I know anyone who likes pancakes as much as you."

I laughed. "Do you think you could drive me back to my place after?"

"Of course."

"Perfect. Hey, do you remember what you said to me last night?"

I needed to know.

"You mean, 'I love you'?"

"Yeah."

"I meant what I said."

I couldn't contain the grin on my face. "Me too," I said.

Rachel stopped me after school one day.

"Hey, I've got a proposition for you," she said.

"Okay, I'm listening."

"What would you think about an after-school tutoring gig? Like what you do currently, but for this you get paid."

"Well, I certainly could use some additional money, but not so sure I'm excited about formally continuing the teaching day."

"But you're basically doing the same thing with those kids you pick up from across the street, right?"

"It's not quite the same. I do whatever I want—I skip it if I want to."

"Well, this gig seems pretty laid back. It'd be at this Youth Center. It's a lot of our students from Carver, but some other neighborhood kids as well."

"Hmm . . . I'd be willing to take a look. How'd you find out about this?"

"Ms. Harper was gonna work there, but decided not to and mentioned it to me. I think they have quite a few openings."

"Cool. I could use the money."

"I'll go with you to check it out after school today! It's super close. I went last week, and think I'm gonna do it. You should do it with me," Rachel said.

Though I had really enjoyed my informal after-school tutoring sessions with my little crew from Ms. Eleanor's, this seemed like a good opportunity—and a paid gig. In addition, I didn't feel as though there was much I could do to support Samuel anymore, outside of the continued classroom work and engagement. If I'd navigated what I did to make an abuse report, only to have it come back unfounded, what was the point? As I was learning very quickly, there was no lack of students in need of opportunities.

The Youth Center offered tutoring, snacks, and mentorship—a sorely needed service—and I'd still get to help support students outside of the formal classroom setting.

Rachel and I made the short drive, and as we pulled into what appeared to be a vacant lot, I asked, "This is it?"

"No, it's in the basement of that apartment complex," Rachel responded.

After walking across the lot and back around the 1920s apartment complex, we came to a heavy black door. I could hear the students inside. Rachel opened the door to a room that looked as I had expected it to: painted white cinderblocks; tiny windows that afforded minimal natural light; folding tables and metal folding chairs; and a small kitchen offering carrot sticks, light snacks, and the same milk as what was included in free-and-reduced lunches at Carver.

As my eyes landed on Izaak and Aiyden, two of my second-grade students, Izaak proclaimed, "Miss C! What are you doing here?"

"Hey guys! I didn't expect to see you here!"

"Are you gonna teach here?"

"I'm trying to get her to!" Rachel said before I could respond.

"Oh, please come teach here after school!" said Aiyden.

"Yes! Please Miss C?" Izaak chimed in at the same time.

I laughed. "I'll have to see, guys! I haven't even talked to—who am I supposed to talk to, Ms. Sothern?" I asked Rachel.

"Jacob," she responded. "He's the founder and executive director. We'll see if he's here."

"Hey, you guys, enjoy those snacks," I said to the kids.

As they focused on their food, I saw a few more familiar faces from Carver's second-grade class, and others I recognized from Carver's middle school. Rachel was right—it was super laid back. Jacob wasn't at the center that day, so I had a phone interview the following week. Due to my credentials and established relationships with Carver students, I was a natural fit for the program.

I was hired to work with kids in all grade levels, kindergarten through eighth grade, after school two to three days a week, depending on who showed up each day. The program was more focused on building relationships with the students than it was on formal instructional support, but I was okay with this. It offered an opportunity for the students to see me in a different light and, at the same time, provided a space for the students to be more relaxed.

I enjoyed working with the older students in particular. I connected with them on literature—*The Giver, The Outsiders, To Kill a Mockingbird, Bud, Not Buddy*—books that were far from accessible to my second graders. It just took a few weeks to get to know many of them well, especially a young woman named Chantelle who was a seventh grader at Carver. We just clicked with each other.

"Miss C, I wish you were my teacher," Chantelle shared as we worked on her English homework.

"Well, I kind of am."

She sucked her teeth. "Nah, like every day, all day. Those teachers we have don't help me like you do."

"Well, it's not quite the same environment. I'm able to help you one-on-one right now. If there were thirty other kids here, maybe you'd feel differently."

"Nah."

I giggled.

"Miss C!" Izaak interrupted. "I wish we had a swimming pool full of candy, with just you, me, and Aiyden, and then we could dive in it and eat all of it."

Aiyden and Izaak, students from my class at Carver, followed me around the center daily.

It was at these moments I could see through the fistfights, and swearing, and defiance—these kids were just yearning to be regular kids, but the experiences and reality around them often stifled it.

"Miss C, does your boyfriend hit you?" Izaak asked.

I paused. "No, Izaak. What makes you ask that?"

"You have a big red mark on your arm." He pointed at me.

"Oh! Yeah, that's big bug bite I just can't seem to stop itching."

The question was one that would have never crossed my mind as a seven-year-old. From a swimming pool of candy to domestic violence.

The conversations I had with students at the after-school program were different than those I had in my classroom. I looked forward to the after-school sessions at the Youth Center, where I felt so much more respected by the students and the staff.

At Carver, the students fell apart if Ms. King was ever absent, particularly kids in the middle school. There was one day that the kids knew Ms. King would be gone for two days at a conference, and the entire school ran amok. There were kids smoking weed in the downstairs bathroom, others using the rolling coat closets to host races in the hallways, and multiple fistfights. Ms. Hartley went downstairs to try to bring order to the chaos.

"Middle school students, I need you to stop this immediately!" she shouted, attempting to assert her authority but looking like a chicken skirting the farmyard as her short legs failed to quickly cut off students from passing her by, her salt-and-pepper bouffant shook, and her cheeks burned red as she pointed her finger in their faces.

Tanisha, one of the seventh-grade ringleaders, was sitting on a table in the hallway, watching the madness, and offered a nonchalant: "Oh, Ms. Hartley. Fuck off."

On the same day, I tried my best to manage my own unruly second graders and had several students walk out of class, broke up two fistfights, and watched in horror as Kahlil exposed himself to his classmates in the library.

After coming back to a thick stack of behavior reports on her desk, I was told that Ms. King suspended more students on the day she returned than she had suspended during the whole school year up until that point.

"Can you believe it? Fourteen seventh graders are gone! That's half the class!" Rachel exclaimed. "It's gonna be an easy rest of the week!"

Ms. King rarely suspended students and, from many teachers' vantage points, rarely provided real repercussions for unacceptable behavior.

Many teachers at Carver struggled, but it really seemed like my experiences were harder than most. It was a vicious cycle: I couldn't effectively manage student behavior, so my second-grade students knew they could get away with walking out of class, swearing at me, or punching a classmate in the face. I was seen as the problem, and it didn't matter that I was trying my best.

Ms. King leveraged fear as her main discipline driver, but the students at Carver weren't afraid of much, especially not a woman in her sixties.

So Ms. King had become a bit unorthodox in her older age. I understood the desire to keep kids in their classrooms—they weren't learning if they weren't in class—but more recently Ms. King had begun to corral all students who had been sent out of class in a newly created space she called the "wellness center," which was actually just an empty classroom with a few tables and chairs and some brochures. This quickly became like a study hall for students in all grades, and it seemed the kids preferred being there over their actual classrooms. Middle school students who had been asked to leave class became the de facto instructors, tutoring and monitoring between six and eight students (sometimes more) of varying grade levels.

The fact that so many students were out of class *every day* shows just how tough things had gotten at Carver by the spring.

Leaving students alone, unattended except for a middle schooler who was the monitor, didn't sit well with me—but I had seen what happened when I'd spoken up in the past and I was going to keep my mouth shut.

On an average day, it wasn't abnormal for me to send at least two or three students to the office—and one Thursday in early April was no different. Seemingly unprovoked, Khalil had slapped Cornell across the face and Cornell, who was typically well behaved, got on top of Khalil, grabbed his braids, and started punching until I was able to physically separate them.

Cornell cried as I sent them both to the office with their write-up sheets; Khalil smirked—this was nothing new for him.

After dropping off my class at the library, I went to check in on the two boys who I knew would be in the wellness center with their middle-school instructors.

"Hi, Miss C!" Khalil said, giggling.

"Khalil, this isn't supposed to be fun, buddy."

"Oh, but *it is*."

I pursed my lips—I didn't have a response.

"Miss C, I need to tell you something." Cornell grabbed my hand.

Khalil looked away from his work, kicking his legs on the oversized chair as he looked to the middle schoolers who were making faces at him.

"What's up, Cornell?" I asked.

He stood and guided me across the room to a quiet corner. "Miss C, Khalil has been playin' too much."

"I'm sorry, bud. I can check in with Ms. King and see what we're gonna do here."

"Miss C, Khalil touched my privates. He was playin' under the table and put his mouth on them."

I couldn't hide my shock and disgust. "Okay, when did this happen?" I asked.

"Just a little while ago. Everyone was playin', and the middle schoolers were busy, and Khalil went under the table and it just happened." He had tears in his eyes.

At this point, I was still holding his hand, which I squeezed. "You didn't do anything wrong, okay? I'm sorry this happened. I'm going to go talk to Ms. King right now and see if we can get you out of here. Do you wanna come with me?" I asked.

"Yeah."

The two of us walked to the office, and I motioned to one of the few chairs that were typically reserved for waiting parents. Cornell sat down.

I looked to our secretary and asking, "Ms. Willis, is Ms. King in her office?"

"She should be back there!" she said.

"Thanks so much!"

I walked back to Ms. King's office and lightly tapped on her door.

As I relayed the story, her eyes got big and she quickly got to her feet.

"I just left them for a few moments while I was eating lunch. I'll make sure I address this right now. No need for any further involvement, Miss C. I'll take it from here," she said.

As I followed Ms. King back to the front of the office, Cornell rose.

"Come with me, Cornell," she said.

"I wanna stay with Miss C, if that's okay," Cornell responded.

Ms. King wasn't used to being talked back to, but she nodded in agreement as she said, "I'll be by Miss C's room to pick you up shortly."

Cornell and I walked back to my classroom, and as Ms. King walked into the wellness center we heard the raucous laughter stop as the room came to attention.

"Ms. King will take care of everything, okay? You didn't do anything wrong," I reassured Cornell, who nodded and looked at the floor as we walked.

But I wasn't sure she would. She hadn't followed through with Samuel, that was for sure. What systems were there to protect Cornell?

"Can I play on the computers?" Cornell asked.

"Just until library time is over, and the rest of the class comes back—deal?"

"Deal," he said with a small grin.

As the day ended, I weighed my options. I could get involved, push to make sure things were handled the way I deemed was correct. But I'd seen what that had gotten me with Samuel: not much except a large target on my back.

I'll let Ms. King handle it, I decided.

But as I packed up to go home for the day, I couldn't let it go. The anger in me swelled—this wasn't right. So I decided to push the envelope a bit.

I slipped on my coat and backpack, and entered the front office through the side door that offered a direct line to Ms. King's office.

I knew she'd still be there—she always was. It was quiet. I lightly pushed the door open, this time without knocking.

"Ms. King?" I said quietly.

"Yes?" She looked up from her paperwork.

"I just wanted to check in on the Cornell and Khalil situation."

"I've taken care of it." She narrowed her eyes, daring me to push the conversation further.

"Okay, well, thanks for your support," I said, pulling the door closed.

There was no way for me to push the matter further. I'd seen what working within the system got me with Samuel. That was the end of that.

Spring break was a welcome intermission as we prepared for the final weeks of school. Mick and I had planned to spend as much time together as possible—movies, lunch dates, going to the pool at his apartment, playing music, and just hanging out. We also had plans to record some music together; I wanted to sing a few Christian songs and put them on a CD to give to my dad for his birthday.

Though I'd been a music minor in college and spent most of my life singing, recording was new, and very fun, territory for me.

Mick had set up a makeshift music studio in his closet, and it was a treat to hear him providing direction from his spot in the studio to me in my booth.

After an afternoon of recording, we called it quits and celebrated with beers on his balcony, where we'd spent a lot of time recently. There wasn't all that much to look at aside from more apartments across a service alleyway, but we'd been enjoying being outdoors there together.

"You have a really great voice," Mick said.

"Thank you!" I couldn't help but blush. "I really enjoy singing, but was only a music minor in college, which I realize is more than nothing but, at my school—which was heavily focused on opera—if you weren't a music *major*, you were nothing."

He laughed. "Well, I feel like I can hear the operatic influence—is that even a word?"

Now it was my turn to laugh. "I really love the song too. My dad got me the Jaci Velasquez CD and I immediately fell in love with 'God So Loved.' I memorized a lot of scripture growing up, and it's always great to hear it set to music."

"Your faith seems to be really important to you."

"Yeah, it's always played a big part in my life. I grew up going to church every Sunday, and largely still do, though I've been going to later morning services on Sunday due to some late Saturday nights . . ." I trailed off and smiled.

"I'm curious—with your faith, do you still believe in evolution then?"

"You know, I don't see them as necessarily conflicting. I think I can believe in both."

"Interesting."

"I'm gonna own I haven't really thought through all the details there, though."

And I hadn't. As much as I wished my faith was a solid bedrock, as I had just sung "God so loved the world," there was a lot, particularly as of late, that didn't sit well with me.

Mick graciously changed the subject.

"Thanks for the willingness to apartment-sit for me. I'm glad someone will get to take advantage of the pool!"

"Are you excited to go home this summer? I'm sure it'll feel good to see your family and friends."

"Absolutely. I'll be excited to be a back in the Bay. I knew I wanted to join the Teach for America Kansas City corps because it would be so different than anything I'd ever experienced, and I was most definitely right!"

"Well, is it clear you haven't been missing much in the Midwest?" I asked.

"Not at all. I've really enjoyed my time here, for many reasons, the most obvious being you."

I blushed again.

We'd exchanged keys for each other's places, which was a first for me, and we had already begun talking about what would happen to "us" once we had completed our Teach for America experience even though that was over a year away. Things were moving quickly, and though I was scared, everything felt so right.

"I know it's a ways away, but what would you think about moving to San Francisco with me after we're done with our second year?" Mick asked.

I couldn't contain my grin. "Seriously? I'd be so excited. I mean, I'd have to think about it—it'd be so different than anything I've ever experienced, but I'd be with you, right?"

"Definitely take your time and, like I said, we've got time, but I'd be excited if we could migrate back there together after our time here. In the meantime, what would you think about coming this summer to visit my family?"

"That sounds like a good start!"

"Let's pick the dates and get you out to visit. I'd love to show you my home and have you meet my family."

"I'd be honored."

The high I'd experienced during my spring break with Mick quickly ended as the apprehension of going back to Carver heightened. Our final days of vacation weren't relaxing at all, and were instead fueled by anxiety as I anticipated the final months of the school year.

My last thirty-six hours before going back to school were filled with uncontrollable crying and panic attacks. On the night before we were scheduled to go back to school, I called Rachel sobbing. She spent the night at my place, ensuring we'd get up together and support each other as we prepared for the final six weeks. It was a sprint to the finish line.

chapter nine

My Success for All reading block (aside from the scripted curriculum and total lack of creative control) had quickly become the highlight of my day, at least from a behavioral perspective. The constant remixing of students kept everyone engaged—until Jabris joined the class.

He would have been a very large third-grade student in his own right, but having been held back a year, his boxlike frame towered over his second-grade counterparts. After a recent reading assessment many of the students moved levels, so my classes looked different.

Jabris was an instigator, grabbing books out of other students' hands as they worked through their lessons, roughly knocking students down with his big frame as we moved to the carpet, throwing pencils across the room, and doing anything else he could think of to disrupt the classroom. Daily, I quickly moved him through my behavioral chart, had private discussions with him during and after class, and even connected with his homeroom teacher to determine the best ways I could engage him. My attempts were largely futile.

As we approached the end of the school year, it was clear Jabris wouldn't be moving up, which meant he'd remain in my class. As time went on, it seemed as though things with Jabris were getting worse, not better.

"I'm going to kick your ass," rang out Jabris's voice from behind me.

"Jabris, that's not—" I said as I heard students' chairs clatter to the ground.

I turned around to see two figures move across the classroom. Jabris looked like a football lineman on a quest for the quarterback. Marquand, one of the students I tutored after school, was the other figure darting around chairs as he quickened his pace and Jabris chased him. As the two made their way toward me at the front of the classroom, I knew that would be my opportunity.

"Jabris and Marquand, I need you to stop where you are right now!" I commanded.

The two continued without acknowledgement. Marquand skirted by me and continued his circle around the classroom. I made myself as large as possible, opening my arms and planting my feet, showing Jabris that he couldn't get through. I'm sure I looked ridiculous, but it was all I could think to do in the moment.

Jabris didn't stop as I had anticipated, and ran into me full bore. I fell hard, landing directly on my coccyx. Even though I'd seemingly been prepared for the contact, it hurt. The class went silent, a few gasps escaping from open mouths.

"Miss C! You okay?" Marquand said, running toward me.

Jabris made it known he wasn't finished and continued his pursuit.

"Jabris, ENOUGH!" I roared.

This time, he stopped.

"I need you to go to the office," I said.

He *tsk*ed his teeth at me. "Aw man, Miss C. You got in *my* way. That's on you."

"I need you to go to the office now. I'll send the referral form in a few minutes, with Marquand."

He turned with a huff and walked toward the door.

Now it was Marquand's turn.

"Aww Miss C, that ain't fair," he said. "I ain't do nothin'."

"Take a seat. The rest of you continue with your partners," I said.

At this point in the school year, there wasn't much that surprised me anymore, but I couldn't believe I'd gotten knocked on my ass by a second grader. Maybe I shouldn't have gotten in front of Jabris, but I didn't know what else to do.

Damned if I do, damned if I don't.

I wrote the two referral slips, one for Marquand and another for Jabris. I'm sure Ms. King would have something to say about this, but I didn't care. I'd taken to writing up everything at this point. If I wasn't going to get the support I felt like I needed from the administration, I was going to at least leave a paper trail, and a big one at that. Ms. King did have words for me later in the day.

"I'm not sure why you didn't just let them run," she said.

"If that's what you want me to do next time, I will."

"I'd rather you have your classroom under control."

I set myself up for that, I thought, not responding.

"Well, I suspended Jabris for three days, but you really gave me no choice, particularly when a teacher is physically involved. But I want you to know this one is really on you."

Now that there wasn't any doubt that this one was indeed my fault, the guilt ensued. But as Ms. King walked out, an unfamiliar face walked in with Jabris in tow.

"Are you Miss C?" she asked.

"Yes, that's me. You must be Jabris's mom."

"Yeah, I just wanted to come talk to you because Ms. King told me what happened in reading class this morning with Jabris."

"Yeah, it was a bit of a tough morning."

"Why you lyin' on him?"

What does that mean? I thought.

"I'm sorry?" I said.

"Why you lyin' on Jabris?" She pursed her lips.

Jabris looked at me, smirking as he watched me squirm.

"I can assure you, I'm not lying. You can ask any of the students in the reading class. They can confirm what happened if you don't believe me."

"Well, I'm fixin' to whoop him," she said.

And then just as quickly as she had come in, she was gone. I hadn't even gotten her name.

I felt so defeated. I didn't even get a say, and every attempt to engage or do what I thought was the right thing was for naught.

Carver was just a cog in the bigger wheels of multiple failing systems. I'd already ended up on my ass and, if I wasn't careful, I knew it could get worse.

With only a month of school left, time flew by with the day-to-day grind at Carver, schoolwork for my graduate program, after-school hours spent at the Youth Center, and carving out time for a personal life with Mick. I continued to live for the weekends, going out drinking with friends and spending the weekends at Mick's—and sometimes even the weekday evenings as well. We couldn't get enough of each other, and would talk about everything from our families and friends to music and our philosophies about life.

I'd really begun to enjoy my time at the Youth Center. I was working after school three days a week, and the different environment had only supported the continued growth of relationships with my after-school students.

Chantelle and I had grown much closer. Initially, I had been driving her home (with permission from her mom and the Center). Upon finding out she was going home to an empty house that stayed that way until late in the evening, I connected with her mom and took it a step further: Three days a week, after our time at the Center, I'd drive Chantelle to my home to eat dinner and do homework with me.

By 9 p.m., Chantelle's older sister was typically home from her National Guard duty. Chantelle's mom worked the late shift, so didn't typically get home until 11 p.m. or later.

"So, it's nothing fancy tonight, Chantelle," I said one night. "We've got Kraft Mac & Cheese and hot dogs."

"Miss C, you funny. That's kid food," Chantelle said, ribbing me.

"And I can still pretend to be a kid, clearly!" I laughed.

Honestly, with only ten years between the two of us, there were times I felt more like a big sister than a teacher—to Chantelle or any of my other students.

This feeling was particularly acute as the water boiled on the stove, and Chantelle's and my collective schoolwork was spread out across my kitchen table. We each had claimed half of the table: my side held curriculum textbooks for my master's degree, copious handwritten notes in my notebook, and my computer, while Chantelle's side was covered with her middle-school textbooks, notebooks, and pencils for her evening homework.

"Miss C, I don't get this. Why are there letters in math? Can you help me?"

"Ooooh! I can help you with that. I don't love math, but I actually don't mind algebra." I poured the noodles from the box into the boiling water and plopped two hot dogs into the other pot. "The most important task at hand though—do you want one or two hot dogs?"

"One is more than enough."

"Done!" I said, pulling up a chair next to Chantelle's. "Okay, whatcha got for me?"

Looking back, I realize I likely crossed some traditional student-teacher boundaries, not only in driving Chantelle home, but also in having dinner multiple nights a week with her. But, at the time, it seemed like a no-brainer. I held her accountable for her homework while I was doing my own graduate schoolwork, and we ate together often in a much healthier manner than I would have done if I was alone, which often involved skipping meals altogether. Then I drove the couple miles to drop her off at a home where the lights were on and her sister was waiting for her. It's unsurprising that the two of us formed a special bond, as we really got to know and depend on each other.

I was grateful for the time with her, and for the chance to form a positive relationship with a student when so much of my day was marred with the negative.

Mick was the first guy I'd taken back to my childhood home in Northwest Iowa. But his first and only experience, at that point, had been at my grandfather's funeral. I knew I needed to invite him back to share what my home truly had to offer, even if it couldn't compare to the California coast.

So I invited him to come to our community's annual Tulip Festival. The Tulip Festival began in 1936 to honor the area's Dutch heritage, and continues today with authentic costumes, music, and dance; Dutch foods; windmills; and, of course, thousands of tulips.

Aside from being the most Republican county in the state of

Iowa, Sioux County is also the most Dutch county in the United States. The first wave of Dutch immigrants established a colony in Northwest Iowa in the 1870s, and these strong ties continue today, with 46 percent of households claiming Dutch heritage,[15] my family included: My dad is 100 percent Dutch and my mom is 75 percent.

There's a subtle beauty to the Iowa farmland and an authenticity to the Dutch people that's difficult to find elsewhere, but the Tulip Festival offered an even better reason to go home.

Mick was in from the beginning.

"You guys have an entire festival focused on tulips? I'd love to go with you. That sounds like a lot of fun," he said.

"It's no Golden Gate Bridge, so please don't get your hopes up. But I'll show you all the fun that Northwest Iowa has to offer."

Mick laughed. "I'm in."

It was a long haul from Kansas City—almost five hours of interstate driving, traversing flat farmland.

At one point, Mick joked, "You could see your dog run away for days."

After lots of easy conversation and a few pit stops, we pulled onto the gravel road that made up the final miles to my dad's home and the farm that had been in my family for more than a century.

I'd grown up on the gravel roads, driving on them before I legally had permission to drive on the pavement. I'd learned about staying on the dirt path created by all the passersby until you approached a hill and about how the tall corn would create blind corners during the summer. I knew well the familiar sound of a car approaching in the distance, and how I'd glance outside to see if I knew who was driving by, and that the driver would always offer a finger-raise in greeting whether I knew them or not. The gravels gave me prairie-flower walks and talks with my dad and terrain to run—four miles total around the farm.

The slight fishtail of the back two wheels of my car slipping over the loose rock was a familiar experience to me, but as I slowed to take the corner I noticed Mick was tense, his hand gripping the door and his knuckles white.

"Are you okay?" I asked.

"Oh—yeah." He paused. "You drive these roads a lot, huh?"

I couldn't help but laugh out loud. "I'm so sorry! I can take it slower. Yes, I'm much more comfortable on these roads than I am driving on the freeway. Seriously though, my bad. I can take it easy."

Mick's hands loosened their grip on the door handle as my speed decreased, and we pushed through the final mile to my dad's home.

"I'm super sorry—we're gonna have to sleep in separate rooms again. It's just the reality of the situation with my dad," I said.

"I totally get it. I absolutely will respect your dad's wishes. I know he has a gun cabinet," Mick teased.

"You're hilarious," I scoffed. "Plus, you get the Ninja Turtle sheets," I joked.

Mick was a natural at engaging with my dad—much more so than I'd anticipated from a born-and-bred San Franciscan interacting with a man who'd spent almost the entirety of his life working in nature and farming.

Our time spent in Northwest Iowa only made Mick's and my relationship stronger.

We spent an afternoon at the Tulip Festival, watching the parade of authentic, Dutch-costumed street cleaners ensuring a path suitable for the tulip queen; the Pride of the Dutchmen marching band; and the antique tractors. We noshed on grilled bratwurst, funnel cakes, and Dutch letters—a puff-pastry cookie with almond-paste filling shaped in an *S* for Sinterklaas, or St. Nicholas.

We perused the art, watched wooden shoes be made, and listened to the antique player organ my grandfather had kept in working condition for more than two decades before he had passed. We saw thousands of tulips in various sizes, shapes, and colors. And we saw friends and acquaintances from my childhood.

More than once, I heard someone ask, "Is that Nicole Cleveringa?" only to find myself engaged in conversation shortly thereafter with elementary school friends, old church parishioners and neighbors, and friends of my dad and grandparents—many whom I remembered and others I didn't.

The small talk was well-meaning, but tedious: Are you still in Des Moines? Oh, you're teaching now—how are you liking that? How's your mom, and those brothers of yours? It's so nice you can be here to visit your dad. How long are you staying?

"Is this your special friend?" asked one old acquaintance.

Mick and I were, unsurprisingly, a hot commodity in small-town Iowa. It had been a while since I'd last been home and, at an event like Tulip Festival, everyone from all the local small towns was in one place.

As Mick and I waited in line for our final funnel cake of the day, we recapped the best parts of the experience.

"That band—the marching band you were in. I can't believe those were middle schoolers. It's clear why the Pride of the Dutchmen is as good as it is, when they're feeding from the middle school like that!"

"Yeah—the high school band has done the Rose Bowl parade multiple times. People always remember them, not only because they're so good, but because they march in wooden shoes."

"The drumline is great too—makes me really excited to work with my students when I get back. *So* many ideas!" Mick's eyes lit up.

"Well, I think that aside from the funnel cakes, my favorite part is when that little old church lady asked if you were my 'special friend.'"

Mick laughed. "I thought you handled that like a pro, but truthfully we are most definitely more than friends."

He slipped his hand into mine and I couldn't contain the grin on my face, looking away to hide any awkwardness. There was a young woman in a Dutch costume in line in front of us, waiting for her food. She had a large symbol tattooed on the back of her neck that was perfectly framed by her collar and the Dutch bonnet she wore.

I leaned into Mick and whispered, "Oh my gosh, look! Do you see that tattoo on the back of her neck? That's an ancient Dutch symbol."

"Whoa, seriously?"

"No."

"Oh my God. You are the absolute worst. You 100 percent had me."

Any feeling of awkwardness was gone.

"Thanks again for coming home to visit with me."

"Absolutely—I'm so happy to be here with you."

"That said, we're probably going to have to get two funnel cakes, because I'm not sharing."

"Deal."

When I'd moved from the small town of Alton to Iowa's state capital, Des Moines, in ninth grade, it was a huge leap to go from a town of 1,200 to a city of almost 200,000. I'd gone from an elementary-school class of forty to a high school class of a hundred and forty. The move to Kansas City after college was another big shift, more than doubling what I had deemed to be a metropolis in Des Moines. Kansas City boasted a population of more than 450,000.

Coming back home to Alton was often bittersweet. And, by coming back with Mick, I recognized things I hadn't been attuned to in the past: Alton was much smaller and quainter than I'd remembered. This was the place that taught blue collar values—the whatever-it-takes work ethic, a tight-knit community focused on compassion, a staunch focus on character and humility.

But I didn't live in the community anymore and, after moving to the "big" city in Des Moines and then the even bigger city in Kansas City, I was left straddling two different experiences. Living in a true city had taught me the benefits of being "unknown," including the ability to get lost in a crowd and the incredible access to opportunity.

A lot had stayed the same in Alton: the little old church ladies getting the pulse on all the happenings, the small-town grocery store where you greeted someone you knew in every aisle, the butcher (yes, Alton still has one), and the single red light down the street from the single bar down the street from the single convenience store.

But there were changes I hadn't expected as well.

The OK Cafe had closed, which had been the town's only real restaurant during my childhood and where I'd held my first real job. And the Highway 60 bypass had been constructed, cutting four new lanes of 65 mph expressway through the Iowa fields and skirting around all of the nearby small towns, including Alton. What little amount of traffic we used to get through town was now nonexistent, and many of the businesses had dried up. Congressional approval of the Keystone Pipeline project was a sore subject with my dad; the small, plastic, orange flags detailed the planned path for the pipeline, adding yet another slice through the Iowa farmland.

There were also a number of new hog confinements across Sioux County, including one about a quarter mile from my dad's farm home. I wasn't thrilled about this and neither was Dad, especially as they had seemingly popped up everywhere. Not only did the smell leave something to be desired, but the confinements were just massive buildings that held hundreds and even thousands of pigs. Workers came in and out daily. The small family farm was becoming a relic of the past.

My aunt and uncle had sold the land that had been willed to them by my grandparents—land that had been in our family for more than a century. My dad had kept his plot around the farmhouse, but he told me he wasn't sure how much longer he could continue to farm the hundred acres that were left. It didn't make sense to maintain all the machinery for such a small plot.

This was becoming the new reality of small-town Iowa. My dad didn't seem too concerned, but I was seeing all these changes at once, which was tough to absorb. Thankfully, Mick was as supportive as always.

The long weekend went quickly. Anticipating the five-hour drive back, we planned to leave before church on Sunday morning so we could get back into the city and still have a bit of time to decompress before beginning the school week.

"Thank you so much for the hospitality, Dwane. I'm so appreciative," Mick said to my dad as we were leaving.

"Happy to have you both. It was great to spend the time. Next time you come, we'll have James and Andrew here and we can do some trap shooting too."

"I'd really like that."

I gave my dad one last hug. "I love you," I said.

"Call me when you get home."

"Will do, Dad."

I'd always get a bit teary-eyed as I drove away from my dad's home because I knew it would be a while until I'd see him again. After I drove my car off the front yard, we were back on the gravel road. We passed the new hog confinement that had sprung up so near our home.

"Ha! Look at the pig out there just chilling," said Mick.

I couldn't help myself—I burst out laughing. "Oh Mick, that pig is dead!"

He looked at me, clearly waiting for an explanation. I realized I may have been a bit harsh.

"They set it out for the rendering plant to come and pick up."

"I don't even know what that is."

"It's a place that processes it for other use—they don't want it inside with the other animals in case it's diseased. That way they can still find a use for it—usually dog food. Of course, I grew up out here. There's no way I would have expected you to know that."

At this point, he couldn't contain his laughter either. He was a California boy, through and through.

Even though the trip home had gone well, and I was enjoying my friendship with Chantelle and teaching at the Youth Center, and the end of the school year was in sight, I could feel the all-too-familiar grip of my depression and anxiety beginning to take a firm hold on my daily life.

Crying on the way to school was becoming more and more

common. Even the promise of the weekend ahead didn't sway my mindset as I walked to my car one Friday morning.

I saw the note on my windshield before I saw the broken glass.

Sorry :(

Then I saw the broken glass in my rear seat, and that my car had been rifled through.

There wasn't even anything to steal—some old CDs? I told myself.

And then the tears came. At least this time I had a reason to cry.

I went through the motions of the day, doing my best with the tools I had available to me and executing some good lessons. Then I said goodbye for the weekend, gave out hugs, and deflected Rachel's offer to go out since it was Friday.

"I'm so tired," I said.

"Rally, my friend. We've got to celebrate the end of the week!" Rachel said, pushing me.

"Tomorrow night, promise. I just need to sleep." I tried to look as tired as possible.

That part wasn't a lie; I was exhausted.

It was tougher to say no to Mick's offer to hang out, but I didn't have the energy to share the whole story with him and I just couldn't pretend to be fine. Thankfully, he seemed to understand as well.

So my night went according to my plan: a bottle of wine to myself and passing out by 8:30 p.m.

I'd been going to my counselor, Shanna, on Sunday afternoons every week, strategically timing our sessions with the hope they would help me push through the mounting anxiety about the week ahead. And though I'd feel better after talking with her, it was only a matter of hours before I was again stuck in the muck and mire.

The only enjoyment I truly got was in sleep, when I felt as though I could hit "pause." I didn't want to think. This was a familiar cycle to me, but somehow this time felt different. The "stuck" was more stuck than I'd ever been before.

Even though I didn't want to go back on antidepressants, I knew it was time to get back on medication. My antidepressant of choice, since fifth grade, had been Paxil.

So after gaining my family doctor's approval, I began taking it again, starting at a dosage of 20 mg. I'd been on and off the drug probably five or six times since I was ten—this didn't feel strange.

But I had always viewed taking medication as a sign of weakness, and felt judged by others, even some people in my own family. As such, I largely kept it a secret when I was on antidepressants, which made me feel worse. I saw the medicine as an emotional crutch and hated that I needed it to feel okay.

Every time I deemed myself stable enough, I would find a way to ween myself off the pills. So for over two decades, I'd bounced on and off the medicine every few years—this time, it had been about two.

The shit show at Carver combined some of my worst nightmares: reminders of my own low-income upbringing, emotional traumas, substance abuse, the inability to protect my students, and, ultimately, an utter lack of control of my environment—the worst case scenario of an adult child of an alcoholic.

Carver Elementary was set up to fail. From funding deficits that meant we didn't have enough chairs and desks, to a lack of computers and an abundance of aging textbooks, which contributed to the constant looming threat of losing funding and autonomy due to No Child Left Behind policies—we were a mess. And that doesn't even include the huge gap in school safety; Carver was one of the few schools without a resource officer or clear guidelines for emergency preparedness. And, of course, we also had grave student behavioral issues, violence, and poverty.

This doesn't even touch on the abysmal salary I was taking

home—the poverty line was easily within reach—or the lack of support for new teachers and disrespect for the profession overall.

Ironically, Wendy Kopp initially founded Teach for America in 1990 to address a national teacher shortage and the lack of innovation within the education system overall, and to place high-performing college graduates and leaders into high-needs schools across the nation.

But it was a Band-Aid for a gaping flesh wound of a problem. Less than a year into the program, it was clear to me that the United States education system was set up to fail.

It was too much—the problem was insurmountable. I couldn't allow myself to become part of this dysfunction, to become so calloused that I would deem a student a lost cause, or worse, to stop caring. I was beginning to question whether I could do this for another year, but I couldn't, in good conscience, leave these kids behind. I was almost halfway done with my commitment, and I couldn't look back—quitting midway wasn't an option.

I tried to see the summer ahead as an opportunity to get my bearings, to focus on what I *could* control, and to make my plans for the coming school year. One day at a time. My students needed me. I couldn't be another person who disappointed them.

But even in the final weeks of the school year, the problems were relentless.

We found out we didn't meet our state testing goals—our Adequate Yearly Progress that Ms. King had been talking about all year. We were required by the state to meet our AYP to re-earn our district-wide accreditation. This was a big red mark against the school, and although it wasn't what we had hoped for I don't think anyone was surprised.

What I hadn't realized before was that this wasn't the first time Carver had failed to meet our AYP—this had happened *five times* before. This is why the school was officially in the "Level 5 School Improvement Continuing Restructuring" phase.

Would the district shut down Carver? I wasn't sure. From my vantage point, it seemed we'd done most of all the recommended restructuring already, and I didn't see it making much of a difference.

Ms. King kept a pretty low profile after hearing the news, which I assumed was because the hopes and dreams she had laid on her Teach for America teachers were dashed.

chapter ten

Late in the year, as I greeted my students while they walked into class one morning, I overheard the mother of a child (who looked like a third or fourth grader) as she yelled at our school counselor in the hallway.

"I'm going to lose my job if you keep suspending her!" the mom shouted, pointing to the young girl standing next to her whose small frame hunched over, looking at the floor as her mother flung her hands about in a frenzy. "I don't know what else to do!"

"Ms. Kennedy, I'm going to need you to calm down," Mr. Kemper said.

I wished Mr. Kemper, as the school counselor, could have seen this was not the best way to soothe an irate parent.

"How are you going to help me?" she pleaded. "I need help before I hurt my daughter. I'm going to hurt her!"

I could hear the sheer desperation in her voice. Mr. Kemper tried to motion the mother into the office.

"I will not go into that office until you help me!" she exploded. "I've asked for help everywhere. I'm going to hurt my daughter if y'all don't get me some help and stop suspending her!"

And this is how we've gotten here in the first place, I thought compassionately.

Growing up in rural Iowa, getting suspended from school was

unheard of. At Carver Elementary School, a student was suspended almost every day. And there were members of my own class of second graders who were on that list.

Students who weren't in class couldn't learn *and* there had to be repercussions for physical violence, stealing, bringing weapons to class, doing drugs in the bathroom—all of which occurred at Carver Elementary.

I watched as Ms. Kennedy, the angry parent with tears in her eyes, was escorted to the office by Ms. King.

I often wondered if the students understood that their actions were wrong, or if dysfunction was just so ingrained at Carver—and they were so young—that they thought this was just how a school operates.

These feelings were confirmed later that afternoon. I was in my only free preparation period of the day while my students were at their art class. Daniel, one of my second graders, peeked his head around the doorway.

"Daniel, my friend. You're supposed to be in class," I said.

It was then that I noticed the tears brimming and realized this was the wrong approach.

So I changed tactics, softening my voice to ask, "What's going on?"

He showed his face more fully, and then the tears spilled over onto his cheeks.

"Hey, bud. Come here. What's going on?" I asked.

He continued to sob. I pulled him close and gave him a side hug.

I gave him a few minutes before asking, "Hey—what happened?"

"Fighting," he said.

"Who is trying to fight you?"

"No one is trying to fight me. It's just that everyone is fighting."

I didn't respond right away, hoping he would continue.

"There's something wrong with this school. Everyone fights all the time," he said.

I let out a big sigh. "Oh bud, I'm so sorry," I said, pulling him closer and giving him a real hug. "I understand," I said.

And I did. I just didn't expect this second-grade boy in front of me to comprehend the dysfunction on the level he did.

"You know what, we can't control other people, but you can control *you*. And you just keep doing the best you can. You can come get a hug from me whenever you want, buddy," I said.

"Okay, Miss C," he said.

"Let me call Ms. Walker and let her know you're here with me. Do you want to stay here the rest of the period?"

"Yeah. Can I play on the computer?"

"Go for it, bud."

He gave me another hug before plopping in front of the computer screen.

At least I know I'm not crazy. Even a second grader understands, I thought.

The schools closed just in time to avoid the Kansas City heat, as June and July made way for one-hundred-degree temperatures and lots of sun. The final days of school were anticlimactic. There were lots of hugs goodbye and even some tears, largely from the students whom I least expected to express emotion.

They always kept me guessing.

It was the most lighthearted and free the school had felt the whole year, as the darkness of the brick walls and lack of windows were enlivened by excited voices reverberating from classrooms and light from the front school doors being flung wide open.

"I'll see you next year, Miss C! Thanks for everything!" said one now former student as they walked out.

In truth, I wasn't sure I wanted to come back to Carver. I felt guilty for the relief I experienced while saying goodbye to my students. Especially because I knew, for many of them, school provided some of the only stability and consistency they could depend on.

And yet, they weren't my problem anymore, and I felt free from the weight of Carver and of my students. After the insanity of my first year of teaching—which was my own personal trial by fire—the hugs goodbye, the empty classroom, all of it felt insignificant.

It was one of the roughest, and yet most rewarding, years of my life, but as I continued to question whether I could do this another year, I pushed those thoughts to the back of my mind.

The focus now was on the rager of a party that was taking place at another Teach for America corps member's home. And of course, on more time with Mick. It was time to celebrate a job well done, or at least a job that was *done*.

I knew the summer was going to be full: I'd be working part-time at the Youth Center as a teacher coupled with graduate school classes. But knowing I'd pepper in days full of spending time with Mick and KC Royals baseball games and cold beer on hot patios—things were looking up.

Working at the Youth Center turned out to be a perfect summer job. I had free rein to teach whatever reading and writing curriculum I chose with the middle-school students. The biggest difference from teaching at school was that the students I taught at the Center were largely students that *chose* to be there, which made all the difference in attitude and engagement.

It meant I could assign fun writing assignments that focused on personal experiences: "Where I'm From" poems and persuasive essays focused on the merits or drawbacks to school uniforms or drivers licenses for young people under the age of sixteen. It also meant sharing short stories I was passionate about and helping to build others' excitement, focusing on analytical discussions on *Flowers for Algernon* by Daniel Keys and "Thank You, M'am" by Langston Hughes. It wasn't the foundational tenet of second grade—the phonics of reading and numeracy, and counting in math. Teaching middle school meant getting to know and understand my students through literature, and I loved it.

I was consistently seeing the lightbulbs turn on for students and was building meaningful relationships with them. With behavioral issues virtually nonexistent, I even began to enjoy teaching. The idea of going back to Carver in the fall didn't seem insurmountable.

I was also learning so much more about teaching methodology and curriculum from my graduate school courses, which I was able to directly apply to my summer classroom.

I was able to finally take some time for myself as well. I had promised two of my second graders from Carver that I would take them on field trips during the summer as a reward for their positive behavior during the school year. Although I didn't have Ms. King's permission to do so, I had discussed these trips with parents before we had entered summer break, promising I'd confirm dates and experiences in the coming weeks.

Rashaad and Efrem had earned coveted tickets to a Kansas City

Royals game with Mick and me. And so, one extremely warm Wednesday afternoon in June, I picked up the two boys, bringing along matching Kansas City Royals hats for them to sport at the game, thinking it was unlikely they had any gear. Both were ecstatic in anticipation of the experience, as neither of them had ever been to a Royals game before.

The two chattered incessantly on the car ride there and, as we walked through the crowded parking lot to the stadium, the excitement was palpable.

"Miss C, I feel white!" Efrem exclaimed.

Though that was not quite what I had expected to hear, I couldn't help but giggle. "Why's that, Efrem?"

"There are just so many white people around me. I feel white too," Efrem said.

What does that mean? I thought.

"Well, that's okay," I said. "Are you having fun?"

"Oh yes!"

"Do you guys wanna go and get some snacks?"

"Yes!" they both shouted.

Efrem and Rashaad continued chatting through most of the game, only pausing for bites of nachos, popcorn, or hot dogs. They were excited by the hits, but less so about the rest of the game.

"Miss C, is Mr. T your boyfriend?" Efrem asked.

I had explained to them that Mr. T was a teacher from another school in Kansas City and that he was my friend, but Efrem saw through it and cut to the chase.

"Yes, Mr. T is my boyfriend." I smiled.

"Do y'all like kissing? Y'all look like you like kissing."

I couldn't contain my laughter at this point. "That's a pretty personal question, Efrem!"

"I bet they do," Rashaad added.

I was not going to answer and looked to Mick, who also burst out laughing.

The sun began to set, and all too quickly the game was almost over. With the Arizona Diamondbacks hitting a home run to our outfield seats and the blowout nature of the game, we decided to duck out a bit early. We would later find out the Royals were handed a loss of five to twelve, so we made the right choice in leaving the game to bask in one another's company.

Rashaad and Efrem continued to chatter as we drove them to Rashaad's home for a sleepover. The drive was short.

"I hope you guys had fun," I said as we got out of the car and began walking toward the light streaming through the screen door.

"Oh yes, Miss C. Thank you so much for taking us to the game," said Rashaad.

"Yes, thanks, Miss C. I wish you could be our teacher next year," said Efrem.

"Aww, thanks, Efrem. I hope you guys have fun at your sleepover tonight!" I responded.

Rashaad's mom appeared at the door and let them in, saying, "Thank you so much, Miss C! You have a good night now!"

I said goodnight to the kids and Rashaad's mom, and then bounded back down the stairs and into my car, where Mick was waiting.

"That was really fun," I said to Mick as I put on my seatbelt and put the car in reverse.

"Thanks so much for inviting me! Hey, it'll be pretty late when you drop me off. You could just spend the night if you wanted," Mick said.

Mick and I were spending as much time together as we could before he left for San Francisco for the final weeks of summer.

"That sounds great!" I conceded, maybe too easily. "I mean, if you want me to."

"That's why I asked," he said.

I could see the white teeth of his grin reflected in the night lighting of my car.

"I'm so glad you get to spend some time at home this summer with your family, but I'm definitely going to miss you," I said.

I was none too good at playing it cool.

"I'll most definitely miss you, too, but I'm really excited for you to come out and meet my family before we head back to school this fall," Mick responded.

I'd dated a lot throughout high school and college, but had rarely made it to the "meeting the family" step. I'd also never dated anyone outside the state of Iowa, so flying to San Francisco to meet my boyfriend's family brought a new level of anxiety.

"I'm so excited to meet them! And to have you show me around San Francisco!" I said.

I was no stranger to California—I'd traveled to San Diego numerous times to visit a high school friend who was stationed in Coronado with her husband who was in the navy—but San Francisco was uncharted territory. And a liberal bastion I had been taught to be wary of.

"But I'm not leaving tonight, so still plenty of time to enjoy each other's company," Mick said.

I laughed as I drove, excited to spend another evening with Mick.

June came and went quickly, and July was seemingly on the same trajectory. With Mick back in San Francisco, I was left to focus on my summer work and graduate school courses.

For year two, I had a new program director for my Teach for America experience: Chris. I can only imagine what my previous program director, Katheryn, had told Chris about my first year of teaching. I knew I had struggled, and was far from the Teach for America poster child many others had become for the organization.

Mick had very quickly become one of TFA Kansas City's favorite teachers to tout, after finding a bunch of old drums in a closet, putting together a drumline, and collaborating with another teacher to organize a step team—a percussive dance team—to incentivize students for good behavior in the classroom. Soon, he (and a few other successful TFA teachers) were rubbing elbows at Teach for America fundraising events and sharing their stories of success with prospective donors. Needless to say, I was not invited.

But Chris was making the effort to get to know me and see how he could support. We met for coffee one day in the late summer.

"So, you've been teaching during your summer break?" he asked.

"Yes, at the Youth Center. I taught there after school two or three days per week during the school year, and I've been teaching middle school English and writing for their summer program."

"That's great! Continuing to build those skills. Would you mind if I stopped by sometime?"

"Of course! I'll double check with Jacob and the team, but I'm sure that's fine."

I could tell Chris wanted to see what he was going to deal with in the coming year, and I couldn't help but be a bit embarrassed. I'd never struggled like this before—my work ethic always made up for any lack of skills, but teaching at Carver was different.

Chris came into my class at the Youth Center the following week and sat in the back of the room. This felt more like a formal teacher observation than a getting-to-know-you situation, but the lesson went exceedingly well, and I was proud of the progress my class had made over the summer.

As the students left for the day, Chris excitedly came up to me and said, "You have the seventh and eighth graders eating out of your hands! You may just be teaching the wrong grade during the school year."

I smiled and nodded, saying, "The thought had crossed my mind."

"Well, I'm not too worried about you for this fall—it looks like you've set and maintained high expectations, and your lessons were great."

It felt good to hear these affirmations—something I heard little of throughout my first year of teaching.

"Thanks so much, Chris. Looking forward to working more closely together in the coming year."

We shook hands and he left; that was the only time I'd see him that summer.

I was done with work for the day and planned to head to Mick's apartment. I was house-sitting for him, which meant grabbing his mail and lying out by the beautiful pool while we texted each other off and on.

By this point, I was counting down the days until summer school teaching and graduate school courses were over, but most importantly, until I'd be in San Francisco reconnecting with Mick and meeting his family for the first time.

I filled the time easily and was even able to include one more student field trip into the mix. I had promised Damian, one of the second graders from my class who was soon to be a third grader, that

I would take him to the Nelson-Atkins Museum, which offered an extensive collection of ancient and contemporary art.

With my dad's plans to be in town over the weekend, the timing was perfect.

I called Damian's home to firm up the plans.

"Hey Damian—it's Miss C! Would you want to come with my dad and me to the Nelson-Atkins on Saturday morning?" I asked.

"Oh my gosh, yes!" He was so excited the words ran together. "Let me ask my mom—*Mom!*" he blared into the phone in excitement.

"Damian, do you think I could talk to your mom too?" I laughed.

After working out the details with his mom, we were confirmed for Saturday morning.

"That's a pretty lucky kid," my dad noted as we drove to pick up Damian on Saturday morning.

"It's no big deal to have him come with us. And, aside from it being fun, I think it'll mean a lot to him in the long run."

"I suppose so," my dad offered pensively.

I pulled up to the curb in front of his house just a few blocks from Carver and, before I could climb his front stairs, Damian was bounding out the door.

"Bye, Mama!"

"Hey Damian! It looks like you're ready to go, huh?!"

He nodded in agreement.

"Thank you so much, Miss C! Y'all have fun!" said Zareen, Damien's mom, waving as she spoke.

"Will do, Zareen! We'll grab lunch after, and I should have him home around one o'clock."

"Sounds great!"

"We getting lunch too?! You're the best, Miss C!"

"Does Gates BBQ sound okay? I'd love for my dad to get to try it."

"Your dad's gonna come too?!"

"Yep! He's in the car!"

"Ohmygosh, this is so great."

Damian opened the back door of my car, crawled in, and began putting on his seatbelt.

"Are you Damian?" said my dad, turning to ask the young boy as he got situated in the back.

"I am! And you must be Mr. C."

My Dad chuckled. "I suppose I am, but you can call me Dwane."

"Okay Dwane. Did you know Miss C is going to take us to Gates BBQ after the museum?"

"Is that a good place to go?"

"It's my favorite." Damian nodded, wide-eyed. "I like to get the mixed plate so I can have a bunch of different stuff. And lots of BBQ sauce. That's important."

"Well, I think that sounds like you know how to do it. I'll just follow you!" my dad affirmed.

"But you're both excited to go to the museum first, right?" I said, noting that it sounded like the highlight would be the BBQ.

"Oh yes," they both agreed.

I think all three of us were pleasantly surprised by the artwork the Midwestern museum had to offer. After growing up in such a rural place, I wasn't expecting much. But the exhibits delivered, even for an eight-year-old.

After perusing the space we were ready for lunch, and Gates delivered too.

From the moment we walked in—and someone yelled "Hi, may I help you?" across the room, as was the custom—I knew it was going to be a good experience. The sliced meats smothered in sauce and array of sides (potato salad, coleslaw, fries, and baked beans) were all delicious. We gorged ourselves and felt good about it.

As we all sat back in silence, unable to eat a bite more, Damian looked to the two of us and said, "Well, y'all ready?"

I burst out laughing. "Damian, that's the sweetest—I think we are! Are *you* ready? Did you get enough to eat?"

"Ohmygosh yes—what a great day, Miss C. And it was great to meet you too, Dwane."

"It was so nice to meet and spend time with you, Damian," my dad responded.

We all moaned and groaned as we walked to the car.

"I think I may have to take a nap now," my dad noted.

"Me too!" Damian added.

We dropped Damian back home, and then headed back to my apartment.

"I'm not kidding about that nap," my dad said.

I laughed. "Well, the couch is all yours!"

My dad and I went to church together the following morning. It was a necessity when he was in town.

We chatted when we got back, before he began the five-hour trip home.

"I'm really glad to hear you've found a church home here."

"Yeah, this one is really community driven, and there are a few other corps members that go too."

"I know this past year has been tough for you. You've just got to keep bringing it to God," my dad said.

"I know. I actually just finished reading the Bible through in its entirety for a second time. There were some psalms that really spoke to me this time, like I felt like I was meant to find them."

"Let's see them!"

I grabbed my Bible, now dog-eared and well-loved, with highlights and notes throughout.

I found the first folded page and read aloud: "'I cried unto the Lord with my voice, and he heard me' is psalm three, verse four. And 'O my God, I trust in thee: let me not be ashamed, let not mine enemies triumph over me' is psalm twenty-five, verses one and two."

"Psalms offers a lot of great prayers," my dad said.

"Reading the word has been good—it's kept me grounded. I've also been going to the International House of Prayer with Mindy—there's 24/7 prayer and worship."

"Just keep at it, Cole. You're always in my thoughts and prayers."

"Thanks, Dad. I love you."

"Love you too."

We hugged and I cried, like always when we said goodbye.

"Let me know when you get home," I said.

"Will do."

I closed the door and was alone with my thoughts again. At least I didn't have to think about Carver yet.

As summer school was ending, I received a phone call from Ms. King.

"It sounds like things went well with the middle schoolers this summer at the Youth Center," she said.

"Oh wow! Word gets around, I guess. Yes, things went really

well this summer. I really connected with the age group, and it was nice to teach things I'm really passionate about."

"How would you feel about teaching middle school at Carver in the coming year? We have an opening, and it sounds like it may be a better fit for you."

"You know, I think I'd like that a lot. We'd have to do some shifting of my paperwork though, right? I don't think my certification will allow me—"

"Yes, but that shouldn't be a problem. Teach for America teachers are already on emergency teaching licenses—it's trading out one emergency license for another."

"Okay, great! What do I need to do?"

"Let's have you come in Monday, and we'll get the paperwork filled out. I should be able to push it through the school district quickly, so it will just mean getting it through at the state level, which should be done in ample time before the school year starts."

"Wonderful. I'll plan on stopping in on Monday then!"

"Sounds good. Thank you, Miss C."

I hadn't really taken much time to think about it, but this meant Teach for America teachers—Rachel, Melissa, and me—would be running the entire middle school at Carver. It had to be better than teaching second grade again. I connected much better with the middle schoolers at the Youth Center.

It was official: I was going back to Carver Elementary School, but in my own way. This was a good thing, and I was excited.

So much so that I called Mick to tell him the good news.

"Guess what!" I said.

"Hey! What's up?"

"I just got a call from Ms. King. She wants me to teach middle school next year!"

"How does that feel?"

"Super exciting! I definitely need a shift from the second grade. Just have to wait for the paperwork to go through."

"Great news! I'm happy for you!"

"I'm even more excited that I get to see *you* next week though."

"I can't wait, love. Just a week away."

It was going to be my first full week of no work, no homework, and no teaching—just relaxation with the man I loved, sightseeing in one of the most iconic cities in the world and staying a few short blocks from the beach.

On the afternoon I flew into San Francisco, we already had plans. So I dropped my bags, freshened up, and was whisked away to a party celebrating the twenty-first birthday of a friend of the family.

Olivia, in true San Francisco fashion, had two loving fathers. Her party was unlike anything I had experienced in the Midwest; I walked into a beautiful, intimate, basement room of an Italian restaurant in San Francisco's North Beach neighborhood and saw prosciutto hanging from the ceiling. It couldn't have been a better kickoff to my time in San Francisco.

The following days were filled with decadent dinners, a San Francisco Giants game, tours of the city sights including Coit Tower, Golden Gate Park, Ocean Beach, Lombard Street, and of course, the Golden Gate Bridge. Mick's family was even more wonderful than I'd imagined. Although his parents were also divorced, his family was idyllic: loud and boisterous, and fun.

The first stop was Mick's mom's home, which was where he had spent the majority of his childhood, in the Sunset District in San Francisco.

"The only place where beachfront property costs less than it does in the rest of the city, because it's so foggy and cold all of the time," Mick joked.

The boxlike homes were lined up one after the other without any space between them. They looked so similar that it almost required you to look for the tiny house numbers to tell them apart.

"This is it!" Mick said.

We walked through the gate, which banged closed behind us, and up several granite stairs covered in plants.

The door was open and Mick's mom, Sharon, was waiting at the top.

"Hi, I'm Nicole." I put out my hand to shake.

"Of course you are. Can I give you a hug?"

"Uh, sure!"

I would quickly learn that in California, everyone hugs.

Sharon was immediately intriguing to me; she exuded warmth and love, was interested in my energy and light, and lived for health and worldly spirituality—such a contrast to my own mother who experienced life in facts and logic.

"We've got a lovely dinner planned for you—I just whipped up a roast with some vegetables. And for dessert, an Italian specialty, cassata."

"That all sounds great."

Joel, Mick's younger brother, was strikingly handsome, but not moreso than Mick. He gave me a hug as well. "It's so great to meet you, Nicole."

"Likewise."

Joel was on summer break after just graduating from college. I was excited that the timing worked out so I was able to meet him as well.

The conversation flowed easily during dinner as we discussed Iowa, our sightseeing plans for the next few days, and the coming school year back in Kansas City.

"So, you grew up in Iowa?" asked Joel.

"Yeah, in a small town called Alton—population 1,200," I responded.

"Oh wow, our high school was bigger than that!" Joel looked at Mick wide-eyed. "What are you most looking forward to doing on your trip?"

"I'd say it's a toss-up between the beach tomorrow and the San Francisco Giants game later this week. I was a softball player and still am a big baseball fan."

"What's your team?" Joel asked with genuine curiosity.

"Honestly, we don't have any pro sports teams in Iowa, so I'm not a die-hard fan of any one particular team. I like watching the Twins, the Cubs, the Royals—the Midwest teams."

"Well, we'll make a Giants fan out of you—they can be your home team," Mick said, smiling. "I'm excited we'll get to go to a game later this week!"

It was clear where Mick had gotten his charisma: his dad. Adam had originally made his way out to California from New Jersey after being drafted as a quarterback for the San Francisco 49ers, but after an injury he was cut.

So he had gone on to law school and stayed in San Francisco.

He was also big into baseball—a huge fan of the Yankees. Mick was named after Mickey Mantle. Due to San Francisco being his home for more than two decades, Adam had also adopted the San Francisco Giants as his team. He attended games quite often and had gotten us pretty good seats, just a few dozen rows behind the third base line.

I'd been to a few Kansas City Royals games, but these were by far the best seats I had ever enjoyed.

"Nicole, I hear you're a ball player?" Adam asked.

"Ah! I wouldn't say actively now, but I enjoy a good game of catch!"

"Well, we'll have to get you playing water wiffle ball at our pool sometime soon. It's tradition!"

"Happy to partake in that fun whenever you're ready! And thank you so much for these amazing seats. Super grateful."

"Absolutely, honey. We've got to make sure you want to come back!"

"I don't think you'll have any problem with that!" I laughed.

I inhaled the city experience and imagined what life could be like living in such a place; it was so different compared to where I was from.

After meeting Mick's family and spending time in his home, our relationship blossomed further. His family clearly approved, which felt wonderful.

As I prepared to head back to Kansas City, I gushed, "I love this city, Mick!"

"I'm so glad you like it. You know, you could live here someday sooner than later if you wanted."

I blushed. "I think that sounds like a really exciting idea."

chapter eleven

The summer had quickly come to a close, and though I was hopeful in many ways that teaching middle school at Carver would be a better fit for me, I was hesitant to embrace anything resembling excitement.

With therapy and medication, I had successfully circumnavigated my anxiety and depression during the summer months and was feeling quite good. But the pending school year brought a heaviness with it.

When I got back to Kansas City after my trip to San Francisco, reality really set in. There were new lesson plans to write: three grade levels of English classes and geography for seventh grade. My second-grade classroom decorations wouldn't quite do either. This wasn't a light lift. On top of that, the sets of books that were available for the class didn't seem as though they'd pique much interest, and there weren't enough copies for everyone.

"Well, I guess we won't start the year by reading a book—there aren't even enough copies for the seventh grade class," I complained to Rachel, who had come over to my apartment to work on lesson plans and drink wine.

We were embracing the final days of summer. Next week, all of the teachers would be back on campus, and students returned the following week.

"What are you going to do?"

"Beg people to fund a couple class sets of books on Donors Choose over the next few weeks, I guess? With the first few weeks being more about procedures and expectations than actual content, I think I'll be okay."

"Brutal. Well, I'm on my second year of teaching science labs without any lab equipment, so . . ." she trailed off.

"Oh my God." I laughed. "How does that work?"

"I was creative with the little bit of stuff we had. I'll do it again, but they're not really getting the hands-on experiences they're supposed to have."

"That doesn't seem fair. I went to public school, and I still had a full lab in eighth grade, but I suppose that was Iowa."

"Me too, in Illinois."

"How are you feeling about this school year?" I asked, hoping I wasn't alone in my dread.

"Honestly, super anxious. But I just keep telling myself it's just one more year—"

"And then we never have to go back," I said, finishing Rachel's sentence for her.

She laughed. "Yeah, and I feel awful for thinking that way. It's not the kids' fault."

"I'm in the same boat," I reassured her. "I have this looming sense of dread, even though I'm so glad to be teaching alongside you and Melissa. I just know it's going to be incredibly difficult. But I guess that's what we signed up for."

"Yeah, I'm not sure any of us really knew what we signed up for."

"Agreed. I guess it can't be worse than my first year?"

"You most definitely had a tough one. And this time we're in it together, just the three of us running the whole middle school."

"In three rooms that don't even have doors, in a basement, and without a bell system."

"Yeah, the passing periods could be interesting."

There was a lot working against us.

We both looked back to our computer screens. A lesson plan framework with the words *I do, We do, You do* stared back at me. Tears began to brim my eyes.

"I can't do this anymore," I said as I shut my computer, wiping my eyes before Rachel could see. "I'm done for the day."

"Then I am too," Rachel agreed. "Wine time?"

"Wine time."

We were back on campus preparing our classrooms when Ms. King walked in and announced, "Miss C, I'm afraid I have some unfortunate news."

"Okay. What's going on?"

"We're in a bit of a waiting game right now. Your temporary authorization certificate still hasn't been approved by the state."

"Okay, well what does that mean for me then?"

"It means, unfortunately, you won't be teaching middle school, at least to start. I still want you teaching middle school English, but your temporary authorization certificate only covers you for the elementary ages, so we'll start you there."

I took the news in.

"So, what grade level do you need me in? Is there an empty teaching position open?"

"Yes, you'll be teaching third grade for at least the first few weeks, maybe the first few months. You'll likely have some of the exact same students you had last year."

My eyes grew big as I stared at her and tried to swallow the lump in my throat. I knew it wasn't hard to tell how I was feeling.

"You'll be fine. You just have to set those expectations high first thing. I think you learned that after the year you had this past year. I'm sure you'll have your third-grade students in shape in no time."

I let out a big sigh. "Okay, so I'm guessing I won't be teaching them in this classroom."

"Of course not, this is a middle school classroom."

"Well, can you show me where I'll be teaching so I can start to prepare?"

"Follow me. We've got you in what was the student support services room last year. It's just around the corner from where you taught last year."

I was able to successfully hold back the tears as I followed Ms. King upstairs and into the small classroom in the corner. The pale-yellow walls were barren, except for remnants of tape showing where posters had hung the previous year. The room was smaller than most, which was fine the year before since it had served as a classroom for a small number of students with special needs. But how was an entire third grade class going to fit? I was starting at square one just a few days before we welcomed students back.

"There's plenty of materials in here for your class, and you know where to find the supplies for any posters and decorating you want to do," Ms. King said.

"I'll see if I can repurpose some of the stuff I had made for the middle schoolers, but I'll leave the rest downstairs."

"I think that sounds like a good idea. You're going to set these third graders up for success up here, and then we'll get you downstairs teaching middle school yet, Miss C. It's just a waiting game right now."

"Thanks, Ms. King."

"I feel it. This is the year we meet our AYP. We're going to do it—together."

I couldn't even indulge her. I was too frustrated.

"Do you happen to have my new class roster?"

I know Samuel is on it, I thought. I could just feel it.

"I'll get it for you. I'll stop by in a bit."

When Ms. King left, I let the tears flow.

What a fucking mess! This is worse than teaching second grade again—it's teaching the same kids as last year.

I decided to call Elizabeth, the lead for Teach for America Kansas City and Chris's boss, to see if she could offer any support. Her response wasn't nearly as empathetic as I had hoped, and she had no patience for my tears.

"You're lucky to even have a job! You're gonna have to let this one go," she told me.

After hanging up, I quietly sobbed as I set up my third-grade classroom two work days before the school year started, moving the desks into pods, organizing the small library of books, repurposing what posters I could from the middle school room downstairs. I began looking through the curriculum and shifting my "get to know you" activities for the beginning of the year to fit third graders.

The worst news was yet to come: In addition to planning for my third grade classroom, I was also expected to create lesson plans for the sixth, seventh, and eighth grade English classes for a substitute teacher to use as they hadn't been able to fill all the teaching positions at Carver.

So much for the high hopes I had for my second year of teaching.

I decided I was going to fake it to make it—no matter what

it took. I'd purchase a pretty new dress to wear on the first day of school. I'd overzealously greet students at the door and welcome them to the school day. I'd put my all into creating fun and interesting lesson plans for both middle school English and third grade. Fuck it—what's the worst that could happen?

And so, on day one, as anxious as I was walking into my third-grade classroom, I put my plan into action. Surprisingly, it worked for a while. Although I felt like I was going to throw up on the daily drive to work, I also caught myself laughing as I welcomed students to Carver.

My fake enthusiasm slowly became real.

Many of my students noticed, but Orion saw right through it.

"Miss C, what is wrong with you?" Orion asked.

"What? Can't I be happy to be at school?" I responded, smiling.

"Ain't nobody happy to be here, Miss C."

I giggled at his brazen truth. "Oh, that's not true, Orion. Clearly, I am!"

Many of my worst fears had been realized as I had a very similar class roster as I did the year before. But it lacked Samuel, which was a relief. And, surprisingly, many of the new faces were great additions who helped to build a supportive and familial classroom culture.

It was a new school year, and a new me, although I applied many of the same classroom expectations that I had implemented in my first year. I knew I needed to remind myself that things had been going really well the previous fall, too, until the incident with Samuel.

As I finished my first week of school, I was incredibly proud of how my kids would stand quietly in straight lines in the hallway, and how they engaged in my "get to know one another" activities and participated in my lessons to build our classroom culture. I set up systems, processes, and procedures that I hoped I wouldn't need for long as I still wanted to move to the middle school. I tried to remain hopeful that would happen, but I knew it was quite possible it wouldn't. Nothing at Carver was predictable.

Though I wasn't getting much sleep or spending much time doing anything other than teaching and attending graduate school classes in the evenings, things were going well. Mick was in the midst of his own first week at a new charter school because his school had been shut down at the end of the first year.

Our established group of Teach for America teachers gathered on Friday to celebrate our first week of year two, and that's where Mick and I finally reconnected. I gave him a big hug, and felt so happy to be in his arms.

"How was week one?" he asked.

"Oh man. Aside from teaching many of the same students as last year, it's gone surprisingly well. I know it could very well just be the honeymoon period of the first days, but I'll enjoy it while I can."

"I can't believe how many shifts you've had to navigate. You got switched to a different school at the last minute in your first year. And now they switched grade levels on you at the last minute. I'm so sorry you've had to deal with this," Mick said.

"Feels surreal that, originally, I wasn't even placed at Carver, but in the grand scheme of things, I'm doing okay. How are things going with you?"

"My charter school is great, actually! Definitely still the same issues as any other district school, but our principal is amazing, and there are so many Teach for America corps members. So far, so good!"

I was glad he was happy.

"That sounds wonderful. Did I mention how happy I am to see you?" I said.

He grabbed me for another hug.

"This year is gonna fly, and then we can do whatever we want. We're already more than halfway done with our commitment—it's all coasting downhill from here!"

"I hope you're right," I said.

By the third week of school, my classroom's culture was well on its way to becoming happy and healthy—at least as well as could be expected at Carver—and lessons continued to run smoothly. I was almost becoming anxious about my pending transition to the middle school since I hadn't been the one to set up the physical classroom nor had I set expectations at the beginning of the year with the thirty-two seventh graders. I had no idea how teaching middle school was going to work.

Rachel and Melissa seemed to be doing alright.

"It's a shit show downstairs, but honestly, what classroom isn't?" Rachel shared one Saturday night over drinks. "We can't wait to have you. Klay is the absolute worst. He just sits and reads to the kids from books they could care less about. Kids walk in and out all day."

"Wait, Klay is teaching my class? I thought it was a sub?"

"No, it's Klay," she said.

Mr. Klay was quickly approaching retirement, and made sure everyone knew it. As such, he had terrible "senioritis," and only did the bare minimum to keep him from getting into trouble with Ms. King or the union. He was a bean pole of an old man, more than six feet tall but with a slight hunch to his shoulders. He was missing teeth, which added even more character to his smile and overall demeanor. One of my most memorable engagements with him was when he shared that to cover the smell of alcohol on his breath, all he had to do was rub garlic on his teeth.

"Nobody'll even come near you when you smell of garlic to high heaven," he'd told me.

Needless to say, I didn't have much hope for the classroom climate Mr. Klay was likely creating with my middle schoolers, and I wasn't excited about taking over for him.

"Great. Sounds like I'll have my work cut out for me. What's he gonna do when I take over the class?" I asked.

"I think he's going to third grade," said Rachel.

"Seriously? How's that gonna work? And why in the hell am I writing his lesson plans for the middle school then?! I thought I was writing plans for a substitute!"

I was fuming. It felt like Ms. King was taking advantage of me.

"I have no idea. That's a question for Ms. King. But he can't do any worse than what he's currently doing," Rachel said.

"How does he still have a job? His teacher observations have to be horrible."

"The union. But speaking of teaching observations, did you get yours?"

"I have no idea what you're talking about. I know we were supposed to have multiple last year, but Ms. King never formally came into my classroom, at least not that I knew about."

"Well, you should ask to see them. I signed mine from last year this past week. She asked me to backdate them."

"Knowing Ms. King's opinion of me, mine probably don't say anything nice. Not sure how I feel about backdating them, especially if I never had any observations, but I guess I'll tackle that if and when it comes. Until then, I think that calls for another drink."

One morning in early September, Ms. King sauntered into my classroom, her old age finally beginning to show physically this school year.

"Miss Cleveringa, I have some good news. Your temporary authorization certificate went through," she said, beaming. "We'll have you downstairs teaching middle school next week. I suggest starting to prepare your class for the transition this week."

This is what I had wanted, but after all the work I had done to set up my third-grade classroom, I almost didn't want to go. Leaving would also mean it'd be harder to keep an eye on Samuel since I'd be on a different floor.

"Oh wow! That *is* good news. I'll begin preparing the kids. Can I tell them who will be taking over for me?"

"Mr. Klay, of course. You'll just be switching places."

"Oh, okay."

I knew I wore the surprise on my face but didn't say anything more. I was skeptical of Mr. Klay's ability to effectively support an elementary-aged class because it was my understanding that he had spent the entirety of his career teaching middle schoolers. I wondered if he had the same issues with an emergency credential that I had had.

"I'm sure you'll be happy to be writing only the middle school lessons moving forward," she said, smiling sweetly.

I nodded, clenching my jaw in frustration. "I'll most definitely be happy to hand over the third grade lesson planning to Mr. Klay."

"Well, you'll have some work to do downstairs, but based on

your performance at the Youth Center, it sounds like you're up for it. Well done, Miss C."

It finally appeared I was in her good graces.

I was anxious about making the move, but was looking forward to being with Melissa and Rachel, especially because, as they had taught these same students last year, they'd be able to share their insight.

I told my class of third graders the news as soon as possible, wanting them to be prepared for the transition. They were not happy about it.

"Oh man, Miss C?! Why do you gotta go teach those middle schoolers?" Damien asked.

"We want you to stay with us. Why do all our teachers leave?" Destiny said.

It broke my heart, but I knew I needed to appear strong for them.

"Guys, what I want you all to remember is that I'm still here! I'm just going to be downstairs. And I promise I'll still come up and visit. You're going to have a lot of fun with Mr. Klay."

"Yeah—fun," Orion scoffed.

I shot him a knowing look. "And I'm going to have fun with your sister downstairs, right?"

"I bet you are, Miss C."

"Well, we'll have a celebration on Friday, and I'll see if we can get Mr. Klay up here so you can officially meet him as well."

"Can you make cupcakes?" Izaak asked.

"I think I can make that happen—if you're lucky."

The irony in all of this is that it was bittersweet saying goodbye. I felt like we had finally hit our stride and understood one another. That's what I had wanted the previous year, but now it was too late.

I was cautiously optimistic that teaching middle school at Carver would be as positive of an experience as I had had working at the Youth Center over the summer. But I didn't want to get my hopes up.

It was official: Three Teach for America teachers were running the entire middle school at Carver. In the previous year, the English teacher had only lasted a few months before she requested a transfer. Before she left, there was an accusation that she had thrown a book at a student. Although it was probably a lie, it had to be taken seriously, which is why she was able to move to another school.

The bar had been set so low I could have stumbled over it. I knew I had to do better than that.

I spent an inordinate amount of time creating new posters and hanging them up, and rearranging the middle school classroom to create the space I had visualized for the first days of school. As I worked on the physical space, I imagined the first days and weeks of teaching middle school going really well.

But there were only twenty-eight mismatched desks and chairs for the thirty-two students I had on the roster.

"Don't worry—you'll rarely have everyone here every day anyway," Melissa reassured me. "I don't have thirty-two seats either, and I rarely have an issue when they're in my class."

"Is there that many students who just don't come?"

"Oh yeah. You'll meet multiple case workers who are working through truancy issues."

"Okay, well that's definitely something I didn't have to worry about last year."

"I think there are some extra chairs that you could have

students pull up to that table if you do end up with a pretty full group. We could always have a couple students carry their chairs to their next class as well." She motioned to the table as she spoke.

"Do you think they can handle that?"

"If we choose the right ones."

And, just like that, on a Monday in September, already more than a month into the school year, I had a new start. I stood at the door and greeted the students who passed by, just as I had done with my second graders last year and third graders this year.

Rachel and Melissa did the same, and nodded to me in assurance. But I could tell my middle schoolers were underwhelmed.

"Hi! I'm Miss Cleveringa, but you can call me Miss C," I said.

"Where's Mr. Klay?" one student responded.

He didn't even tell them about the shift? I thought.

"He was transferred upstairs to teach third grade," I explained.

There were bursts of laughter.

"Klay is teaching third grade?" one child asked.

"Yes, and now you've got me for English, homeroom, and geography."

"This oughta be good," said a voice from the back.

I steeled my eyes in response.

"The first thing we're going to do is talk through expectations. I have a feeling mine may be a bit different than Mr. Klay's."

They listened and seemed relatively engaged. Nobody walked out of class, and nobody told me to fuck off. It was the same for the eighth graders, and then the sixth graders as well. This was the get-to-know-you period—they were feeling me out—but I still considered my first day with my middle schoolers to be successful. I could do this.

As we moved through our second, third, and fourth days together, the middle school students began to test me.

"Where are you going, Shakur?" I said as a boy walked toward the doorway.

"I need to go to the bathroom."

"Then you need to raise your hand and ask—Asia is already out. Please wait until she gets back."

He put his hand in the air as he stood there and practically shouted, "CAN I GO TO THE BATHROOM?"

"Take a seat."

He sucked his teeth at me but sat back down. Another win.

By Friday, I was feeling pretty good about how this first week had gone. I was connecting with a number of my students on a personal level, we had begun preparing to read our first books together—all of which were brand new thanks to a Donors Choose drive I had created online—and I had only had to send one student to the office for slapping another across the face.

I wasn't quite having fun, but as my farmer father had always said, "They don't pay you to have fun. They pay you to work."

"Work" most definitely described the entire Teach for America experience.

The second week of teaching middle school was much more eventful: Two students were caught smoking marijuana in the restroom and two other middle schoolers got in a fistfight.

Then, before I even understood what was happening, a quarter of my class was out the door and in Rachel's classroom.

"What just happened?" I asked Tanisha, who looked to me nonchalantly.

"Someone's fighting next door, isn't that clear?"

I grabbed my classroom phone and called the office, but they'd already been told about the fight and Ms. King was on her way to take care of it.

"Well, I guess we'll continue," I said to the kids who'd stayed in my room.

"The others won't be back until they know who won," one student said.

"You triflin' bitch!" rang out over the cheers and laughs.

The oohs and grunts continued as fists landed, and yelps were heard as hair was pulled.

"Alright, alright! Everyone get back to their classrooms!" shouted Ms. King, who had suddenly appeared.

It was like she'd sounded the ring of a bell signaling the end of the fight.

My students filtered back into my classroom to my disapproving looks as I continued the lesson. I'd discuss their actions with them later when I could speak to them one-on-one. For now, we had a lesson to get through.

For some of our students, school was a safe haven. Those kids were a consistent presence, always there as the school building was open. I learned very quickly who not to expect to show up.

In these first weeks, I also learned very quickly, from the diagnostics, that most of my students were reading and writing well below their grade level. It seemed impossible to find books that were accessible to all of them, let alone interesting, but I was up for the challenge.

I was teaching literature and short stories I was passionate about: *Where the Red Fern Grows*; *Roll of Thunder Hear My Cry*; "The Monkey's Paw"; and "The Lottery." And though we had been advised against it in my Teach for America training, I was leveraging sarcasm as a tool for engagement and, honestly, a defense. Shockingly, it had proven quite effective. When students would talk back to me or refuse to do what I asked, I would quip right back.

"I didn't ask what you wanted to do today—this is the expectation," I said once.

"I know your mom may help you when you're at home, but

you've got to do this on your own like a big kid at school," I said another time.

When I caught a student on his cell phone, I said, "There's no way you have a girlfriend to text—I need you to focus now."

When I'd be really snarky, I'd elicit various responses of glee from students.

"Ooooh! Miss C gotchu!"

It was a remarkable relationship-building tool, and turned into a bit of a game to see if I could at least get one good quip in each day.

As my third week with my new middle school crew came to a close, I was proud of the progress we had made. After wrapping up our day, my students lined up at the door—even in middle school, we were expected to walk our students to the door, and I was about to find out why.

I pushed the silver bar that opened the heavy, blue, steel doors to the outside, and the blacktop and playground came into view. I stood holding the door open as we began our goodbyes, and suddenly heard a sound I had only heard before on my family's farm in a controlled environment. I looked to Brexton, one of my new seventh-grade homeroom students, who had stopped midstride. We locked eyes.

"Is that what I think it is?" I asked.

"Yeah," Brexton said as he was pushed from behind by Shakur, who was impatient with him blocking the doorway.

"Dude—you gotta go, man," Shakur scoffed.

I put my hand on Shakur's shoulder.

Before he could protest further, I said, "There were gunshots. Get back downstairs."

As the news traveled down through the hall, I ran outside a short way and grabbed the kids who weren't already headed back into the school, yanking backpack handles back toward the school and disregarding protests until they were safely inside.

"Guys, get back in the building! Shots fired!" I yelled.

In hindsight, I realized I could have reacted better as my words created panic as older students scrambled to find their siblings and get back inside the school. But, then again, shots *had been* fired—so panic seemed like an acceptable response.

The school went into lockdown for a short while, which frustrated students and staff alike because no one wanted an extended school day or the violence that was erupting. Once we received the all clear, we walked our students back to the main school doors and let them back out. It felt wrong to let them go, but what else was there to do?

Once the students had all filtered out for the day, I went back into my classroom and cried. Having grown up in an Iowa farming community, I wasn't a stranger to guns—the sounds, the smells, the power you felt when you held one in your hand. My grandfather had been a champion trapshooter, and I felt pride when we'd go shooting together. But I was new to hearing gunshots in a city setting. It was completely different and in the worst way.

I knew the neighborhood around Carver Elementary was violent from my experiences of the past year, including when I'd picked up the bullet from the playground. But it wasn't until years later, when I read about the history of Kansas City, that I learned exactly how violent it really was.

Carver was on the east side of the city. This area is not only where three quarters of Kansas City's crime takes place, but it also has one of the worst murder rates in the United States.[16]

Violence was seemingly ingrained in this community, and over the weeks to come I'd further understand how much a part of my students' daily reality these experiences really were. Somehow it had felt more distant with my second-grade class, whereas my middle schoolers lived in it more fully.

By September, I'd learned the following about my students:

Ariel had lost her twenty-year-old brother to gun violence—a memorial with candles, flowers, and balloons decorated the spot where he took his last breaths.

Christian shared that he had spent the last week living on the street after his mom kicked him out, and had only recently been let back in his home.

Destiny hadn't had running water for months and was made fun of for coming to school smelling of urine.

Jamar rarely came to school but when he did, as a seventeen-year-old eighth grader, he really stood out. He was forced to wear an electronic ankle monitor as one of the terms of his probation. I only saw him four or five times during the month-long period he was at Carver, and never got the full story as to what he had done to warrant the monitor before he violated the terms of his probation and was back in a detention center. Another student come and gone.

Many of our middle schoolers' attendance was inconsistent, and though I was sad to see things turn out so poorly for Jamar, the truth was that one less student meant my job got easier.

It was all getting to be too much.

chapter twelve

Wine was becoming an all-too-welcome friend in the evenings—even during the week. And the weekends didn't hold any promise of relief anymore as I'd spend the whole time stressing out in anticipation of the coming week.

One Saturday, after I'd been ignoring Rachel's texts all day, I finally responded.

> Hey, I don't think I'm going to make it tonight. I'm not feeling well.

BOO. Are you ok?

> Yeah, just need to sleep.

Need me to bring you anything? I've got a can of chicken noodle? Sour Patch Kids? Dr. Pepper?

> Haha. You're great. I'm good.

Feel better!!

Mick was a tougher sell.

> Hey. I think I'm going to stay in tonight. Not feeling well.

Oh man! Can I come over? I'll keep you company?!

> You are really sweet. I think I'm just going to sleep. You should go enjoy a night out.

Are you sure? I don't feel right about that.

> Please. Let's see each other tomorrow—maybe lesson plan?

Ok–feel better and I'll see you tomorrow.

I had good friends and a sweet boyfriend. I was the one who had cancelled my plans, and yet I was feeling sorry for myself.

Rachel and Mick had their own burdens to carry, and I did what I could to find release without adding to theirs.

Anna was at her boyfriend's place, so I had the apartment and a bottle of wine to myself. I didn't even bother with a glass—I twisted off the screw cap and tossed it on the counter, taking a swig of Chardonnay straight from the bottle.

I carried the bottle into the living room with me and pulled up my pants on my thinning frame before dropping down on the couch as I took another pull of wine. I flipped on the TV and found a movie. I knew I wouldn't watch much of it as I continued to swig the wine. The plan was to drink until I passed out, to shut off my mind for at least a little while.

Seemingly in direct contradiction to my blackout night, I went to church the next morning. The sermon focused on spiritual warfare.

I was already in my own battle: at school, with my mind, and with what felt like the whole world. There was nothing about this world I saw as kind. Everything felt so, so heavy.

The grief came from the ultimate realization that the problem was too big to fix. I'd cry on the way to school, and I'd cry on the way home. I'd cry in the shower and as I went to sleep—really any place where I was alone.

That day, as I cried while driving to see my counselor, the tears became anger.

The huge homes on Ward Parkway used to make me daydream about what life must be like for people who lived in such luxury. Now my face flushed as I felt rage rise. As I looked at the thick-columned mansions, perfectly manicured lawns, and black wrought-iron fences, I was disgusted. My students came to school with empty stomachs, some without running water or electricity, others squatting in vacant homes. The differences between the haves and the have-nots had never been so clear to me, and it was so clearly aligned by the color of skin. The dichotomy was stark. If we all got what we deserved, we'd live in a very different world. Where was God in all of this?

I was a recipient of the free-lunch program while growing up and a Pell Grant to go to college, and was given hand-me-downs from various cousins and family friends as a child. I'd gone to public schools for almost my entire education and, despite them being just a few hours away from Kansas City, I'd had a vastly different experience from my Carver students, being offered choices for which courses and electives to take, and band and sports and school dances.

I was seeing, every day, the systems of oppression and violence that the state and country provided these Black students. And I was part of it. They deserved better than this.

Worst of all was the realization that I was failing them.

I tried to cling to the small differences I could see I was making. With work at the Youth Center starting up again, I had checked in with Chantelle and her mom, and we planned to continue the same setup as we had arranged earlier in the spring. I'd take her after the Youth Center closed, we'd eat dinner, do our homework, and then I'd drop her at home as soon as her sister was home for the evening. At least I was making a difference to Chantelle.

Right?

It was only October. I anticipated the marathon of teaching that loomed in the coming months, the anxiety rising as I thought through how many more days of teaching were left, how many more fistfights there would be, how many more battles I would fight. It was overwhelming.

All I wanted to do was sleep. I didn't want to go anywhere or see anyone. I wanted to push pause, take a break. But there wasn't any place to go. Usually, therapy and medication could pull me out of whatever hole I found myself in. It wasn't working this time.

I knew I'd been isolating myself, but I didn't see any other way to protect those I loved from my heaviness.

―――――――

It was another late afternoon at the Youth Center. I continued to enjoy working with students in a more relaxed environment while supplementing my incredibly modest, second-year teacher income.

"Stupid white ni★★ers," Lontrell said.

For obvious reasons, my ears piqued at the words. The phrase had come from a small group of middle schoolers who were huddled together around a table in the corner of the basement room.

"Hey Lontrell—that's not okay," I said.

"Sorry, Miss C."

"And what color is my skin?"

No one said anything for a moment.

Then Aniyah chimed in. "But Miss C, you ain't white. You can't be. You just light skinned or Mexican or something. You ain't white."

Now it was my turn to pause as I tried to comprehend the weight of what she'd just said.

"Aniyah, with my Dutch blood, I'm about as white as they come."

The group went back to talking, and I went back to the fourth-grade student in front of me.

"Miss C, can I do your hair?" Kallisha asked.

"Well, are you done with your homework?"

"Yes!"

"Let me see," I said, taking her math worksheet and reviewing her answers.

"This looks really great, Kallisha. Do you have anything else you need to finish today?"

"That's it, Miss C. Promise."

"If you can fix number seven, you can totally do my hair."

"Oh yes! Imma give Miss C braids," she announced to anyone that would listen.

The fourth-grade girl quickly corrected her answer and put her materials away. It was strangely comforting to feel her run her hands through my hair.

"Miss C, your hair is so soft. I wish I had hair like you."

"I think you're so lucky to have such beautiful hair! Mine's pretty straight and boring."

"I don't know, what you think?" She held up my long hair to the side of her face.

I wasn't the only one who burst out laughing.

"I think your hair is gorgeous exactly the way it is, my dear. I'm excited for you to give me some braids, but somehow I don't think I'll look quite as pretty with them as you do. Maybe I could get some beads like you too."

"Oh Miss C, you funny."

As she continued portioning off sections of my hair, I allowed myself to really think about Aniyah's words.

You ain't white.

I'd never been ashamed of being white before, though I'd spent most of my life in a place where everyone looked like me.

Had my students' lived experience taught them that white people did not care about them, about Carver Elementary, about their circumstances? And because I had earned their trust and demonstrated I had their best interests in mind, did that then mean I couldn't possibly belong to the white demographic? It would seem so.

I was beginning to more fully understand and empathize with this conclusion. Looking back now, I wish I'd had a direct conversation with Aniyah, Lontrell, and others in the small group, allowing her, and them, to explain her conclusions more fully. But I didn't, so I can only speculate.

But the statistics need no speculation. To this day, Black students in Kansas City fare far worse educationally than their white counterparts.

White students in Kansas City have more access to highly qualified, fully certified teachers, in addition to more access to higher quality and a wider breadth of course offerings.[17]

In Jackson County, Black students are three times more likely to be suspended from class for ten or more days than their white counterparts. And they are two to three times more likely to live in poverty and live in a household without a parent in the labor force.[18]

In the city council district where Carver Elementary resides, 15 percent of households lack a home internet connection and 11 percent lack access to any computer at all.[17]

This may help explain why, in 2022, the average composite ACT score for Black students was 13.7, while for white students it was 19.4.[17]

More than 70 percent of murders in Kansas City occur within the Black population, with 52% of all homicide suspects being Black.

Hell, even the vice principal at Carver, in my first days of teaching, predicted that many of these students would live a life full of violence.

I was doing what I could. The people I surrounded myself with were doing what they could. But, all too often, it didn't seem like enough.

One of those people was Jacob—the founder of the Youth Center. Over the past year, we'd built a good rapport filled with respect for one another. We were both working to make a difference to Kansas City students during their after-school hours and in the summer months.

After engaging with a few students, Jacob stopped by the table where Kallisha and I were sitting.

"Wow—your hair is looking really great, Miss C," Jacob said.

I laughed. "Thanks, Jacob—I'm lucky to have Kallisha making me look so good."

"Most definitely. I wanted to check in with you quickly. I'm planning to come and visit Carver tomorrow and would love to drop by your classroom in the afternoon, if that's still okay!"

"Of course! You can just check in at the front office like normal, and then I'll see you downstairs. I'm sure my students will be excited to see you."

"Great, I'll see you then!"

There was nothing to be concerned about with Jacob visiting my classroom. He had no authority at Carver, so I knew this was not a formal observation. But I was still anxious about having anyone come into my classroom, though embarrassed may be a more accurate word.

"How are we doing on those braids, Kallisha?"

"Oh, we've got lots more to go, Miss C."

I laughed. "Well, we've only got about ten minutes left today, so let's see how far we can get."

At Carver the next day, I thought through my lessons to figure out where I would be when Jacob arrived at my classroom in the afternoon.

I thought highly of Jacob and the Youth Center. My lessons and student engagements had always gone well at the Youth Center, and I didn't want his view of me to change based on what he saw in my classroom at Carver. My days at Carver were so unpredictable, which made me nervous.

Of course, students tend to act differently when a visitor is in the classroom—they're typically on their best behavior. But I felt like my barometer for determining acceptable student behavior had definitively and significantly shifted after my previous year of teaching.

I hadn't received much feedback over the past few months either. Chris, my Teach for America program director, hadn't been around much as he had added several other first-year teachers, who theoretically needed a lot more support than I did, to his docket.

And Ms. King had never shown up for the formal teacher observations that had been scheduled.

Although there was no formality to Jacob's observation, and the likelihood of it affecting my employment at the Center was minimal, I had anxieties nonetheless.

I had placed a chair near the back of the classroom, which Jacob slipped into quietly.

We were just beginning reading *A Christmas Carol,* and I had set the stage with vocabulary and what I deemed to be a pretty good incentive: After we finished the book, we'd watch the movie.

"Can't we just skip the reading and watch the movie? I'm sure it's better anyway," said Keith soon after Jacob arrived.

"Haha, very funny, Keith," I deadpanned. "Here's the deal, I can't make any promises, but I know the new Jim Carrey version of *A Christmas Carol* is coming out soon. I'll see if I can get us a field trip at the new IMAX theater to go see it."

I'd struck a chord.

"You can do that, Miss C?" Keith asked.

"Well like I said, I can't make any promises, but I can sure try. At the very least, you know I'm good for popcorn and snacks in the classroom."

"Okay, let's get at this then," Keith said, speaking for the whole class.

I'd created packets for the book that we would work through

together—some of the lessons and activities were to be done individually, others in pairs or small groups, and others as a full class. I'd spent hours poring over the activities and vocabulary, determining which questions to ask from comprehension to higher-level thinking.

"This is too much, Miss C," Christian said, flipping through the pages.

"My friend, I know it seems like a lot right now, but just focus on this first page. We're going at this together. We don't have to do it all today."

"I ain't doing this right now," he insisted.

"Okay, well take a break if you need it, and then come back to it."

"Nah, I'm not doing this at all." He set the book down.

Student defiance was not quite what I'd hoped Jacob would experience. I walked over to Christian to have a private conversation.

"Hey, how can I support you?" I asked.

"I'm not doing this today," he responded.

"Well, what can you focus on instead then?"

"Putting my feet up on this desk."

"Not the decision I would hope you'd make, Christian. This is not how you earn going on a field trip to an IMAX theater."

He sucked his teeth at me, a sound I was becoming all too familiar with, but he also picked up his pencil and wrote his name at the top of the page.

It was a start.

By the end of the period, nobody had cursed at me or walked out. My class had maintained a dull roar as they worked in small groups, and though it wasn't a perfect experience, all in all, I thought things had gone well. Sure, there was some speaking out of turn, and a few kids had put up a fight as we worked through the lesson, but I was looking forward to checking in with Jacob the next day when I was back at the Center. He'd slipped out toward the end of the lesson.

The rest of the day continued uneventfully, until a run-in with a cockroach during a seventh-grade geography lesson.

I'd been fortunate to have never seen a real life cockroach until that moment, but I immediately knew what it was. I had been writing some notes on the chalkboard when I heard the squeals of the girls. I followed the pointing fingers to the reddish-brown bug skittering across the floor.

Given my farming community upbringing, I wasn't one to be afraid of bugs, snakes, manure, dirt—the list goes on. But the size of the cockroach, its long antennae, its hairy legs and large wings made me tense up as it slid behind a bookcase.

"Oh, Miss C. That is disgusting," Tanisha wailed.

"I couldn't agree more, but there's no getting it back there. It's probably in Ms. Irving's room by now. Let's stay focused on the lesson."

So I continued with our discussion until the cockroach provided a short intermission by popping out at the back of the room and skittering through the middle of the floor. This time students were on top of desks, pushing chairs over as they avoided the two-inch pest.

I did my best to feign indifference.

"You guys, it's a bug. A nasty one, but a bug."

But even I couldn't help myself and quickly leapt to the other side of the classroom, annoyed that the roach had made its way over to my desk.

"I got you, Miss C. I'm on the hunt," Ja Khel promised me. "I'm gonna stand right here till he pops out again."

"You know what, I appreciate that Ja Khel, but I think I'll be okay. You can go back to your seat."

And then I heard the squeals again as the roach ran across the chalkboard. Ja Khel was poised in the right position and jumped at the chance. He smashed the roach against the yellow dust of the chalked notes, making a satisfying crunch against his hand.

There were groans and shrieks all around the class. Tanisha gagged. Even I was disgusted.

"Oh, Ja Khel. Appreciate you taking care of that, buddy. Here's a box of tissues. That was—disgusting." I handed him the tissue box.

"Foul, man, that was foul," Shakur said.

I was lucky there were only ten minutes left of the day because there was no coming back from a cockroach smashed by hand. As the day came to a close and I said goodbye to my students, I grabbed my bag and walked through the school to the parking lot.

"Hey, Miss C! How goes it?" said Ms. Fantay, the art teacher.

She also worked at the Youth Center, but on opposite days than when I did.

"Oh hey! Not too bad! Another day closer to Friday!"

She laughed. "I just wanted to check in. Jacob was in my classroom today, too, and mentioned that you may have had a tough day."

So much for thinking it had gone well.

"Yeah, the normal ups and downs to be honest. You know—middle schoolers."

"Totally get it. My lesson most definitely wasn't pristine either. And it's not like he really evaluates us, so who cares."

"Can I ask what he said that made you say something?"

"Oh, just that he thought the students behaved really poorly."

"Oh."

Really? I thought.

"But honestly, that's all of us, right?"

"Yeah, I suppose so."

By this point, we had made it to the parking lot.

"Well, I hope you have a good night. We'll see you tomorrow," Ms. Fantay said.

"Why are the two of you not planning on spending Christmas together?" my mom prodded me about my holiday plans with Mick.

"Because he wants to spend Christmas with his family, and I want to spend Christmas with you, the boys, and Dad."

"Well, I just think you should be with someone that makes you the priority."

She didn't have to say the second part, I could fill in the blanks: the way Tom does for me.

My mom had started dating Tom at almost the exact same time Mick and I had gotten together. She had never been one to lose herself in the relationships she had, but Tom was different. He showered her with flowers, jewelry, lotions, and perfume. And for the first time that I'd ever seen, my mom actually seemed to like it.

But I had always been incredibly independent. The fact that Mick and I didn't plan on spending the holidays together hadn't even registered as problematic until she'd said something.

"Are you still thinking you're going to be moving to San Francisco with him in the spring?" she asked.

"Well, yeah, but one step at a time."

"And you're going to move halfway across the country without a ring on your finger?"

"It's ultimately my decision. I'm not going to do anything I don't want to do. I'd like to live in San Francisco."

"I just don't think that's smart."

"Clearly."

My dad wasn't much more supportive when it came to the idea of me moving to San Francisco.

He even shared the old, problematic adage: "Why buy the cow when you can get milk for free?"

"Dad, I am not talking about my sex life with you."

"I sure don't want to talk about that with you. But if you're going to move in with him before you're married, and live as though you're married, why even get married?"

"First, we're not ready to get married. And second, I love him, but just because you love someone doesn't mean you're a fit for living together. I want to know that we can live together *before* we get married."

"Well, you know how I feel about that," Dad said.

"Clearly."

Although I disagreed with them, I took my parents' feedback to heart. I knew Mick wasn't using me—our relationship was much more than that. But were they right that I should not move across the country without a real commitment?

I decided to talk to Mick about it during our next date night. He was a fantastic cook and made dinner for me often. His latest creation was rosemary pork loin and polenta—a far cry from the tuna noodle casserole dinners I grew up making. We said our cheers and clinked our wine glasses, and I posed the question.

"Where do you see us going at the end of Teach for America? You know it'll be here before we know it. Am I really going to move across the country with you?" I asked.

"Well, only you can answer that question. Of course, you know how I feel. I want you to come with me, but I want you to move out there because that's what *you* want to do, not because of me."

"But it's false to think that I'd have the balls to move out to San Francisco on my own. Of course, I'm going because of you."

"That's a lot of weight to put on me. Your happiness in San Francisco shouldn't depend on me."

"Am I really going to move halfway across the country without a commitment? Without a ring on my finger?"

That escalated quickly, I thought, kind of surprised at myself.

"Whoa." He paused. "Do you really want to get married right now?"

"Well, no."

"Do you think we're ready to get married?"

"No. Not tomorrow, but I don't want to be your girlfriend for ten years either."

"Where is this coming from? This seems so out of left field."

He wasn't wrong.

"I've just been thinking a lot about the potential for next steps."

"We *do* have next steps. San Francisco seems like a pretty good one."

"It is! But like I said, there's no way I'd move to California by myself, so it's false to think that I'd be making the move for ulterior motives, aside from being with you."

"I don't know that that's fair," Mick said.

We sat in silence.

"How are you doing, really?" Mick asked. "I see you, skipping out on nights out. You may be pretty good at keeping that front up for everyone else, but I'm worried about you."

"I'm okay. I'm really trying to take better care of myself. I hope this doesn't scare you off, but I'm thinking about making an appointment with a psychiatrist. I'm just getting medication from my normal doctor at home. I think seeing someone with that specialty may be able to ensure I'm on the right medication."

"Well, I want you to do whatever you think is best to take care of you. You can't continue to give and give without taking care of yourself."

"I know, and I'm doing my best."

By this point, dinner was over. I hadn't eaten much, but I was sure enjoying the wine.

"Any chance we can open another bottle of red?"

"You know it," Mick said.

The rest of the evening was more awkward than I would have hoped, but I dulled it with red wine before flopping into Mick's bed for the night.

But the next morning, as I drove home, I couldn't hold back the tears.

It was complete overwhelm. I couldn't shut my mind off, couldn't stop thinking about my problems, Carver Elementary's problems, the world's problems—nothing was fixable. So what was the point in trying?

I parked my car and just sat there, looking at the keys in my lap. Everything felt heavy.

I called my dad crying, which had become a common ritual at this point.

"What's wrong, Cole?"

"I don't know."

"What can I do to help you feel better?"

"I don't know. Just knowing that you're there right now is helping." A sob escaped. "You don't even have to say anything," I said, sitting in my car in front of my apartment, just crying to my dad as he listened.

After a few minutes, I was able to get control of the tears.

"I can let you go, Dad. I just needed to know someone was there."

"Are you sure, Cole?"

"Yeah. Thanks, Dad."

I needed groceries and was already in the car, so I turned the key in the ignition, continuing to cry as I drove to Target. I wiped the tears as I pulled into the parking lot, made myself as presentable as possible, and went inside to shop for my essentials.

I would have preferred to use the self-checkout—the less engagement, the better—but with alcohol in my cart I was forced to exchange niceties with the store clerk. After I unloaded my purchases in my car, I got in the driver's seat and began crying again. I cried as I drove home, as I unloaded the car, and as I put my items away. I called my dad back and cried to him some more.

Why so many tears? I wasn't entirely sure, but I couldn't get it together.

I called my mom, who I was learning very quickly was not helpful when I found myself in these situations.

"You've got to understand that Mick doesn't treat you well. You want to be with someone who puts you first and wants to be with you all the time," she told me.

"Thanks for the insight, Mom. I'm not crying because of him."

"Are you sure?"

"Yes, I'm sure."

"Well then, you just need to get out of that school."

"But I'm so close to done. It seems so stupid to quit now, and nobody else has quit. I can't imagine being the only one."

As an objective observer with an intimate understanding of the goings-on with my family and with Mick, my roommate Anna often offered sage insight.

"I just think your mom doesn't want you to move to California," she said when I told her what my mom had said.

"I think you're probably right," I agreed. "But I've never felt this way before. What do I have to lose? What's keeping me here? My job? I will be *so* excited to leave that behind."

I only had six months of Teach for America left, and my

commitment would be fulfilled. There technically wouldn't be anything keeping me in Kansas City. There was a light at the end of this dark tunnel.

But I was afraid I was putting too much faith in this golden road to California where I could start over with a clean slate in a new state. Running away sounded so good.

chapter thirteen

One Saturday in mid-October, I spent the entire day in bed.

As I slowly awoke, I could tell I had slept in by the beam of light streaming through the opening in the curtains. My head pounded as I gained consciousness, having overindulged in white wine the night before. I forced myself to sit up, glancing at the red glow of the digital clock across the room: 10:07. I rubbed my eyes and allowed my body to drop back into the comfort of my cocoon before nature pushed her own plans upon me. I begrudgingly put my legs over the side of the bed before forcing myself up and opening my door. I stumbled over my own feet as I made the short trek to the bathroom where I relieved myself.

While I was up, I toyed with the idea of getting some water. But going to the kitchen meant I might run into Anna. I decided to wait until my thirst situation was more dire, and snuck back to my room, quietly closing the door behind me.

I walked over to the window to pull the curtain fully closed before plopping back down on the bed. I didn't have any plans for the day. I felt like shit. Alcohol undoubtedly played a role, but I knew it was more than that. I didn't want to do anything, so I pulled my covers back up to my chin. I didn't have to think when I was sleeping. Sleep was easy.

But often it felt too brief.

I woke again, giving myself a moment before I sat up, this time the red lights of the clock offering a dimmer glow in the full light of midday: 1:54.

I'd successfully slept away half of the day. But now I was thirsty. I knew I should be hungry but I wasn't, and I had no plans to force the issue.

But getting water meant I might have to see Anna, if she wasn't at her boyfriend's place. I cracked open my door and headed down the stairs and into the kitchen.

"Hey!" I heard as I approached the final stairs.

I knew Anna knew I'd been avoiding her.

"Hey! How are you?" I said as I walked into the kitchen in my pajamas.

"I'm doing well! Rough night last night?"

"Yeah, but not feeling great overall." I moved toward the sink to get my water.

"Anything I can do to help?" she asked, her eyes hopeful as I refused eye contact, forcing her to stare at my back.

My eyes brimmed with tears.

I grabbed a water glass and filled it, wiping the tears that had threatened to make their presence known.

I turned around with the full glass and took a swig before I said, "You're really sweet. I'll be okay." My eyes were still glassy with emotion. "I actually think I'm going to go back to bed."

"Oh wow, you must be sick! Let me know if I can get you any food or anything."

"Thanks, love. I'm just going to go get back to it!"

I climbed the stairs, bringing my water with me. I knew I wouldn't be able to fall right back to sleep, but reading would get me there shortly. I set the water on my nightstand, turned on my lamp, and grabbed *Crime and Punishment*. I pulled my covers back over me, rolled to my side, and started reading. Before I knew it, I was waking after another nap. It was 7:02.

I grabbed my phone, realizing I hadn't checked it the entire day. It didn't matter—I probably wouldn't have answered anyway.

The only message I would care about would be one from Mick. And there it was, waiting for me, from thirty minutes before.

Hey! You coming out tonight?

I hadn't even gotten out of my pajamas or taken a shower. I wasn't going anywhere.

> Hey! I've actually been in bed all day– not feeling well. I'm so sorry I'm not going to make it.

I'm sorry. If you're up for it, maybe we can get together tomorrow before we start the week?

And there was the reminder. Only one more day stood between me and another week at Carver.

> Let's check in tomorrow. Hoping I feel better by then.

Feel better, Cole.

> Thanks, love.

I was flaking on him, and he was still sweet.

I cried as I let my head hit the pillow again. I had wasted a Saturday. Sundays at this point were always awful as I spent them in anticipation of the school week; now I'd ruined a Saturday as well. It was the only day of the week that had the potential to be good.

There was no magic moment when I realized the depression had set in so fully. It had felt gradual, and then all at once. It came in like the tide, waves crashing closer and closer to shore, sneaking in further and further without me even noticing until it was upon me. Overwhelming me. Drowning me.

This tide of anxiety and depression had come in and out through the different seasons of my life. It started at the age of eight, waxed and waned through adolescence, and now fully engulfed me as I moved into adulthood. It like I lived life at the beach, enjoying the water and the surf, the feeling of the sand between my toes, the small crashes of the waves, and then, as the sneaker waves found their way in, I'd get deeper and deeper into the surf until all at once the water would be over my head, sweeping me off my feet. In the past, I'd been able to right myself pretty quickly; my feet were able to find the wet sand and dig in as the next wave came.

In the past, the right antidepressants and therapy had more than provided me with what I needed to feel better, to navigate the difficult seasons of my anxiety and depression.

But this time was different.

This depression wasn't like the others. I couldn't find the ground. And although I was scrambling, reaching for the surface, I was unable to decipher which way was up. Before I knew it, I was gasping, begging for air, a lifeline, anything so that I could breathe.

Shanna wasn't enough anymore. My weekly counseling sessions were helping, but not enough. And the Paxil didn't seem to be working either.

I hadn't seen a psychiatrist since I was in elementary school, aside from the short hospital stay in middle school. Maybe it was worth exploring again. I'd do some research and see if I could identify someone who it would make sense to go to.

By November, I felt like I was understanding the norms of what it meant to teach middle school at Carver. I'd had fistfights in my classroom and there was the occasional student who walked out. But I hadn't seen anything as blatant as I did when I turned to see Derreck slap Mahlik across the face.

"Derreck! What are you thinking? Dude, you need to go to the office right now."

"Ah, Miss C—he deserved it!"

I looked to Mahlik, who offered no response. Given his lack of explanation, I assumed he probably did deserve it, but I obviously couldn't say that out loud—and I also couldn't let a blatant, hard slap across the face just go unpunished.

"Okay, so then what happened?"

Derreck sucked his teeth at me and looked away. "I ain't no snitch," he said.

In my first year as a teacher, I had written up students for anything and everything; with my middle schoolers I had taken a different approach. There was nothing worse than a "snitch" in their eyes and, in this case, I was a snitch without all the facts.

"I'm sorry then. If you can't help me fill in the blanks, then I can't help you. I need to you to go to the office."

He elbowed me as he pushed past me in the close quarters of our classroom, making his way out of the small room. He shoved over his desk before he left, which made a loud crash as the metal hit the floor and papers and pencils scattered—a final punctuation as he walked out the door.

"Grand," I said under my breath.

As Tanisha helped me pick up, I prodded Mahlik further.

"Mahlik, what happened?"

He looked away. He wasn't snitching either.

As I looked to the others in the class, they uncharacteristically focused on their work, refusing to make eye contact. I righted the desk and stacked the materials on top. Then I went back to my own desk, pulled out a referral slip, and filled it out with the details that I witnessed, making sure to note I didn't have the full story. I hoped Ms. King would be able to fill in the blanks.

"Tanisha, can you take this to the office?" I asked.

"You got it, Miss C," she responded.

The retaliation was swift. Just a few periods later, I walked into my classroom to see it was completely torn apart. I immediately knew what had happened: Derreck's brother and his friends—some of whom were my students, but most of whom were eighth graders—had gotten involved.

It was well known that Derreck's brother, Ja Khel, was involved in gang activity. This wasn't speculation—Ja Khel himself talked about it often. Although I wasn't sure if Derreck was also involved with the gang, I knew he could very well be on his way, even at just twelve years old.

I tempered my anger with this in mind as I viewed my destroyed classroom. Almost all the desks and chairs in my room were overturned. There were materials—folders, worksheets, pens and pencils, art supplies, torn workbooks, entire class sets of books—strewn about everywhere, and especially on the floor. The bulletin boards and posters I had meticulously handmade were torn down, no longer usable.

I didn't need to report to anyone that this had happened—it felt like all my students knew, and that meant Ms. King would know soon enough. And besides, I'd seen what snitching had gotten me in the first place.

"Oh my God, what happened?!" Rachel asked as she peeked into my classroom.

"I wrote up Derreck."

"Oh."

That was enough explanation.

"Any chance you'd want a wine date after grad classes tonight?"

It was only Wednesday.

"You know I'm game."

This wasn't anything a bottle of wine couldn't numb.

Derreck was suspended for a day, and back at school on Friday. He largely stayed clear of me, until the lunch period. I was sitting in my classroom by myself, eating a cold can of Chef Boyardee ravioli, when Derreck poked his head into my room.

"Miss C, can I talk to you?" Derreck said.

"Of course, Derreck. Pull up a chair."

As he came closer, I could see he was in distress. His eyes were teary, and he seemed almost frantic. His tears spilled over as he explained.

"Miss C, Ms. King said I assaulted you. I didn't mean to elbow you when I walked out the other day. I was just angry."

"Wait. Hold up. Say again?"

"Ms. King wrote me up, saying I assaulted you the other day. She said I could be expelled."

"I never said you assaulted me, Derreck."

The sense of relief on his face came quickly, but the tears remained.

"Can you talk to her, Miss C? Explain what happened? I own that I shouldn't have hit Mahlik, but I didn't assault you."

"I'll talk to Ms. King. I know when you went to move past me the other day that you were just upset. There was no intention to hit me, or even elbow me."

"Oh, thank you, Miss C. I really appreciate it." He wiped the tears from his eyes.

"And hey, I hope you see where I was coming from the other day too. I know I didn't see everything that happened, and I know that Mahlik may very well have deserved to be smacked. But I also couldn't just pretend I didn't see that happen. If I didn't write you up, the other students would think it's okay to go around smacking people too."

"I know, Miss C. I'm sorry about everything."

I never thought I'd see Derreck be so vulnerable.

"I'll take care of Ms. King."

"Thank you, Miss C."

"Are we good then?"

"Yeah, we good."

I squeezed his shoulder as he wiped away any trace of tears, steeling himself to go back to the lunchroom. It was something I, too, was becoming all too accustomed to.

After my most recent counseling session with Shanna, I had felt a lot better, but working on school preparations the next Sunday afternoon led to more than two hours of crying.

I'd hidden as much as I could from Mick, but we'd gotten too close to really keep the depth of my depression to myself. He was as supportive as he could be, and I did my best not to unload on him, but my coping mechanisms—sleep, alcohol, and newly added long runs at the track across the street from my apartment—weren't working. Mick had the insanity of his own classroom to deal with.

His new charter school had many benefits, including a majority of Teach for America teachers and a super supportive administration. Yet it was still the same school district.

I knew how bad my depression had gotten when I found my mind wandering to particularly dark places. I wasn't certain I wanted to be dead, but I surely didn't want to be here, or really anywhere. I wanted to push pause, and in a way that was more than staying at home and blocking the world out. I didn't want to be.

Sleep was that out for me. It was my shutoff. I came home and went to sleep. On the weekends, I was sleeping fifteen hours in a day. Then I'd wake up, drink wine straight from the bottle, and go back to bed. Rather than an embarrassment, the fact that I could put away a full bottle of wine became a bit of a badge of honor to me.

As I continued down this path, a plan came to light. Though I had no intention of carrying it out, I knew how I would do it. There was a perfectly placed tree on my route to school, situated just so that I thought I would have enough runway to accelerate at what I thought would be an opportune speed. All it would take was a slight turn of the steering wheel of my car.

But if I was going to do it, I wanted there to be certainty I'd die. A car accident wasn't a sure thing. I wasn't ready to go yet, but I sure did look at that tree every single day on my drive to work.

Recognizing the abyss I found myself in, I finally made an appointment with a psychiatrist. Ironically, the act of going to see Dr. William McKnelly was the sanest I'd felt in months.

He was an eighty-year-old man who was a bit rotund and commanded authority while sporting a soft smile. The fact that he was eighty and still working told me almost everything I needed to know about him: He was experienced, good at what he did, and wanted to help as many people as possible.

His round, gold-rimmed glasses and salt-and-pepper beard lent themselves well to his role as an aging professor of psychiatry; he'd served as both a faculty member at the teaching hospital and a practicing psychiatrist for almost fifty years.

I'd been to many therapists and psychiatrists in my short life, but he was the one who made me feel most at ease, most seen, and most understood.

"Some people are more susceptible to being depressed by the mere fact of being born. This is not your fault. It's biological, and there's absolutely nothing you could have done to prevent yourself from being depressed," he told me.

I stared at him, not fully buying what he was selling, as much as I wanted to. I'd been made to feel this was my fault—a weakness that I should be able to conquer. Depression was my dirty secret that I strove to keep hidden at all costs, and I'd done it pretty well for the past thirteen years. But this time was different; I couldn't hide anymore.

Dr. McKnelly continued, "This sort of depression in particular happens to high achievers. One of those high achievers happened to be Abraham Lincoln. Did you know Lincoln dealt with depression the majority of his life?"

I shook my head no.

"His gloom was familiar to everyone who knew him well. He often wept in public, talked of suicide in his life more than once, and saw the world as a pretty miserable place."

"Well, maybe we should start a club."

Dr. McKnelly chuckled. "My dear, I'm going to help you. We're going to figure this out."

From the very first session with Dr. McKnelly, I knew I was in good hands, and that I would be lucky to be called one of his patients.

I would find out later Dr. McKnelly was truly ahead of his time. He was the founder and director of a methadone clinic for opiate addiction, and the director of the lithium clinic at the University of Kansas Medical Center. Both are controversial treatments still today, and he was met with criticism when he worked to make them available in the conservative Midwest.

It wasn't until later in my life, as I've become more open and honest about my experiences, that I fully understood how prevalent anxiety and depression is: In a typical year, more than sixteen million adults in the United States experience a major depressive episode,[19] which translates to almost 8 percent of the general population.[20]

And depression isn't a recent development. The first chronicles of depression were found in the second millennium BCE in Mesopotamia, when it was believed depression was a spiritual problem versus a medical one. Many of the initial treatments focused on driving demons from those it afflicted, and included beatings and starvation.[21]

In the Middle Ages, Christianity drove the narrative, and exorcisms, drownings, and burnings were done to rid people with depression of Satan's grip over them.[21]

By the eighteenth and nineteenth centuries, depression came to be seen as a hereditary weakness, causing those who experienced it to be locked up or shunned by the community, something that arguably continues to this day.[21]

I had always felt guilt and shame about my depression, which is why I'd learned to hide it so well. But it had gotten so bad recently that I was no longer hiding it well.

"Okay, so you're on 50 mg of Paxil right now. We're going to bump that to 60 mg, and we'll add 10 mg of Wellbutrin on top of that."

This would be the first time I'd be on two medications, and the highest dosage of Paxil that I'd ever tried. But this was also the first time I had a plan for how to kill myself.

It was worth a try.

Given my penchant for books, I'd already done a large amount of reading about anxiety and depression, so I knew that, to this day, experts still don't understand how antidepressant drugs work. But they'd helped me before, and I hoped that adding a second one would help me again.

My mom wasn't thrilled that I was back at a psychiatrist. I think, for most of my life, she has thought I should be able to handle my depression and anxiety myself. But even she knew this time was different.

As I fully embraced seeing a psychiatrist and acknowledging my depression, I worked to take care of myself in other ways as well. I was working out multiple times a week, forcing myself to eat even when I had no appetite, and had even started to reengage with my faith.

I'd often wondered if my bouts of depression were God's way of testing me or punishing me for my lack of faith.

There was a passage in the first chapter of Peter that said "the trial of your faith is more precious than gold." I didn't see it that way.

My weekly church-going was only happening because of my childhood friend, Mindy. After seeing Dr. McKnelly for the first time, I began attending additional prayer sessions at the International House of Prayer, or IHOP, participating in their live worship and listening to the testimonies of their members.

Knowing I was in a dark time, Mindy invited me to IHOP often, and as I was seeking supportive fellowship, I accepted. With 24/7 streaming, there was never an excuse not to go to church.

I felt a little out of place with these girls who were so much more connected to Jesus than I was, but I knew I couldn't get close to Christ without work, so that's what I thought I was doing.

I was proud of the steps I had taken to manage my depression and to take care of myself better. I felt that I was on the right path.

But even if I felt I was taking positive steps, it didn't mean others hadn't been affected. A few weeks later, Mick and I had a really difficult conversation.

"You're not the same person anymore in going through this depression," Mick told me.

"I realize. I'm doing my best to take care of myself."

"I just don't think I can do this anymore."

I couldn't even pretend to hold it together anymore—the tears came fast.

Mick continued, "You're a shell of a person right now. You've given so much to others, you're so worried about others, that you don't have anything left to give."

I didn't know how to respond.

"Look, I wasn't given a choice in this," Mick said.

"And I was?!" I said in anger. "You think I *like* being like this? I'm doing the best I can. And you're going to leave me *now*? When I need you most?"

I could tell I'd struck a nerve as the tears began to fill his eyes.

"You're not the same girl I fell in love with. You need a friend more than a boyfriend."

"Oh, really. Well thanks for being my friend," I said, the sarcasm thick.

"If we break up now, is there a chance we can get back together down the line?" Mick asked.

"What kind of question is that?"

"I just need you to be able to take care of yourself. I can't do it for you. It doesn't make me love you any less."

"I honestly can't wrap my head around that right now."

"Look, let's just sleep on the idea of taking a break."

"It sounds like you've already made up your mind, Mick. I don't want to be with someone who doesn't want to be with me."

That was a lie. I wanted to be with him more than anything. But it really did feel like he was leaving me at the very moment I needed him the most.

I cried as I sat on his futon, unwilling to look him in the eyes.

"Can I hug you?" he asked gently.

I nodded, ashamed at how much I still needed him, and even more so that I agreed to spend the night so we could "sleep on the idea of taking a break." Though, in reality, neither of us did much sleeping as we spooned each other.

In the morning, we made our split official, after I'd thought all night about what I wanted to say—to hurt him in the way he was hurting me.

"I feel like you're leaving me when I need you the most, and my thought process is if you can't handle me at my worst, you don't deserve me at my best," I said.

It worked. I could see he was holding his breath, willing the tears not to spill over. I started taking his apartment keys off my key ring.

"Keep them, in case there's an emergency."

"What is that supposed to mean?"

"Just keep them, okay?" he insisted.

I said nothing and walked out the door, holding back the sobs until I was in my car.

I don't think I'd ever hurt so much in my life. The tears poured out of me as I made the short drive home. I pulled into the dark garage, turned off the ignition, and let the sobs rack my body. I don't know how long I sat in the car by myself, just crying. When I found an intermission, I wiped the snot and wetness away, grabbed my bag, and beelined for my apartment. I bound up the stairs, shut the door, and crawled into bed, willing sleep to come. But I was only left with my tears.

If there was any lucky part about my breakup with Mick, it was that he did it before Thanksgiving break. Aside from the swollen eyes that I blamed on allergies (I'm sure the kids totally saw through the lie), I was able to make it through the two-day work week at school easily, and then it was time to head home to spend time with my family.

The almost five-hour drive provided more than enough time for me to stew in my thoughts, and the more I thought, the angrier I got.

My friends and family had varying responses—from "let's go get a drink" to "fuck *alllll* of that" to a not-so-veiled "I told you so."

Anna had taken a less aggressive approach, saying, "I'm so sorry, Cole."

She'd hugged me as she ran her hand up and down my back.

"It's going to be okay. I know it might not feel like it right now, but it's going to be okay."

It was good to get away for a bit. I was grateful to be on the farm with my dad and my brothers, just us. I didn't have to put a show on for anybody and could let my emotions flow freely.

There were multiple times I sat on the couch and just cried as my dad held me. At least, with Mick dumping me, now I had a reason why I was a wreck.

As I finally began to make sense of our breakup, even I had empathy for Mick. I wasn't the same person. He's only human. I can't say I wouldn't have done the same thing. And I still loved him immensely, as painful as that was to admit.

I was back in Kansas City and preparing for the final weeks before Christmas when I hit a breaking point. It was the first time I had cried publicly during a church service. I did my best to hide it, but I felt the eyes of other parishioners. As soon as the service was over, I beelined out the door and walked the few blocks home where I crawled into bed and bawled.

Not knowing what else to do, I called my dad.

"Dad?"

"How're you doing, Cole?"

I choked on a sob. "Not so good."

"I'm sorry to hear that, Cole. What can I do to help?"

"You're listening. Thank you."

"I'm so sorry, Cole Rae."

"Dad?" I sobbed some more. "I don't want to be alive." More sobs came after I admitted the truth out loud. "I think I need to go to the hospital."

"Oh Cole, I think that's a good idea. Do you have someone you can call to help?"

"I can call Dr. McKnelly."

"I think that's a good idea. Keep me posted on what's happening, okay?"

"Okay."

"I love you."

"I love you too."

I couldn't help myself. I had to call Mick. He had been my lifeline through this whole Teach for America experience. I needed him.

"Hey, I'm really sorry to bug you," I said when he answered.

"You never bug me. What's up?"

"I was hoping we could just talk." I didn't really know what I wanted. Validation he still cared? To be told that I was worthy of his love?

"Absolutely. Let's meet at Starbucks."

My voice shook as I admitted, "I'm actually—not doing so great. I'd rather not be in public."

"Come over." There was no hesitation in his voice.

"Are you sure?"

"Yes—I'm here."

During the short drive to Mick's house, I called my dad to let him know my plan.

It felt strange to see people going about their daily lives as I was literally falling apart. People continued with their trivialities while I drove and contemplated the meaning of life and whether I wanted to continue to live.

I parked in the parking garage in my normal spot, but this time I didn't use my key to enter. I lightly knocked to announce my arrival.

Mick opened the door. I could see the concern wash over him as he took in the disheveled girl in front of him. He opened his arms for a hug, and I couldn't hold back the tears as I fell into him.

I was honest about where I was at mentally. I told him I wasn't eating, couldn't stop crying, was contemplating suicide, and was planning to go into the hospital.

"I'll take you if you need to go, but let's just see how this afternoon goes."

"Okay."

"I'm guessing you have prep work to do for the week. Let's go get your stuff and you can plan here."

I nodded in agreement.

"And if you want, grab your swimsuit and we can go down to the sauna for a bit as well, if that sounds good."

"That actually sounds really good."

I worked at Mick's place all afternoon, and we spent some time in the sauna and took a steam together as well. Mick may not have understood fully what I was going through, but he knew exactly the support I needed. As we walked back to his apartment, I realized the afternoon had quickly become evening.

Mick said, "You know, you're welcome to spend the night."

"I'll be fine."

"Let me rephrase. If going to the hospital this afternoon was really an option, I'd be more comfortable if you stayed."

So, I stayed, but set clear boundaries. We weren't together, and I made it clear he wasn't going to get the benefits of being together. But the comfort of falling asleep in his arms was just what I needed, even though I knew it might not serve me well in the long-term.

chapter fourteen

As I woke to Monday morning, I was able to get the crying under control before school, even better than I had anticipated. Though my alcohol intake in the evenings was increasing overall, I felt like I needed it to get me through. The end of the semester was in sight, and after that, there was only one semester left. Then I'd be done with Teach for America.

But then what? Mick would go back to San Francisco, and without me? I didn't even want to think about it.

I threw myself into the final weeks of school before the long holiday break. We were wrapping up *A Christmas Carol* in my seventh-grade class, and even I was surprised at how engaged the students were.

Dewayne was not usually one of my most committed students, but at the end of the class period, he asked, "Miss C, do we have to stop reading? Just a little more?"

"That's it for today, my friend. But we've got more tomorrow. We're almost done!"

I didn't fully anticipate how much they would appreciate the story.

"And what about that movie, Miss C?" Shakur asked.

"It's in the works—that's all I can say for now."

I had been working with a school board member in hopes he could help me get IMAX movie tickets donated for the Jim Carrey version of *A Christmas Carol* that had just been released. He'd been successful—we had just been given the green light for a noon showing on a Tuesday. We'd have the whole theater to ourselves, and the best part was that we had enough tickets for the entire middle school to attend.

I anticipated the tough part would be convincing Ms. King that this was a good idea, but even she was on board.

"Oh, that's great news. You organize the chaperones, get those permission slips, and I'll help with the transportation," she'd said.

And so, with Ms. King's blessing, Rachel, Melissa, and I found a few additional chaperones and planned our trip to the IMAX theater.

The movie didn't go off without a hitch. We'd set the expectations as well as we could, but it was still sixty Carver middle-school students feeding off one another's energy—running through the theater in excitement, calling out at the movie, screaming in laughter, and throwing popcorn buckets.

But it was a memory I hoped they would take with them. And it brought me joy that I was able to make good on a promise that was quite special, rather than having to fall back on playing *The Muppet Christmas Carol* on a TV in the classroom.

It was some happiness to cling to, and I needed more of that than I cared to admit at this point.

I had another session with Dr. McKnelly to check in on how the shifts in my medication were going. Before he could even ask me how I was doing, I was crying.

"I'm sorry, Dr. McKnelly," I said between sobs.

"You have nothing to be sorry about. What's going on?"

"My boyfriend and I broke up."

"Ah. I'm so sorry. I'm sure that adds fuel to the fire. And that's okay. We're still going to get you through this."

"I've just never hurt so bad. I don't think the increase in meds is helping all that much."

"Well, we can absolutely bump the Wellbutrin up to 20 mg and see if that helps. But my dear, there's no cure for a broken heart."

That made me cry even harder.

We talked about coping mechanisms, and how I could potentially take my focus off the day-to-day. I'd started going to a hot yoga class with Melissa, which was something Dr. McKnelly highly approved of.

"Time—you've just got to give it some time. And keep your mind focused on other things in the meantime."

"Thanks, Dr. McKnelly."

"And you know you can always call me, day or night. If I can't immediately help you, I'll find someone who can."

"Thanks."

I was lucky to have such a fierce advocate in my corner.

I'd been blowing off Melissa and Rachel, but had been keeping myself busy with anything and everything else, and sleeping every moment I could in the interim.

And I was seeing Mindy quite a bit again, attending the International House of Prayer multiple times a week. When I had told her about the breakup, she held me as I cried. And then she cried with me.

Having grown up together, she knew me well. I'd shared everything with her about my relationship with Mick, and I didn't feel judged.

After leaving a prayer session at IHOP one afternoon, Mindy

and I connected with a few of her friends from her community as we walked to our cars.

It was clear she had shared my story with the three of them, and as we stood in the parking lot chatting, one of them asked, "I'm really feeling God's presence here. Mindy has shared with us that you've been having a tough time, and that you and your boyfriend recently broke up. Would it be alright if we prayed over you, Nicole?"

"Uh, sure," I said.

I didn't know what else to say, but figured I'd go along with it, even if prayer in a parking lot didn't quite seem like the right time or place.

The four girls formed a circle around me, first holding hands and, as they continued to pray, holding their hands up as if taking in my energy.

"Lord Jesus, be with us here today as we support Nicole. Let us feel your presence. Give us your grace, your love, your vision. Be with us now," one of them said.

I largely kept my eyes closed as I stood in the center of the circle, but I peeked to see one of the girls whispering under her breath, while others swayed, arms outstretched toward my body.

"Father God, be with us. Give us your light."

A few minutes passed.

"I'm seeing a deep, beautiful blue," one of the girls said.

I kept quiet, not knowing what to say. I assumed I was supposed to be praying as well but was more interested in what these girls were doing around me.

A few more minutes passed.

"I'm having a vision of a wooden trough. It's muddy and filled with nasty garbage and slop. There are pigs eating the nastiness, greedy for more."

"What else?" Mindy asked.

"As I look closer, there are three beautiful pearls in the muck and mire. A hand is plucking them out and has begun polishing them."

It was quiet again.

"Where the spirit of the Lord is, there is liberty. Father God, thank you for Nicole, thank you for these visions. Help us to keep your word in our hearts that we may not sin against you. Help us to be more like you. In Jesus's name, amen."

We all opened our eyes.

"Oh, that felt so good. We love you, Nicole," one of the girls said.

"Love you guys too. Thanks."

I did feel supported and loved, but honestly, I was wary. As much as I'd tried to be a good Christian, I continued to be a skeptic. I'd grown up with Mindy, but only recently met the others. They didn't know me, and I wasn't sure how I felt about their "visions" and what felt like proselytizing.

There were lots of hugs before Mindy and I went our separate ways.

"Those pearls are you, Nicole. I know it," Mindy said. "And those hands polishing, that was God. He loves you, Nicole."

"Thanks, Mindy."

"I think there are a few more things you can do that will help you to release Mick and be even closer to God," she said.

After we climbed into her car, she took out a notebook and began writing.

The enemy has stolen, and he owes me seven-fold and restore to me what is rightfully mine.

"You'll need to repent for your physical relationship with

Mick, and to take back and give back your soul, mind, heart, and body to Jesus," she said.

"Okay."

Mindy was one of my lifelong friends, but this didn't feel right.

"Ask God to break your soul tie with Mick. Bless him when you release him, and receive from the Lord all you will be."

"Okay."

"And then if you're not already, pray regularly, out loud if you can. I start each day by saying, 'Jesus, I want joy today.'"

I giggled.

"Seriously. It works. And as you talk to God, you'll get to know him better. You may not be able to hear him at first, but you'll learn to hear his words, his will."

She tore the page out of the notebook with all the notes she had made me.

"He'll get you through this, Nicole. Jesus loves you."

It sure didn't feel like it.

Christmas had always been a magical time for me. I quite literally wrote and sent more than a hundred holiday greeting cards as a college student, and yearly thereafter, often bought from the dollar store as to not break the bank. I baked and sent dozens of cookies to family, friends, and even a few elderly folks in the local nursing home. I was thoughtful and strategic about the Christmas gifts I chose, spending an entire day wrapping the presents in different shades of holiday paper, stacking some under my own personal Christmas tree in my room and others downstairs under the communal one I shared with my roommate.

As I approached Christmas that year, I refused to see it any differently. I'd arranged a holiday cookie decorating session with Chantelle, four girls from Carver's middle school, and four other teachers including Rachel and Melissa.

I posted the photos online, intentionally wanting Mick to see I didn't need him to be okay or to have a good time.

And though I wanted to show Mick I was doing just fine without him, I have to admit it was quite cathartic to throw myself into the holiday spirit—which is why my friend Andrea's invitation couldn't have been better timed.

I had inadvertently met Andrea through a friend who recommended I do some self-care through massage therapy. Although I hadn't had many massages, I figured out very quickly Andrea had a gift. In addition to the immense gratitude I had for her giving me a "teacher discount," the hour I spent each month on her massage table was one where my anxiety and stress melted away.

It was these monthly encounters that led to a somewhat unconventional friendship—I was in my early twenties and Andrea was middle-aged—but my old soul knew no boundaries. I had shared many stories about my Teach for America experience with her.

Knowing many of my students went home each week with a backpack of food from the local nonprofit program, it was unlikely many of my students would have numerous presents under their respective trees, so she asked if she could do something about it.

"What would you think if I mobilized my friends to put together small gifts for your homeroom students? It could all be the same thing. I'll take donations, see how much we amass, and then I could get thirty-two of the same thing and you can pass them out on the last day of school before the holiday break."

"I don't think there's any reason to say no to that!"

And with that, Andrea was off to the races. The idea blew up more than either of us could have ever anticipated. Andrea recruited a few friends to join the initiative, who in turn easily convinced others to share the love.

The donations were overwhelming, taking over our living rooms as we organized the gifts and determined recipients, which was clearly going to be more than my homeroom students. We ended up with gifts for all of the middle schoolers and kids in numerous other grades at Carver Elementary.

There were school supplies and craft materials—glue sticks, construction paper, and coloring books—notebooks, pencils, erasers, Post-it notes, more than a hundred books, and even balls for the playground. There were food items: macaroni and cheese, trail mix and Teddy Grahams, bags of animal crackers and plastic containers of peaches, four hundred granola bars, three hundred bags of potato chips, more than a thousand bags of fruit snacks, cans of chicken noodle soup, oatmeal, Oreos, Pop-Tarts, Apple Jacks, milk, fruit, pudding, and popcorn. There were more practical items like boxes of Kleenex and hand sanitizer, toothbrushes, fuzzy socks, soap, and more than two hundred and fifty pairs of hats, gloves, and blankets for the cold winter. There were less practical, but incredibly important, "fun items" like sparkly nail polish, rings, perfumed lotion and lip gloss, bouncy balls, frisbees, Hot Wheels, Star Wars toys, Silly Putty, and the crucial candy canes and chocolate Santas.

And then, of course, there were the thirty-two backpacks that had spurred the idea. These were for my homeroom students, and we strategically filled each of them with forty-five different items, including ten dollars in cash and ten dollars in McDonald's gift cards for each of them.

It was more than we could have ever imagined.

It felt amazing to pass out the gifts to classes throughout

Carver, and then to give the overflowing backpacks to kids in my homeroom. I wasn't going to let a chance for a short speech pass.

"I know we all have our ups and downs—that's to be expected. But if there's any point during this holiday break or even in the future that you're feeling low, I want you to think about this backpack and remind yourself that every single item in here came from someone who cares about you. These individuals care about you, without ever having even met you," I said.

I let the idea sink in with a few moments of silence.

"Now, get out of here. Have a great holiday break!"

The room came alive with energy as some students pulled items out of the backpacks and examined their loot while others took my advice and ran out the door with their bags, ready to start the two weeks of holiday vacation.

"Thank you, Miss C." Brexton came to give me a hug.

"You're so welcome—this has so little to do with me."

"But you made it happen."

"I only helped. This was a lot of other people who, like I said, care about you."

"Merry Christmas, Miss C," said Brexton.

"Merry Christmas, Brexton."

The classroom continued to buzz with excitement as the few volunteers who had been part of the initiative and decided to join in the distribution watched in awe as students expressed their delight about their gifts.

"That was a really great speech," Andrea said, leaning in for a hug.

"You made this happen," I said.

"We both did," she responded.

I stood back to watch as some students squealed in delight and others looked quietly in awe as they pulled item after item out of their new backpacks.

And just like that, my first semester of teaching middle school was over. Only one more semester at Carver and I'd be done with my Teach for America experience.

Little did I know, my biggest battle was left to fight.

I always cried after Christmas. It was nothing new. For me, the season had always been associated with a magic no other time could replicate. With Christmas cards, holiday cookies, copious presents, and extended family, I'd always found people were kinder—more focused on generosity and gratitude—during the holidays.

But after reveling in the magic of the tree, family time, and opening presents, the abrupt shift to normalcy afterward was always too much to bear.

As had been the case since middle school, I split the holiday time between my mom and dad, first spending a few days at my mom's house in Des Moines, opening presents with her and my brothers, and Tom and his two boys, who were similar in age to my brothers.

Then my mom's extended family gathered at a rental space to spend time with one another—nobody's house was big enough to accommodate my grandmother, seven aunts and uncles, twelve cousins, and many of their kids. It was always an intense experience—from the over-the-top potluck to cookie-decorating contests and games that involved stealing presents from one another.

I then drove four hours with my brothers to our family farm where we spent a few more days in Northwest Iowa with our dad.

We split wood—despite it being frigid, which had somehow become Cleveringa family tradition—and enjoyed the fruits of our labor with multiple fires in the fireplace and eating too much food before opening too many presents.

But the afternoon of the twenty-fifth, after all the wrapping paper had found its way into the garbage bags, the space under the tree was barren, and family members had gone their separate ways to enjoy their gifts, year after year I'd sit next to the tree and cry. I'd hug my dad, embracing the calm after the build-up of the previous month, not wanting to let the magic slip through my fingers.

That year was worse than usual. It was another holiday without Mick. I purposely wasn't engaging with him because I knew doing so would make letting him go impossible, but I was secretly hoping he would at least text me to say Merry Christmas. As much as I wanted a future in San Francisco with him, that didn't look too promising at the moment.

By the next day I was restless and not finding all that much comfort in my dad, my mom, or my brothers, so I drove back to Kansas City. However, I hadn't fully thought through what it would feel like to sit in my apartment by myself.

Anna wasn't home yet, so I found myself alone with my thoughts. And then I found myself contemplating how easy it would be to just "be done"—no worrying about going back to school or about what came after Teach for America. There'd be no need to worry if there wasn't an after. Then I found myself thinking through where I could buy a gun. I certainly wasn't afraid of them. I knew how to load them, how to hold them, and what to do with them. And that's what scared me most.

I had only been home alone for half a day, but I knew if I didn't call someone, I was going to find a permanent solution to my problems.

I didn't feel like my family or friends could do anything for me. I had Dr. McKnelly's personal number, so I called him. The University of Kansas Medical Center was a short drive away, and he said he would meet me there.

"This isn't your fault," he said after meeting me at the door.

The statement brought tears to my eyes.

As we walked into the hospital, I asked, "What can you even do for me at this point?"

"Honestly, we can monitor you, have you engage in some group therapy, and, of course, work with me and a few other doctors."

"That's it?" It wasn't the answer I wanted to hear.

"You've maxed out your medication. I really can't give you any more. We can shift things around, but I know Paxil is what has historically worked best for you."

I looked to the ground, defeated.

"Unless you're willing to try something different."

As we continued walking down the hospital's hallway, I looked up and into his eyes. It had seemed to be a gradual, and yet sudden, descent into the abyss I found myself in. I didn't fully recognize it until I was already waist deep in the muck and mire. The struggle only seemed to increase the rapidity of my descent. I'd pretended everything was fine, forced myself to go out, faked laughing at jokes, feigned interest in the things I used to care about. That is, until the weight and heaviness of life started crushing me, and it became unbearable even just to simply *be*. I was willing to try anything.

"What's different?"

By this point, we'd walked into his office and both took a seat.

"ECT. Electroconvulsive therapy."

I paused. "They still do that? Like shocking my brain? Seriously?"

"Yes. And I think you're a prime candidate."

"Why?"

"Recurrent major depressive disorder. This isn't the first time you've experienced these lows, even if they are the worst they've ever been. And it's very possible it won't be the last."

"Well, that's not very optimistic."

"I get that, but to be honest, other than monitoring you and therapy, I don't have much more to offer. And I realize that's not very optimistic, but I think ECT is something you should really consider."

"I've seen *One Flew Over the Cuckoo's Nest*."

"That's a movie. More than 75 percent of my patients I recommend this treatment for have substantial improvement when dealing with the type of depression you've been navigating much of your life."

I let the recommendation sink in. "Otherwise, the option is to stay here and have you and the nurses and doctors monitor me? And do more therapy, with a new counselor?"

"There's really not much else we can do at this point."

"Then sign me up."

I didn't need to think about it. If my options were staying in a psychiatric unit or trying something that could ultimately "fix" my state, I wanted the latter. I trusted Dr. McKnelly.

"Are you sure? You can take some time to think about it. It's something you may want to talk with your family about."

"Yes, I'm sure. I can make my own decisions. Besides, I'm not sure my family would be too thrilled about it."

"Well, there are a few things to go over. There are some potential side effects—short-term memory loss during your treatment being the most important one. This potential loss of memory typically includes several weeks before your first few treatments. Sometimes there's jaw pain and headaches after the treatment, but those usually go away in a day or two. And then, of course, there are the risks that come with going under general anesthesia during each treatment."

"How many treatments would I need?"

"I'd recommend eight to twelve. We'd assess how you're feeling as we move through the full course of treatment."

"Well, even with those side effects, I'm still in. I don't want to sit here without any real course of action to get better. And honestly, I wouldn't be totally opposed to losing many of the memories of my time teaching or of the last few weeks."

"You're not the first person to say something like that. And if that's your mindset, I'll see what I can do to get you scheduled for your first treatment in the next day or two while you're still here in the hospital."

"Sounds good. In the meantime, I'll be here!" I joked.

Dr. McKnelly didn't laugh.

I was desperate to get my life back. Sitting in the hospital without a plan of action wasn't an option, so I didn't feel like I really had any other choice.

"Let's get you checked in to the hospital, and then I'll plan on checking in with you tomorrow morning regarding the timeline for ECT."

"Sounds like a plan."

I stood and followed him out the door, back down the hospital corridor, through two double doors, and into a new wing I'd never been in before.

I called my dad first to share the news that I'd checked myself in to the psychiatric unit at the University of Kansas Medical Center. I knew he'd be supportive of whatever decision I made, even the extreme choice of undergoing electroconvulsive therapy.

"Can I come and visit?" he asked.

"Yeah, I don't see why not? I'd really appreciate it."

He'd later share that, in that moment, he was fearful of how ECT would affect my health and whether it was safe, and that although he would have preferred for me to make a different choice, he did not tell me any of this in that moment because he believed I ultimately knew what was best for me.

My mom took a very different approach.

"I don't understand why you couldn't handle this yourself," she said.

She sent flowers to my hospital room, but didn't come to visit while I was in the hospital over the six days I spent as an inpatient. And when she found out that I had chosen to undergo ECT, she was wholly unsupportive.

"Do you understand the potential repercussions? Especially the short- and long-term memory loss?" she asked.

"Would you rather have me dead?" I shot back.

"Of course not. You just need to quit that job and take better care of yourself."

I wished it was as simple as that.

"I'm trying to do what's best for me, Mom. I really don't know what you want from me."

"With those treatments, you wouldn't remember if I told you."

That's when I hung up.

My time as an inpatient at the psychiatric unit at the University of Kansas Medical Center was uneventful. I read, I wrote, I engaged with some of the other patients who didn't seem too different from me.

I spent most of my time in my room—the TV was blaring at all times in the communal area, which was far from relaxing.

Due to an auspiciously timed snowstorm, I had yet to miss a day of teaching. That allowed me to only share my situation with those whom I wanted to know: my mom and dad, my brothers, my roommate Anna, and Rachel and Melissa from Carver. I didn't want anyone else to know, so I didn't tell them.

Like Dr. McKnelly promised, I had my first ECT treatment two days after checking myself into the hospital.

I wasn't allowed to eat or drink after midnight and woke up at 5:00 a.m. to prepare for the hour-long experience.

I was very apprehensive about the treatment, but Dr. Mc Knelly had made me feel seen, heard, and understood, and he hadn't steered me wrong yet. After changing into a hospital gown, I sat on the uncomfortable hospital bed and was set up with my IV. My anxieties were compounded by the unfamiliar faces—additional psychiatrists and doctors—in the procedure room who were involved in my case. I was on my own—my family and friends weren't there. This was my challenge to weather.

"Hi Nicole. I'm Frank and I'll be your anesthesiologist today," a man said.

"And I'm Katherine. I'll be your nurse," a woman said.

The psychiatrist I'd seen before, Dr. Ardestani, asked, "How are you feeling today, Nicole?"

"I'm doing okay."

"On a scale of one to ten, with ten being the worst, how is your depression today?"

"I guess an eight," I responded.

"We'll be checking in with you each time with this survey to monitor how the course of treatment is progressing," said Dr. Ardestani.

"Okay."

I watched as they began to set up the materials—I couldn't believe I had signed up for this, but I was desperate. I wanted my life back.

I lay on my back, staring at the small holes in the white drop-ceiling tiles, and began counting the rows of squares.

The anesthesiologist explained the procedure, saying, "We'll be giving you a muscle relaxant so that there are no real convulsions with the treatment, and you'll be under general anesthesia so you won't feel anything. You'll only be asleep for five to ten minutes."

"That's it?" I asked, feeling surprised and taking a deep breath.

"That's it."

Dr. Ardestani continued, "We're going to put these electrodes on your chest to monitor your heart, and we've got four electrodes we'll be putting on your head, to both monitor your brain activity as well as to deliver the electrical pulses. We'll also have you put this bite block in your mouth, as stimulations typically cause jaw clenching and we want to protect your tongue and teeth."

I took another deep breath. "Okay."

Katherine jumped in, telling me, "I've seen this therapy help so many people. I'll be here with you when you go to sleep, and I'll be here when you wake up. You'll spend another ten to twenty minutes with me after the procedure. Sometimes you may be a bit confused right after, and we'll just want to make sure your heart rate and breathing return to normal. Then you can go back upstairs. Short and sweet."

"Okay. I'm ready," I said.

Looking to Katherine for assurance, she nodded her head and smiled at me. She provided the affirmation I wanted when I needed it most.

The bustle around me continued as the anesthesiologist put together the cocktail of drugs, and Katherine began connecting the machines that would monitor me as they delivered the treatment. I lay there quietly and let it happen.

"Alright, Nicole. I'm going to go ahead and give you the muscle relaxant, followed by the anesthesia. I'm going to count down from ten. Ten, nine, eight, seven . . ."

And then I was out—in a delightful, drug-induced, brief sleep. I woke to a woman holding my hand.

"Hi, Nicole," she cooed softly. "How are you feeling?"

I took a moment to look around.

Why am I in the hospital? Who is this woman? I thought.

"I'm your nurse, Katherine. You're just coming out of your first ECT treatment. You did so great."

I let her guidance sink in, grateful Katherine had filled in the blanks for me.

I had a headache, but I felt empowered. I was doing something to put the depression and anxiety I had coped with all my life behind me.

It felt like a fresh start.

I'd gotten my first ECT treatment. This was my path to recovery—the path that I had chosen.

chapter fifteen

During my six days in the hospital, I had two electroconvulsive therapy treatments and was discharged on the same day of my second one. I didn't feel any immediate relief—in fact, I didn't feel much different at all, but I was at least mentally stable enough to go home.

With the holiday break and snowstorm, I'd managed to only miss one day of school. I had called in sick, and nobody was the wiser about my status. I wanted to keep it that way.

I was lucky that, moving forward, the early-morning scheduling of the ECT procedure allowed me to keep my secret. I'd wake around 4:30 a.m. to be at the hospital at 5:30 a.m., receive my ECT treatment, allow the team to monitor me to be sure there weren't any immediate adverse effects, and then be released to whomever was willing to pick me up, as it wasn't safe for me to drive immediately after the treatment.

This meant I shared my quandary with my shuttle drivers. First it was my roommate Anna, then Rachel, and finally, after sharing my need, two pastors from my church.

After the procedure, I'd be wheeled out in a wheelchair to the waiting car. They'd pick me up at the hospital doors and make the short fifteen-minute drive to drop me off at Carver Elementary, where I began teaching just a few hours late. I told Ms. King I was having outpatient medical procedures. She couldn't legally ask for more detail and I didn't share any additional information.

Looking back now, I see the insanity of going in for ECT treatment and then going to teach in the same day. But I didn't feel as though I had a choice.

I wasn't going to quit my job—I couldn't. These kids hadn't done anything wrong. I couldn't be another person who had failed them, abandoned them.

So my classes continued as normal, working on a project comparing the story of *A Christmas Carol* to the Jim Carrey IMAX movie we had seen just a few weeks before.

I acted as if everything was normal. My family wasn't the picture of support, so I didn't expect that from anyone else. I didn't tell anyone at Teach for America what was happening, and the number of friends I felt comfortable sharing with was limited as well—both because of the stigma around depression and because I felt desperate in seeking this extreme of a treatment.

According to most recent available data, 970 million people around the world live with a mental health disorder,[22] and yet only half will seek treatment, largely due to the stigma associated with it.[23]

The craziest part is that, for those that ultimately *do* seek treatment, on average it will take them a decade to do so.[24]

I think it was only because of my mom seeking help for me so early, and then encouraging me several times throughout my life to seek antidepressants, that I was able to have the strength to ask for help when I did. The irony was that, this time, the type of help I chose wasn't to her liking.

I wanted to have my life back, and I didn't care how that happened. But even so, the stigma remained strong—I sure wasn't going to share the details of my psychiatric hospitalization with anyone who didn't have to know, even with Mick. It didn't matter that I had made the decision voluntarily.

Ultimately, this was something I knew I needed to do by myself. I'd gotten myself into this mess—I was the only one who was going to get me out. I'd made it this far. I could push through these final months.

By the fifth ECT treatment, just two weeks after my hospitalization, I had hoped I'd be feeling better. I'd put the work in: ECT treatments, medication, therapy with Dr. McKnelly and Shanna.

But I didn't feel better. In fact, I felt worse. It had been five days since my last treatment, and the tears budded at my eyes again. I didn't want to be alive and told the psychiatrist, who was new to me, how I was feeling.

"I thought this was supposed to make me feel better," I said.

"We're only partway through the treatment," responded the new-to-me psychiatrist. "I'll talk to Dr. McKnelly. It's possible we just need to increase the frequency—maybe a Monday, Wednesday, Friday schedule would help. I'll suggest we do that, and then reassess."

"Okay."

"In the meantime, with your suicidal thoughts—do you have a plan of action?"

"No."

"We could get you a bed upstairs if—"

"No." I let my annoyance show.

I was angry that the treatment wasn't working. I was angry with my family—that they weren't here supporting me—and I was angry that Mick had abandoned me. I was angry that when I'd called out to God to help, he wasn't there. I was angry with the world. None of it was fair, and this new approach to life not only allowed me to feel it but name it.

The next three ECT treatments were in much faster succession and brought the relief I sought.

Katherine was a consistent presence during many of them, offering a smile as the drugs put me to sleep, and then again as I awoke. She not only served as a constant face in a really difficult time, but she provided me with a support I didn't know I needed.

By my eighth ECT treatment, she told me, "You look so much better than when you first started."

It helped me to believe that I was getting better. I didn't just feel better, but I looked better too.

I'd started eating and sleeping a healthier amount, adding to the scale the pounds I had effortlessly dropped over the last nine months. The black bags under my eyes faded to gray, and even my eyes had life coming back to them, a willingness to laugh and play. The stress from teaching was manageable, and the end of teaching at Carver was coming closer.

I only had two more ECT treatments scheduled. I went in for my ninth treatment on Friday, February 5. By this point, I felt like a pro and was very comfortable with the procedure.

I disrobed and ensured no jewelry or anything else was on my body; my hospital gown opened to the front for monitoring purposes. The nurse took my vitals and then found a vein for the IV. After getting poked so often, I was now able to direct them to the best spots to access my small veins. Then they put the pulse oximeter on my finger and a constant beep aligned to my heart rate, and readied the oxygen.

Then came the scarier part: placing the electrodes on my head to measure my brain activity through an EEG, and others on my chest to monitor my heart.

I'd begun to enjoy the slow fade to black the anesthesia brought. While I was asleep, I knew the doctors and nurses would give me additional muscle relaxer to keep my body still, and then a bite block in my mouth to protect my airway, teeth, and tongue.

And this is the part I didn't really think about until much later in life: Next came the "small amount of electricity" and then a grand mal seizure that lasted up to a minute.

As I awoke, there was a nurse like always, but this time a doctor was there too.

"Hi, Nicole. It's Dr. Janssen."

I nodded. I knew where I was and what had happened.

"Nicole, we weren't able to do the treatment today."

Now I was confused, and I'm sure it was written on my face. "Why not?"

"There was a malfunction with the machine, and we couldn't get it working in time before your muscle relaxer wore off. It's not safe to give you more than one dose of the relaxant in a twenty-four-hour period."

"What a waste of time," I said angrily.

Ever since I'd started ECT, my emotions were much more visible.

"Yeah, I'm really sorry about that. We'll make sure to get you rescheduled before you go today."

"Okay," I scoffed, annoyed at the setback that meant I'd need an additional session, which came with an additional day I'd be late for school.

A nurse I didn't recognize handed me a glass of water. I wished Katherine was there with me.

"Small sips, okay?"

I nodded my understanding.

I found out later the ECT machine had exceeded safe voltage levels by three times the recommended dose, and they couldn't get it working correctly. Scary.

I didn't wholly examine the process or the repercussions of ECT largely because I couldn't. I was focused on finishing the treatment. I didn't want to know the details of ECT in the moment, because it didn't matter. This was my only way forward. I didn't want to sit in a psychiatric ward—I wanted to do something to overcome the depression that had overtaken my life.

The final two ECT treatments thankfully were completed without any issues. My tenth and final ECT treatment was on March 1, 2010, with only three months of school left.

"I'm so glad this worked for you, Nicole," said Dr. McKnelly.

"I'm so grateful, Dr. McKnelly. I'm almost done teaching and then I can do whatever I want. No ties to hold me down."

"I'm really proud of you—of what you've overcome."

My eyes brimmed with tears of happiness, which hadn't happened in a very long time. "You're going to make me cry."

"Sincerely, well done. But I'd be remiss to portray that your continued experience will always be easy. I need you to know this may be a continued battle. If you ever choose to have kids, you'll be a prime candidate for postpartum depression. I know you know the signs and signals. If it starts creeping back up, you'll know what to do. You may need ECT for long-term maintenance."

"I know what to do. I know I'll need to respond quickly, and I obviously am very aware of the symptoms. Thank you, Dr. McKnelly."

I gave him a hug and felt the white starched coat contradict his soft enveloping arms. He felt more like my wise, eccentric grandfather than my psychiatrist.

"We'll check in a few more times in the coming weeks and months, but I think you're well on your way."

I felt *so* much better than when I had begun. With Dr. McKnelly officially signing off, I had completed my treatment. This seemed like cause for celebration, but because so few people knew

I'd been undergoing ECT, the evening of my final treatment was anticlimactic and I just went home.

I was reflective as I crawled into bed with my book, curling up to reread one of my favorites: George Eliot's *The Mill on the Floss*.

The piano chords of Elton John's "Someone Saved My Life Tonight" began playing in the background of my mind.

Like antidepressants, doctors don't fully understand why ECT helps, but 70–90 percent of patients experience improvement, and usually much more rapidly than seen with antidepressants. ECT remains a viable treatment option even now, particularly for those who, like me, have exhausted all other options.[25]

Medically induced grand mal seizures may seem like a pretty extreme measure to take, but it wasn't a punishment like how media has portrayed ECT for decades in books like *One Flew Over the Cuckoo's Nest, The Changeling,* and even *Zen and the Art of Motorcycle Maintenance.*

ECT saved my life.

The crash of desks flipping next door was a tell-tale sign that a fistfight was about to begin. Everybody tensed as a hush came over the classroom, anticipating the first punches as students prepared to launch from their seats to cheer on their chosen competitor. I was so tired of being able to hear everything that happened in the adjacent classrooms.

I wasn't surprised by the familiar sound in Melissa's classroom next door, but my own cool and collected reaction was almost unsettling. I quickly made my way to the classroom entryway before any of my students could get there, and in a guttural, authoritative voice bellowed, "Sit down!" before movement could even really start.

It was even more surprising that my thirty-two seventh-grade students listened, slowly lowering their bottoms back into their seats as we listened to the grunts and cheers from the fight next door.

"Ah Miss C, c'mon—can't one of us go over just to see who it is?" said Shakur.

"I'm sure you'll find out soon enough. In the meantime, keep working in your small groups. We'll be sharing out shortly," I said firmly.

Romeo and Juliet was going surprisingly well. With some donors' help, I'd purchased a class set of books that offered a side-by-side comparison of the Elizabethan and modern English text, which made it more accessible. Coupled with the promise of another movie, as well as an intramural sports program and a school-garden incentive, student behavior was on the right track as we closed out the school year—with the exception of the fight next door, that is.

I kept my place in front of the doorway, as a soldier keeps his guard, as we listened to the grunts and punches. There were groans from my classroom this time as we heard Ms. King enter the classroom next door to scold the two offenders, signaling the end of the fight.

Just another day at Carver Elementary.

As I stood in my doorway, watching Ms. King take the two offending students up to her office, I clenched my jaw. It had been a long time since I'd looked up to her. But I found myself begin to soften. I felt sorry for her. Carver Elementary, this school district, this system had chewed her up too.

I was brought back to the moment at hand when Ja Khel asked, "Who was it, Miss C?"

"Nobody."

He sucked his teeth at me. I tried to hide my grin. It didn't matter who it was. My thirty-two seventh graders were in their seats quietly working.

The fog that had hung over so many of my months at Carver had lifted thanks to the ECT. With the end in sight, it felt manageable, but even with the new incentives, Carver still didn't function like a normal school. And with this new emotional clarity from the ECT, I was feeling the ups and downs more acutely.

I was successfully able to compartmentalize these fights—and the daily experience at Carver. But the impact on the day-to-day culture of the school—of it being my students' norm that they were trying to read *Romeo and Juliet* as we listened to grunts and cheers from the fight next door—was still a lot.

I was winding down my second year of teaching, with only a couple of months standing between me and the completion of the Teach for America program. I truly cared about my middle school students, but as I began preparations to close out the school year, I felt a tug to do the same with my third-grade babies.

I was strategic about my asks, gaining insights from current and former teachers at Carver, and even from Miss Eleanor. I couldn't be seen as rifling in other people's business, but I also needed to try to get as much insight as I could, particularly regarding how Samuel was faring.

I knew Khalil and Orion hadn't changed much—I often got reports from their current teacher. I'd never know for sure what happened with Nolan. Cornell and Destiny were thriving.

"Samuel has been doing really well, Miss C. He's been minding his mama and Ms. Washington well," Miss Eleanor told me when I asked how he was doing.

"That's great to hear!"

"He sure misses your classroom though."

The surprise was written on my face.

"Oh, Miss C. Of course he misses you! You always took real good care of those kids."

"Thanks, Miss Eleanor."

I knew I wouldn't get much more than that, and I wasn't expecting it. I made eye contact with Samuel as I left Miss Eleanor's and gave him a brief wave. I got a wave back.

I didn't want to overstep. That was enough.

If it wasn't a fight next door or in my own classroom, it was something else—we were already on to new business.

"Girl, I don't care what she says. Her skin is ashy, and her hair? Don't get me started," said Tanisha.

"Tanisha, I'm going to need you to refocus your energy on your group and what you're supposed to be working on right now," I said.

"Miss C, I ain't about this right now."

"I understand you may not want to focus on this right now, but we've only got fifteen minutes of class left. I need to see at least three questions done."

She sucked her teeth at me and rolled her eyes, muttering under her breath just loud enough for me to hear, "You see this trifling teacher, think she know me."

I ignored her comment.

"I see you don't have a book. Let me grab mine for you," I said, walking to my desk to grab my copy.

Tanisha shared her frustration with my persistence, raising her voice to say, "Miss C, I told you I wasn't doin' this today!"

By this point, I showed my frustration as well.

"Here!" I said curtly as I slid the book across the group of four desks. "I didn't ask what you wanted to do. I need you to focus for what is now only ten minutes. Get to work."

"Did you see that?" Tanisha said, looking at her tablemates. "Miss C threw a book at me."

Daija, Tanisha's counterpart, grinned. "I saw Miss C throw that book at you, Tanisha," Daija said.

And just like that, I found myself in the same exact place as the previous middle school English teacher, being accused of throwing books at students. It was Tanisha's word against mine. I doubled down.

"Did I throw that book at you, Tanisha?" I clenched my jaw. "Go on ahead and go tell Ms. King. Feel free."

We stared at each other, each refusing to budge.

"Miss C? Can you help me with this question?" Brexton broke the tension exactly when we needed him most.

Tanisha remained seated, but put her feet up on the desk as she began doodling in her notebook. I didn't even care about the classwork fight at this point. I was still comprehending the idea that, on paper, I could very well be seen as a teacher who had thrown a book at a student. At least Tanisha wasn't acting on her threat.

We broke our standoff, and I walked over to Brexton.

"Whatcha got for me?" I asked.

Only eight minutes of class left. It was an empty threat. It had to be. I focused on the task with Brexton, which only took a minute, and then began milling about the classroom, monitoring students' work.

Tanisha's feet were still on the table, and my *Romeo and Juliet* book was still unopened.

There were just a few minutes left in the period.

"Alright guys, go ahead and start packing up your things," I said.

The classroom began to bustle as students gathered their belongings.

I slowly made my way over to Tanisha.

Loud enough for only her to hear, I said, "Hey, let's try to have a better day tomorrow." I grabbed my book from the desk. "I wouldn't want to have to throw a book at you—again."

She looked me in the eyes, a playful grin on her face. "Ah, Miss C, I was just playin'. You know I wouldn't do you like that."

I had established some really good relationships with my students, but trust at Carver didn't come easily from either side of the table.

I raised my voice to address the full class. "Alright all, go ahead and head to lunch."

"See you later, Miss C," Tanisha said, smirking as she headed out the door.

Thankfully, there were only a few months more of this.

I hadn't seen all that much of Mick in the early months of the year, both because of my hospitalization and treatment, but also because I knew, if I was going to get over him, it sure didn't help to see him.

But one Friday in late March, as we celebrated the launch of spring break, I found myself at Mick's place with a group of friends. Being in the same teaching program made it hard to stay completely out of his orbit.

On this particular night, it was difficult to see him, and I'd had too much to drink as a result. As the group dwindled, and people began peeling off to head home, I found myself too comfortable in his space where I had spent so much time and so many nights before. Finally, by 1:30 a.m. it was just the two of us.

"Do you mind if I hang just a bit longer? I think I just need thirty minutes and another glass of water and then I can drive," I said.

"Of course, you know I love talking to you." He smiled.

And talk we did—for hours. We shared that, despite our best efforts, we'd both spent the past four months unsuccessfully trying to get over each other. Both of us had been on dates, and I admitted I'd joined Match.com to prove that I still had "it," but found I was ultimately completely annoyed by those I was connected with.

We shared that we still loved each other, just as before.

We shared how normal and good it felt to talk to each other, to hug each other, and then, at first timidly, to kiss.

We both knew that if we were going to continue being broken up, this evening sure wasn't going to help. I wondered if I would regret the kisses and being physical.

By 4 a.m., it seemed logical to spend the final hours of the early morning at his place. Falling asleep for a few hours, and then waking up next to him, felt so normal.

As I softly kissed him goodbye, he said, "I love you."

I regretted nothing as I walked to the door, looking back to say, "I love you too."

Not wanting to seem overzealous, I let Mick text me first. As we corresponded, it felt like things were almost back to normal, like we'd never broken up at all—except for the looming deadline of him heading back to San Francisco in eight weeks.

I tried not to think of him over the spring break, but we ended up spending more time together. We talked about our future.

"I love you, Nicole. I want you to move to California," he said.

"You realize how scary that is for me? With less commitment than we had before. We're not back together, Mick."

"I get that, but I ultimately want you to move to San Francisco because *you* want to."

"And as I shared before, I don't think I would be going if you weren't in the equation. I don't know that that's a fair request."

But as I weighed my options, I realized there wasn't really anything keeping me in Kansas City. I wasn't going to be extending my time at Carver Elementary, that was for sure.

I toyed with the idea of moving back home to Iowa. But I was afraid that if I went back, I'd be too afraid to leave again.

I knew that Mick loved me—he told me so. But it was even more than that—I could tell by the way he looked at me, and the way he held me, kissed me, touched me.

"Do you want me to move to California?" I asked.

"I feel like I've done everything but beg you," he said, breaking any remaining tension.

I couldn't help but laugh.

"Did I say that out loud?" he said, and began laughing as well.

"Well, *if* I move to California, would we live together?" I probed further.

"Yes." There was no hesitation in his voice.

The worst of it was the unknown. I was still so in love. But only a few short months before, I'd felt as though I'd been cast aside during a time of need. Could things ever go back to normal? It was tough to ricochet between these two feelings. I had gone four months without him, and gone through my lowest of lows on my own. And yet it felt like no matter how much time went by, it wouldn't change the way I felt about him.

It was a difficult realization that the decision lay with me—if I didn't go with him to San Francisco, he was going to move back without me.

And yet, I acknowledged and leaned into this potential loss. The path wasn't clear. But at least with the clarity the ECT had provided, I felt in control now.

Easter came early, and with it another trip home to Iowa. As had been the case in college at another key decision-making point, I wasn't really looking forward to going home as I knew my mom would focus on my plans for my life after Teach for America was done.

As we finished Easter dinner, Mom had a captive audience as I had been recruited to help clear the kitchen table and load the dishwasher.

"Well, I'm glad you're not continuing teaching, but what are your prospects for what's next?" she asked.

This was it. The moment of truth.

"I know you're not going to like it, but I really am contemplating moving out to San Francisco."

"I just really don't think that's a smart idea."

"You've made that very clear, Mom. But I don't have anything keeping me in Kansas City. What do I have to lose?"

"Time, money, your happiness with Mick toying with you."

Do not respond, I told myself.

My mom refused to look at me, and was laser focused on rinsing the dishes. She didn't say anything more as she carefully lined up the plates on the bottom shelf of the dishwasher, and I noticed the dishes already appeared clean given the intensity with which she was rinsing them. I put down the stack of plates I was carrying on the counter, and wrapped my arms around her, hugging her from behind. She kept rinsing the dish she had in her hands. It wasn't until she shut the water off that I realized she was crying.

"I just want you to be happy." She grabbed my hand.

"I know, Mom."

"And I really just wish you'd move back home." She choked back a sob.

"I know, Mom. But I can't. I'm afraid if I do, I won't be able to leave again."

She raised one of her wet hands to wipe away the tears, releasing my hug. "And would that be so bad?"

I paused. "I'm not ready to come home yet."

Now it was her turn to pause. "Well, I guess you've gotta know."

She turned back to the sink, lifting the handle of the faucet and beginning to rinse the dishes again as the steam rose from the sink. And with that, the conversation was over. We put the final glasses and silverware in the dishwasher in silence, wiped down the table and chairs, and joined my brothers, who were watching a movie downstairs.

The conversation was closed with my mom, but the assault on my decision-making process continued as I drove back to Kansas City, this time via a call from my grandmother. She typically only called for on my birthday or if she wanted something. I knew as soon as I saw the caller ID that my mom had shared my intentions with her and that she was calling to talk about it.

"Hi Cole! How are you doing?"

"I'm good, Grandma. How are you?"

"Oh, I'm good! I just got back from the boat with Father Jansen. I won two hundred dollars on the slot machines, so I took us all out for dinner."

"Sounds like fun, Grandma."

"Oh yeah! You'll have to come with us sometime."

"Maybe bingo, I'm not so much into the slots."

"Well say, your mom was telling me you're thinking about moving to California. All the way to San Francisco, is it?"

"Yeah, I'm contemplating it."

"Well, I know your mom is concerned that Mick doesn't treat you so well."

Brutal. She's shaping the narrative for everyone without even allowing others to get to know him, I thought.

"She's made it very clear she's concerned, but ultimately it's my decision."

I couldn't help but be a little short, even if she was my grandmother.

"Oh, I know that. I think I'm just concerned too."

"I appreciate that, but if I don't take a chance now, when? And Grandma, I love him."

"Oh, that's nice. I just hope he treats you the way you deserve to be treated."

"Thanks, Grandma."

"Well, I'll support you whatever you decide. I love you, Cole."

"I love you too, Grandma."

With the objective completed, the call was over, but at least I understood her support wasn't circumstantial.

I'd get the chance to further think through my decision, as I was having Easter dinner with Mick when I got back to Kansas City. He put on a show with his cooking: hors d'oeuvres, including bruschetta and cheese with wine pairings, and the main course being my favorite meal, rosemary pork loin, polenta, and green beans—and cheesecake for dessert.

"Thanks so much for hosting me for dinner."

"I was glad you said you would come. Would you like another glass of wine?"

"Always. Speaking of wine, have you ever read Peter Meinke's poem 'Advice to My Son'?"

"That is not one I've heard of."

"It's a beautiful piece overall, sharing all these tidbits of wisdom about life, but ends with 'But son, always serve wine.' I feel like that's totally you."

He chuckled. "It sounds like my type of poem! I'd love to read the whole thing. Maybe it's something we could share with our kids someday."

I blushed, taken aback. "You know, I've been thinking a lot about a potential move."

"Yes, and?"

"What have I got to lose? And so much to gain. No matter how crazy people think I am."

"I don't think anyone would think you're crazy."

"I'd beg to differ, but I'd love to plan what it would look like."

Because really, what *did* I have to lose, other than potentially the love of my life if I didn't go?

And so, we made plans for next steps, together. I'd stay through the summer to finish out my time at the Youth Center while he went home with the intention of finding a job and a place for us to call home. It was the beginning of building a life together, and I was excited to do so.

chapter sixteen

"Your life is in God's hands. You have nothing to fear," Mindy said.

The prophesying with her friends had made me somewhat uncomfortable, and after taking matters into my own hands with ECT, I'd largely stopped going to church.

But Mindy was so religious that I didn't feel comfortable admitting this to her, so I just nodded in agreement. We were on our way to another worship session at the International House of Prayer, but my heart wasn't in it anymore.

I'd had a bit of reckoning with my faith. I'd prayed for God's guidance through my depression. I went to church every Sunday, and multiple worship sessions each week with Mindy at the International House of Prayer. I'd read the Bible through in its entirety for the second time over the past year. I'd tithed, even with my meager beginning teacher salary.

But over these two years, I'd ultimately come to the realization that God wasn't here.

When Samuel was beat in my classroom. When I made the report and was threatened by his mother. When my students didn't have enough to eat, were squatting in vacant homes, and didn't have running water or electricity. Through scripted curriculums, fistfights, gunshots, and finding bullets on elementary school playgrounds, we were on our own.

I was on my own.

But I couldn't tell my friend that. I didn't want to hear her response because I wouldn't believe it anyway. We pulled into the strip mall that housed the International House of Prayer.

I grabbed my Bible, worn from my highlights and notes. It was strange, thinking about how much time I'd devoted to this labor and while receiving nothing in return. Too much of my experience with religion had been focused on false promises—prayers and testimonies, worship services and songs, the divine word in the Bible—that never delivered.

All too often I had experienced judgement upon my students, the families, and the communities Jesus had pledged his love and support to. With the hypocrisy made real, I couldn't be a part of it anymore.

I slung my bag up on my shoulder and walked toward the prayer room with Mindy, toward two double doors in a columned strip mall with all the curtains drawn in the rectangular windows—an apt space for prayer.

I was giving it one last go, more for Mindy than me. I didn't want to spend my time in worship anymore. So I stopped going.

As we closed another month of school, leaving only four weeks before summer break, things really began to fall apart.

There were numerous fistfights, sometimes multiple in a single week, the worst of which took place between a seventh grader and an eighth grader—both boys.

Dewayne and Lontrell had planned the brawl, meeting in the hallway during class and absolutely whaling on each other. It didn't take long for others to form a circle around them even though class was still happening.

But what was different about this fight was that only the hoots and hollers of the student viewers were heard. With the way the two boys looked at each other, I could tell they were out for blood, and they got it.

Melissa, Rachel, and I knew better than to get in the middle, which left little to do other than call the office and yell at them to stop, which is what we did. They continued to square off, pacing and walking around each other, Lontrell's cut above his eye and Dewanye's fat lip both dripping blood and leaving multiple trails of blood on the hallway walls and floor.

When Ms. King finally made her way to the middle of the circle, all involved knew the fight was over.

The next week brought new insanity: a "kill list" written by one of the sixth grade boys that was visible through his binder. I was on the list, along with Melissa and a few students. The young man was promptly removed from the school.

On another afternoon, I went to pick up my seventh-grade students from PE class. I walked into the gym to an absolute free-for-all, balls flying everywhere, screams from students running amok, a group of girls gossiping in the corner, and two boys bumping chests, ready to come to blows over a basketball game.

I walked across the gym to the teacher's office at the back, dodging errant balls being tossed directly at me.

I came to the doorway where our gym teacher, Mr. Evans, was sitting at his desk. He glanced over to me and said angrily, "I don't know how you teach those kids. They won't listen. I had enough."

"Okay?" I said, not knowing how else to respond.

I turned around and walked back to the door, herding the kids I walked by and then calling the rest of the class to the door.

Then there was a parent who was irate due to her son being bullied. She wasn't afraid to share her disdain for the white women running Carver's middle school.

"I don't want my child being taught by a bunch of Caucasian, associate's degree-holding teachers," she said with malice.

I knew I should have kept my mouth shut, but with so many nights and weekends spent on my master's degree, I couldn't help myself.

"I'll actually graduate with my master's degree in secondary education next month," I said.

"Oh honey, your degrees mean nothing," she spat back.

As we moved into the first days of May, the entire school had another brief taste of the threat of violence going on outside our doors.

Two of our students, brothers Ja Khel and Derreck, were the targets of a rival area gang. A credible threat had been made so, for two school days, everyone in the school stayed indoors—no recess, and no going in or out aside from the beginning and end of the school day, and even that was staggered.

My experiences during the last two years had been life altering. I didn't have any memory loss from the ECT, but there were things that happened at Carver that I anticipated even ECT couldn't help me forget. But the difference between my students and me was that I was able to leave these experiences at the door. I got to go home at night to my nice apartment in a decent neighborhood, make my dinner, have a glass of wine, and not have to worry about where I was going to sleep. Many of my students didn't have that luxury.

As we approached the end of the school year, it was almost as if the students felt the impending news of Carver Elementary's closure before it was even announced.

The school board's decision was final, albeit controversial. A split 5–4 vote approved the superintendent's plan to close twenty-nine of the school district's sixty-one total schools. Carver Elementary was one of them, and would close permanently at the end of the school year.

I couldn't help but think the fact that we hadn't met our AYP for so many years played a role in that decision.

The school closures made national news—which was unsurprising considering they were shuttering almost half the schools in the district. And yet, on paper it made sense. Why have schools operating at half capacity across the city, particularly when money was tight due to the economic downturn?

But from a relational standpoint, the plan was much more complicated—with schools consolidating, it was almost certain there would be students from rival gangs wandering the same hallways. And of course, student-to-teacher ratios would be "right-sized," meaning there would be teacher layoffs to accommodate dwindling student enrollment. The plan was to cut seven hundred of the district's three thousand jobs, with 285 of them being teachers. The majority of the members of the first-year Teach for America Kansas City corps would receive pink slips on our final day of teaching.

Given the district's revolving door of superintendents, it's no surprise that the school district continued to lose students to private and suburban schools. By 2021, the district had just over

14,000 students, well under half of its 2001 enrollment, and 25 percent of its peak enrollment in the 1960s.

When the news about the school closures was formally released, the feeling of an impending shift became absolute for Carver students.

With nothing to lose, the kids' behavior tanked, and getting anything academic accomplished was impossible amidst the fistfights and students floating in and out of classrooms, if they showed up at all.

In our final weeks, there were multiple physical fights a week, sometimes even more than one per day. Typically, the boys were more inclined to use their fists, but one particularly violent fight took place between two girls in Melissa's class. I wasn't as successful as I had been a few short weeks before in keeping my students in their seats during the fight, but many remained seated, apathetic to the violence that had become the norm.

The hoots and hollers coming from next door were louder than usual, matching the intensity of the two foes. This fight was so raucous, Melissa was hit in the face, which gave her a black eye. I'd never heard a hush come across the classroom in the way it did when Melissa went down. I was told Derreck rushed to her side to ensure she was okay, yelling at the other students to give them space as he wrapped his arm around her and helped her up.

There were questions about whether the student intended to hit Melissa. But none of that was reflected in Ms. King's punishment for the girls, who received a mere three-day suspension, which was, in my opinion, a pathetic consequence for giving a teacher a black eye.

Melissa was obviously extremely upset—so much so that she decided to do something about it. She took the information about what had happened downtown to the school district's administration office. After hearing the details, the district leadership promptly extended the girls' suspensions to ten days each.

Even Ms. King had been stretched to her breaking point as we approached not only the end of the school year, but the end of Carver Elementary. Nobody could say for certain what happened, but after the fight, Ms. King suddenly stopped coming to school. The interim principal who had been placed at Carver Elementary for its final weeks was flabbergasted at what she saw.

The young blonde voiced her exasperation, saying, "This is insane. Has it been like this all year?"

"It's gotten markedly worse with everyone knowing the school is closing, but this is my second year at Carver and, yeah, it hasn't been a calm place for learning."

By the end of her first week, the interim principal had lowered her standards as well, telling students to "just try to make sure there's not any more blood on the walls from fighting."

I hit my own breaking point as well.

It was only a Wednesday, but I couldn't handle it anymore. The class wouldn't listen and we weren't accomplishing anything.

And as I made my foolish plea to bring order to the chaos that was currently my classroom, I heard someone say, "Shut up, bitch."

I didn't know who had said it, and I didn't care. I worked too hard to deserve this.

I felt my face flush. So many times in my first year of teaching I had been embarrassed, ashamed, desperate. Now, I was angry. So much so, that I whipped the piece of chalk I was holding against the brown chalkboard, the small yellow cylinder exploding into tiny shards.

The class went silent, and so was I. It was one of the first times I really showed some real emotion in front of them.

My breathing was heavy, and my chest was rising and falling much more quickly than normal. Tears sprung to my eyes.

"Get to work," I growled.

"Miss C," someone said.

"I don't want any excuses. I don't want to hear anyone say anything. I want you to get to work. *All* of you."

I didn't even know what they were working on, but each of them needed to find something. And they did.

The next morning, I had a bunch of flowers waiting for me on my desk. Without asking, I knew it was from my seventh-grade class. I thought it was sweet, until I realized they had clearly been taken from someone's front lawn. But even that made me smile.

The misbehavior followed by sweet gestures continued.

Derreck in my sixth-grade class flipped me the bird as he walked out of third period. At the end of the day, I found a handwritten note on lined paper.

I'm sorry. Will you forgive me?

It felt like one of those elementary school notes you received from an admirer. *Do you like me? Circle Yes or No.* But even this was better.

It was exhausting, those final weeks and days.

Chris, my Teach for America program director, made his final visit to my classroom during the second-to-last week of school.

"Hey! You're almost there! How do you feel?" he asked.

"It's been rough, to be honest. Even with the end in sight."

"Aw man, I'm sorry to hear that."

"To be honest, I know I'm not a first-year teacher—none of us at Carver are. But it felt like we've been left on our own a bit."

"Well, that's up to you to advocate for yourself. If you needed me, you could have told me, and I'd be here."

"I hear you."

"But honestly, we knew the schools that were slated to close, and Carver was one of them. It didn't make a lot of sense to spend a bunch of time creating new systems and structures for a school that's on the chopping block."

"It could have potentially made our lives easier."

"I suppose so, but now you're in the single digits of days left. You're almost there."

"I know. I just need to say that I feel like we were left out on our own here. Carver didn't really stand a chance. We never got invited to the fundraising parties—it's not a story anyone wanted to hear."

"Your story is very much the untold story of Teach for America."

"I guess so."

"But you got it done. Nobody can take that away from you. You'll be inducted as an alumna of the program, and then you get to decide what's next. Hope you're able to bask in all you've accomplished."

To be honest, it didn't feel like I'd accomplished all that much. My aim was to make a difference—I wasn't sure I'd done much more than finish the program.

With Carver closing for good, that meant cleaning up involved more than just taking down posters and ensuring our textbooks were returned and organized for the next class. It meant packing boxes for the items deemed salvageable by the district, and disposing of *lots* of trash. And this was happening at twenty-eight other schools across the city.

Students were encouraged to take many items home if they could be put to use.

I'd enlisted the help of my class to support in the cleaning, and many were excited about their finds while others utilized the time to catch up on gossip. It was clear that keeping them busy was important, and pushing academics wasn't worth the fight in the final week.

"Miss C, with Carver closing, what are you going to be doing next?" Brexton asked with genuine curiosity.

"Well, I'll be teaching at the Youth Center this summer."

"And then what?"

"You know, I'm thinking I'm going to be moving out to San Francisco."

"Wow! That sounds exciting. California always seems so cool." He didn't pry further. "I'm really going to miss our class. I've really learned a lot this year."

"I'm glad to hear it, Brexton. Truly, that means a lot."

"You don't get mad at stupid stuff, and I can tell you really care about us."

"I do! And I hope you'll keep in touch, Brexton. Can't believe you'll be in eighth grade next year! Do you know what school you'll be at?"

"Not yet."

"Well, wherever you go, know that you're capable of great things, and I can't wait to hear about what you accomplish."

"Thanks, Miss C."

He gave me a hug.

Saying goodbye to the numerous other students over the next

few days was more difficult than I anticipated. It was unlikely I'd been able to support all of them in making the "significant gains"—1.5 years or more growth in a single year—that Teach for America pushed us to attain. But I didn't do them a disservice either.

If there was one thing they knew about me, it was that they knew I cared, and that I showed up, day in and day out, no matter what barriers I had come up against.

As I walked my students to the door on that final day, it was anticlimactic. I gave lots of hugs and made promises to keep in touch—knowing full well the likelihood we'd keep track of each other was minimal—and offered love and well wishes that were nothing but genuine.

I walked back to my classroom to grab my things, hearing the hoots and hollers of the students saying their final goodbyes reverberating off the empty walls. I grabbed my backpack, put my hand on my desk, and took a moment to stand in the empty space that had held such a tumultuous experience over the last year. It was bizarre to see it as just a hollow room with a brown chalkboard, boxes against one wall and mismatched desks and chairs stacked against another.

"You ready to go?" Rachel was leaning against the doorway.

"I can't believe it, but yes."

It was over too easily.

We walked in silence as I tried to figure out how to embrace a moment we had pined for for so long.

"So, drinks tonight?" she asked.

"*Yes*. Just us to start, and then head to the party?" I responded.

"Sounds like a plan."

The charter corps would be celebrating the completion of their two years in epic fashion, with all fifty of us that had started together completing our two-year commitment.

I can't fully describe the feeling of what it meant to walk out of Carver Elementary, knowing I didn't have to go back.

And the irony of receiving news just a few weeks later that Carver had finally met its AYP, after closing the school doors for good, was not lost on me.

I felt so many emotions: There was guilt for the glee I felt in saying good riddance to the school. Pride for having completed the program, which I wasn't sure I was going to be able to do. Sorrow in saying goodbye, probably forever, to students I'd built relationships with. Passion for having learned so much about myself and who I wanted to be. And introspection as I looked toward the future.

I was excited for the summer at the Youth Center, but even more about the potential for the fall. I'd be saying "see you later" to Mick in just a few days, as we'd made plans for him to drive back to San Francisco and for me to join him that fall.

My family wasn't thrilled about my decision to move to California, but in the same way ECT had been my decision to make, this next pathway was mine to take as well. Beginning a new life in San Francisco with Mick would be a new world.

I wrote down my feelings in my journal:

I have a feeling the best is yet to come, and I know I deserve it.

epilogue

Today, I live in the Pacific Northwest with my husband, Mick—the same man I fell in love with during Teach for America—and our two young children. I have continued to work in education and then moved into the nonprofit space, ultimately seeking to increase equity in opportunity. I've been a fundraiser for more than a decade, working on behalf of several deserving organizations doing incredible work to impact people and communities around the world.

I credit the late Dr. William McKnelly and ECT treatments with saving my life. I don't know that I ever properly thanked him, and unfortunately, I'm not able to share my gratitude, or all of the positive things in my life, as he passed away in 2012, just two years after I left Kansas City for the West Coast. He died suddenly as he was preparing to go to work—even at eighty-three, he continued to help others up to the very last moment of his being.

Though I've anticipated going through additional bouts of depression, particularly after welcoming two little ones and living through the postpartum phases, I've been very lucky to navigate these life events without medication or additional ECT treatments. In a slow process in preparation for having children, I weaned myself off of antidepressants with my doctor's guidance, and have managed my anxiety and depression without medication for more than seven years.

And then, during a major life transition, I needed to go back on them. I've done my best to take care of myself through my diet, exercise, and self-care, but even then, the balance isn't always there. I tried not to beat myself up for needing that additional support. I won't have to be on antidepressants forever, but they are another tool to use when needed.

There have been potential long-term repercussions of choosing to undergo ECT. I don't have a lot of clear memories of the months when I was receiving treatment and the final months of school at Carver. But I do have a journal where I detailed my experiences faithfully, multiple times each week. And although it's frustrating at times, the blank moments are filled in by my loving partner and friends who shared these experiences with me.

In the past few years, I've also lost some vocabulary, and memories of many books and movies I know I've read and seen. It's become more and more common for me to be unable to find the words I'm wanting to say, and sometimes I fumble through my stories and thoughts. Some may simply attribute this to the aging process, and it's possible. But there is very much part of me that believes there could be more to it.

And so, I've learned it's okay to admit, "No, I don't remember when . . ." Or to stumble over my words, unable to recall the exact expression I'm seeking. Because I'm still here now, alive, and able to recognize hope and experience a zeal for life I had never been able to embrace before. Before ECT, I didn't have a vision for the future. Depression had lied about it. I remain incredibly grateful for the life I've been able to lead because I was not only able to ask for help when I needed it, but I was also able to find it and make the right decision for me. I know so many others seek help, get entangled in a system that is all-too-often destined to fail, and don't get to wake to another day.

I have known I needed to share this story since it happened more than a decade ago, but it was difficult for me to re-examine all that happened over those two years at Carver Elementary. I share to not only bring to light the continued ails of our education system—so little has changed since then, more than fifteen years later—but also to show others you can navigate through the turmoil anxiety and depression brings, and go on to live a happy, healthy, and fulfilling life. I continue to reflect on my experiences as a teacher in Kansas City and leverage my learnings to inform my daily life. I know what it's like to want to die, but I also know what it's like to come out on the other side and to go on with a renewed desire to experience the ups and downs of life.

The students of Carver Elementary have fared variably. Those whom I've stayed in touch with include a nail technician who has since moved to Dallas, an aspiring dancer who moved to Atlanta with his family and never looked back, and a medical assistant who paved her own way in Kansas City. Numerous others remain in Kansas City, many in the same neighborhoods they grew up in, and include aspiring rappers, college basketball players, dog groomers, and so much more. Many of them now have families of their own and continue to navigate and take advantage of the opportunities Kansas City can provide, striving to provide more for their children than what was available to them.

This story is not meant to be a condemnation of the Teach for America program. The program is a Band-Aid for a gaping flesh wound of a problem, like so many other nonprofit organizations that are seeking to effect change. I credit my own Teach for America experience with my passion for education, and my continued work to ensure equity. I can assuredly say I wouldn't be where I am today without having taught at Carver Elementary School and working with my classes in Kansas City, Missouri, and Oakland, California.

And yet, the failures of the American education system, our vastly unequal society, and the elusive American dream were never so stark to me than during my time teaching. There was no opportunity to "pull yourself up by your bootstraps" for the students I worked with—many did not have boots, let alone bootstraps. These problems stemmed from much larger issues: the historic, economic, and cultural systems and policies in place, and the intergenerational poverty and racism that continue to shape our American society. My students at Carver had outdated textbooks, limited computer access, and I was writing on a chalkboard—which was archaic, even in 2010.

I've been fortunate to learn and collaborate with so many incredible changemakers who are seeking to ensure equity in opportunity for children around the world. And that sense of urgency has only increased after having children of my own. Together, we must continue to cultivate this vision for change with a focus on impact. As we look to the future of education, we must ask ourselves what the next right thing is to do, and how we can get involved.

A portion of all sales of this book will be donated to a subset of the organizations listed below.

Holistic Wrap-Around Service Supports with a Focus on Social Emotional Health

Mindful Life Project: www.mindfullifeproject.org
Student mental health is a vital part of the student support system. JG Larochette, the founder and executive director of the Mindful Life Project, asserts, "If we're going to create a society where everyone has an opportunity to thrive—mentally, socially, academically—mental health must be seen as physical health. We need to provide all students, all educators, all families, mental health programming that is scientifically proven to benefit the biological, physiological, physical elements of wellbeing." Schools can play a critical role in destigmatizing mental health supports, in addition to providing a vital component of student health that ultimately supports students' academic success.

The Mindful Life Project transforms schools from the inside out with innovative and comprehensive mindfulness-based, social-emotional learning programming. Their comprehensive approach supports the mental and emotional well-being of students, teachers, staff, community leaders, and families, with the intention to create cultures and climates where mental and emotional well-being is the foundation of everyone's experience. More than 25,000 students are served each week through in-person direct services, while an additional 30,000 are reached through Mindful Life Project assemblies and virtual services. Their services result in an average gain of an additional nineteen minutes of quality teaching time each day.

World Being: www.worldbeing.org
For millions of young people around the world, aspiring to leave behind poverty, discrimination, and inequality, the skills of mental

health and inner well-being are critical to positively transform their life trajectories. At WorldBeing, they believe that inner well-being is key to global well-being, and their goal is to support marginalized and vulnerable youth, particularly girls and young women in low- and middle-income countries, to build the skills to access their inner well-being. With over fifteen years of operations, innovation, and rigorous research, WorldBeing has well-documented impacts on Sustainable Development Goals (SDGs) such as SDG3: GoodHealth and Well-Being; SDG 4: Quality Education; and SDG 5: Gender Equality.

"We need to be thinking more about students' wellbeing, as opposed to diagnosing and treating mental illness after it happens. Schools should be centers of well-being at every level, supporting students in cultivating mindsets, agency, and outlook in life, grounded in the very real challenges they have, but supporting in the creation of the self-confidence and skills to problem solve, set goals, and deal with conflict in a peaceful way," said Steve Leventhal, founder and CEO of WorldBeing.

AssistHub: *www.assisthub.org*
Finding the right public benefits is tough. Applying for them can be even harder. AssistHub streamlines processes and access to public assistance programs like SNAP, federal financial aid, unemployment insurance, utilities and home energy assistance programs, and more. Systemic barriers can exclude families from critical resources. Ultimately, we know that gaining access to these foundational physiological needs support students' success. An estimated $60 billion of assistance goes unclaimed every year, with barriers that are particularly difficult for parents, women, and Black, Indigenous and people of color. AssistHub ensures that everyone can find and claim resources with dignity and without frustration.

Smile Programs: www.mobiledentists.com
Parents often find taking their children to the dentist to be a challenge—from taking time off work to barriers with transportation. With the convenience of an in-school dentist, the comfort of the familiar surroundings of the school, and a local, state-licensed dentist, children receive the highest level of dental care. The program accepts Medicaid, CHIP, and private insurance, which means treatment is almost always covered at 100 percent, while grant programs ensure no child is turned away due to an inability to pay.

iMentor: www.imentor.org
iMentor builds mentoring relationships that empower first-generation students to graduate high school, succeed in college and in their career, and achieve their ambitions. iMentor harnesses the power of long-term, personal relationships to help students succeed. Partnering with high schools in communities in which a majority of students served will be first-generation college graduates, each year they recruit thousands of volunteers who commit to mentorship for two years. Almost 36,000 mentors have been matched with students since the program began in 1999, with iMentor students outperforming their comparable peer groups in college enrollment by 17 percent and college completion by 20 percent.

Strategic Innovations with Technology-Led, Research-Based Outcomes

HundrED: www.hundred.en
HundrED is a global mission-driven organization specialized in K–12 education innovation. They identify, amplify, and facilitate the implementation of impactful and scalable education innovations that help every child flourish by giving them access to a quality education. Believing that education innovations can transform

school systems and equip students with the skills to thrive as global citizens, HundrED knows the world is full of hardworking educators who are driving innovative, impactful, and scalable approaches in education. HundrED seeks to give them the recognition and visibility they deserve. "We recognize that when scaling an innovation, the aim is not simply to spread the innovation, but to scale the impact of the innovation, with the ultimate goal of transforming education systems so that all children and young people have access to a quality, future-ready education."[26] Innovation must not only support scaling of these proven interventions, but must scale the outcomes as well.

LeanLab Education: www.leanlabeducation.org
LeanLab Education is a nonprofit research organization with a mission to study and grow transformational education innovations that have been co-designed with school communities, melding education technology with the classroom environments they seek to serve and ultimately accelerating impact. They engage in a collaborative process that unites critical insights from school communities with technical expertise from researchers and domain knowledge from product developers. Their belief is that when power is shared in the research and development of innovative products, these solutions have the potential to transform education for all learners.

Talking Points: www.talkingpts.org
Any teacher could speak to the importance of family engagement and its relationship with student success. According to Heejae Lim, founder and CEO of TalkingPoints, family engagement is two times more effective in predicting a student's success than a family's socioeconomic status. TalkingPoints is an education technology nonprofit with a mission to drive student success through effective

family-school partnerships. Teachers can confidently engage with all families with an easy-to-use, two-way messaging system that seamlessly translates communications into 150 different languages. With student success at the center of their work, they empower families to have meaningful engagement and support positive relationship building. TalkingPoints provides an intuitive, multilingual family engagement platform with built-in best practices for educators and families, empowering engagement that builds relationships and trust that enables student success.

Proximity Learning: *www.proxlearn.com*
Another technological innovation mainstreamed during the global pandemic was virtual education. For Proximity Learning, livestreaming teachers into classrooms and homes across the nation was nothing new. Founded in 2009, Proximity Learning has partnered with more than 750 schools to offer certified teachers that teach daily classes, offer tutoring supports, and more. "It's not just online instruction—it's what the teacher does with that time. We utilize artificial intelligence for students to gain support outside of class, leverage new ways to teacher through interactive online learning experiences, and deliver content and new and different ways to keep students' attention," said Evan Erdberg, founder and CEO of Proximity Learning. As the teacher shortage affects school across the nation, we'll need more innovation to ensure students have access to quality instruction.

With a mission to connect all learners with the expert teachers they deserve, Proximity Learning seeks to increase educational equity, enabling every child to realize their potential. As the teacher shortage only compounds year over year, Proximity Learning places certified virtual teachers in front of the students across the nation, increasing equity in education and opportunity.

A Choose-Your-Own-Adventure School Experience

Genesys Works: www.genesysworks.org

Genesys Works was founded to provide pathways to career success for high school students from underserved communities through skills training, meaningful work experiences, and impactful relationships. They envision a future where all young adults are equipped and empowered with the knowledge and skills required to achieve career success, upward mobility, and a lifetime of economic self-sufficiency. More than 90 percent of those students go on to enroll in college, earn a college degree at almost three times the rate of their low-income, first-generation peers, and, seven years later, almost 60 percent earn more than at least one of their parents. By providing skills training, counseling and coaching, and paid internships for high school seniors, they not only help employers fill critical talent gaps, but enable sustain economic mobility for the students and families they serve.

BUILD: www.build.org

BUILD is a nonprofit organization that empowers youth through entrepreneurship, igniting their ability to build career success, entrepreneurial mindsets, and opportunity, enabling them to become the CEO of their own lives. They envision a world where all students—regardless of race, socioeconomic status, or neighborhood—develop the skills and connections needed to achieve economic power and freedom. Through their high quality curriculum, BUILD enables students to engage with and have fun in project-based learning experiences where they discover their personal strengths and passions.

New Schools Venture Fund: www.newschools.org

NewSchools is a venture philanthropy that builds a better

education system by connecting people, resources, and ideas. Believing that entrepreneurship can drive change in education, New Schools Venture Fund seeks to improve outcomes for all students by funding early-stage, innovative schools, education technologies, and diverse leaders. In the past three years, New Schools Venture Fund has reached 23 million students and 42,000 teachers annually, invested in women-led ventures at a rate of 62 percent, and invested $113 million in 421 ventures. They believe that every child deserves good choices in life—and a school that will open the door to these opportunities.

Sora Schools: www.soraschools.com
Sora is the virtual private middle and high school making today's students into tomorrow's changemakers. They believe that students should be in the driver's seat of their education, learning in order to answer the questions they care about. Most schools enforce a standard set of courses with a few electives sprinkled at the end of the program. This approach is insufficient for our global knowledge economy. At Sora, they believe that students should own their own education, flipping the curriculum and scheduling process to allow students to choose their learning experiences based on their interests.

XQ Institute: www.xqsuperschool.org
XQ is one such organization that acknowledges the needs to transform the high school experience, putting the onus on the communities—schools, districts, states, nations, local organizations and institutions—to identify the educational pathways that put students first as they "rethink high school." XQ Institute is the nation's leading organization dedicated to rethinking the high school experience so that every student graduates ready to succeed in college,

career, and real life. From schools co-located within community spaces, to student-led project-based learning, and experiences focused on entrepreneurship and community engagement—high schools can meet and shape the future by equipping learners with the knowledge and skills to succeed in changing the world.

Teach For America was an incredibly innovative organization at its start in 1990, and has continued to impact the communities in which it works in the United States. Today, its approach has also inspired similar organizations in more than sixty countries that are part of the Teach For All network.

I was fortunate to have a conversation with Wendy Kopp, founder of Teach For America and CEO of Teach For All, about the beginnings of the organization and her feelings about the state of the education system more than thirty years after its founding.

"The challenge is massive because we all attended and were shaped by the system we need to change . . . we need to unlearn how we were taught and internalize a different way of being and looking at the world. I've really come to deeply believe this is a very long game, and I've come to see the negative effects of a lack of understanding of that. There is still so much more work to be done."

Let's get to work.

ENDNOTES

1. Nelson, Sean, Huffman, Aaron, Sult, Evan, and Lin, Jeff. "Flagpole Sitta," Where Have All the Merrymakers Gone, Arena Rock Recording Company, June 1996. (Song lyrics utilized with permission of Jeff Lin and Harvey Danger).
2. "Jackson County Vacant Homes." 2021. Jackson County Vacant Homes. https://www.jacksongov.org/591/Vacant-Houses.
3. Stark, Cortlynn. 2021. "Yes, Kansas City's Troost Avenue was named for a slaveholder. And that's not all we found Read more at: https://www.kansascity.com/news/your-kcq/article251695313.html#storylink=cpy." *The Kansas City Star* (Kansas City), May 28, 2021. https://www.kansascity.com/news/your-kcq/article251695313.html.
4. Swaminathan, Nikhil. 2017. "This Kansas City neighborhood wrote the blueprint for transforming a community." *Grist*, July 25, 2017. https://grist.org/justice/this-kansas-city-neighborhood-wrote-the-blueprint-for-transforming-a-community/.
5. Reuters. 2000. "Kansas City Schools Lose Accreditation." *LA Times Archives*, May 4, 2000. https://www.latimes.com/archives/la-xpm-2000-may-04-mn-26560-story.html.
6. 2025 IHOPKC. 2025. "About IHOPKC." International House of Prayer. https://ihopkc.org/about/ihopkc.
7. Hughes, C.R. 2021. "Surviving "Killa City."" Humans. https://vocal.media/humans/surviving-killa-city.
8. Ryan, Kelsey, and Ian Cummings. 2018. "Crime statistics reveal Kansas City's disturbing homicide trend." *The Kansas City Star*, December 29, 2018. https://www.kansascity.com/news/local/crime/article159204444.html.
9. Harrison, Eric. 1989. "Drug-Dealing 'Posses' : Jamaicans: New Faces in U.S. Crime." *Los Angeles Times*, January 3, 1989. https://www.latimes.com/archives/la-xpm-1989-01-03-mn-46-story.html.
10. Blackwood, Kendrick. 2005. "When Moody Ruled." *Pitch Weekly*, August 4, 2005, 17.

11. Rizzo, Tony, and Glenn Rice. 2019. "KC's most-feared street gang finally may be history." *The Kansas City Star*, February 22, 2019. https://www.kansascity.com/news/local/crime/article63070377.html.

12. Reuters. 2000. "Kansas City Schools Lose Accreditation." *Los Angeles Times*, May 4, 2000. https://www.latimes.com/archives/la-xpm-2000-may-04-mn-26560-story.html.

13. Missouri v. Jenkins, 515 U.S. 70 (1995). https://supreme.justia.com/cases/federal/us/515/70/

14. Ciotti, Paul. 1998. "Money and School Performance: Lessons from the Kansas City Desegregation Experiment." *Cato Institute* 2098, no. March 16, 1998 (March): 1-35. https://www.cato.org/sites/cato.org/files/pubs/pdf/pa-298.pdf.

15. Klumpp, Andrew. 2020. "Colony before Party: The Ethnic Origins of Sioux County's Political Tradition." *The Annals of Iowa - State Historical Society of Iowa* 79, no. Winter 2020 (12): 1-34.

16. Alcock, Andy. 2019. "More vacant homes, more violent crime? Small area of Kansas City sees most homicides." *41KSHB - Scripps Local Media*, February 25, 2019. https://www.kshb.com/news/safe-kc/more-vacant-homes-more-violent-crime-small-area-of-kansas-city-sees-most-homicides.

17. The Urban League of Greater Kansas City. 2023. "From Redlining to Chalk Lines: The Costs of Economic Injustice." Urban League of Greater Kansas City. https://www.ulkc.org/2023-state-of-black-kc.

18. US Census Bureau. 2024. "KC Connectivity Report." mySidewalk. https://reports.mysidewalk.com/46060aa3cd.

19. Centers for Disease Control and Prevention. 2023. "Mental Health Conditions: Depression and Anxiety | Overviews of Diseases/Conditions." CDC. https://www.cdc.gov/tobacco/campaign/tips/diseases/depression-anxiety.html#four.

20. National Institute of Mental Health. 2023. "Major Depression- National Institute of Mental Health (NIMH)." National Institute of Mental Health. https://www.nimh.nih.gov/health/statistics/major-depression.

21. Schimelpfening, Nancy. 2023. "The History of Depression." verywellmind. https://www.verywellmind.com/who-discovered-depression-1066770.

22. World Health Organization. 2022. "Mental disorders." World

Health Organization (WHO). https://www.who.int/news-room/fact-sheets/detail/mental-disorders.

23. American Psychiatric Association. 2025. "Stigma, Prejudice and Discrimination Against People with Mental Illness." American Psychiatric Association. https://www.psychiatry.org/patients-families/stigma-and-discrimination.

24. Wang, Philip S., Patricia A. Berglund, Mark Olfson, and Ronald C. Kessler. 2004. "Delays in Initial Treatment Contact after First Onset of a Mental Disorder." HSR Health Services Research 39, no. 2 (April): 393-416. https://pmc.ncbi.nlm.nih.gov/articles/PMC1361014/#:~:text=The%20vast%20majority%20(80.1%20percent,needed%20to%20decrease%20these%20delays.

25. Yale Medicine. 2025. "Electroconvulsive Therapy (ECT) > Fact Sheets." Yale Medicine. https://www.yalemedicine.org/conditions/electroconvulsive-therapy-ect.

26. Green, Crystal, and Lauren Ziegler. 2023. "The Messy Middle: Implementing Education Innovations at Scale." HundrED Research Report 2023, no. #032 (September): 70. #032 Helsinki: HundrED, 2023. https://doi.org/10.58261/KGIC1847

ABOUT THE AUTHOR

Nicole Terrizzi has devoted her life to equity in opportunity, beginning her career as a Teach for America teacher in Kansas City and spending more than a decade collaborating with local, regional, national, and international organizations. She has worked as a fundraiser, grant writer, and consultant to nonprofits, corporations, and foundations, and is passionate about ensuring students have access to the resources and skills necessary to their ongoing success—from highly effective instruction in the classroom, to career-based experiences and mentorship supports, to opportunities to explore their passions in music, art, and beyond.

Nicole is originally from a small farming community in Northwest Iowa, has lived in the San Francisco Bay Area for more than a decade, and recently moved to the Pacific Northwest with her family. She is a graduate of the University of Missouri–St. Louis, where she received her master's in secondary education, and Simpson College, a small liberal arts school in Iowa, where she majored in English and journalism/mass communications. Nicole's hobbies include solo travel; numerous park visits and hikes with her partner, two young children, and dog; and reading creative nonfiction whenever she has a spare moment.

I'd love to hear from you!
www.nicoleterrizzi.com
contact@nicoleterrizzi.com

www.ingramcontent.com/pod-product-compliance
Lightning Source LLC
Chambersburg PA
CBHW040555010526
44110CB00055B/2750